100

GOLDEN WALL AND MIRADOR

Also by Sacheverell Sitwell

THE BRIDGE OF THE BROCADE SASH

TRAVELS AND OBSERVATIONS IN JAPAN

Sacheverell Sitwell

GOLDEN WALL

CLEVELAND AND NEW YORK

AND MIRADOR

Travels and Observations in Peru

THE WORLD PUBLISHING COMPANY

PUBLISHED BY The World Publishing Company

2231 WEST 110TH STREET, CLEVELAND 2, OHIO

Library of Congress Catalog Card Number: 61-12015

FIRST EDITION

CONTENTS

BOOK ONE

ILLUSTRATIONS

COLOUR PLATES

The illustrations numbers 33–45 were taken by Miss Joya Hairs, numbers 47–54 by Mrs Swadener, number 32 by the Museo Nacional de Cuba, numbers 5, 6 by Graphischen Sammlung, Munich, number 46 by Pan American Airways and number 7 by Martin Chambi. Numbers 2, 8, 23, 30, 31 were taken by Mr W. von Hagen and numbers 24–29 and colour plates II and III by Georgia Sitwell. Numbers 1, 3, 4, and colour plate I are from the collection of H.E. The Peruvian Ambassador in Washington.

To

Fernando and Claribel Berckemeyer

INTRODUCTION

THE PROJECT OF SETTING OUT for Lima and attempting a book on Peru has been made possible by the encouragement and help of Don Fernando Berckemeyer, late Peruvian Ambassador to the Court of St. James's, and now representing his country in Washington. This book is dedicated in gratitude to him. In Lima, and throughout Peru, our wishes were facilitated and our journeyings were made easy through the good offices of the Alcalde of Lima, Don Hector García de Ribeyro to whom to whom it would be impossible for myself and my wife adequately to express our grateful thanks. During the first part of our stay in the Peruvian capital we were the guests of Sir Berkeley Gage, the British Ambassador, and Lady Gage, and we would like to thank them for the happy time spent in their company of which we hope some pages of this book may serve for remembrance. During the second part of our stay we were the guests of the city of Lima. My wife and myself will always look back on our weeks in Lima in the light of friendships found there with the Alcalde and Doña García de Ribeyro, with Don Oscar Berckemeyer and his wife and son in their Peruvian home, and with Don Alfredo Porras and his wife with whom we stayed at La Onda. Also, with Don Enrique Pardo and his wife who took us to the Guano Islands. We enjoyed our meeting with yet another Anglophil, Don Benjamin de la Torre in Cuzco; and would give grateful thanks to Brigadier Gardiner of the Peruvian Corporation who sent us in a private car along the railway line; not forgetting the kind services of the district managers at Sicuani, at Juliaca, and at Guayqui in Bolivia.

Now that the experience is over I think that one realizes more than ever the extraordinary tenacity of the Spaniards and the mark they have left in places so far away from Spain. Knowing the Spanish cathedrals it is a moving experience to have stood in the Cathedral Square at Cuzco with the churches of the Spaniards at every hand. But the megalithic walls of the old Inca capital tell a still stranger tale, and one goes back in mind from them to the yet older culture of Peru; to the golden masks and ornaments of the Chimú, the Chavín, the Nazca, and to the wonderful textiles, the mantles from Paracas and ponchos of Tiahuanaco. The writer is very conscious that he has but scratched the surface of this enormous and strange country; only enough to savour the Sevillian airs of Lima and to have some little experience however tenuous of the high plain or Altiplano. There is enough here for a lifetime when we consider the archaeological sites along the coastal desert, add in the highlands, and include the forests and jungles of the Amazonas. Indeed the only excuse for attempting to write of Peru at all on such short acquaintance is a quick response to works of art.

Peru has to face the same problems which beset most Latin-American countries and which are now beginning to present themselves in acute form, but in some senses they apply more particularly to Peru. The infant mortality and the illiteracy of the Indian population are at last in process of being conquered, and soon the Indians will begin to swarm. How to house them, and find food and work for them, is the big problem, and its difficult and enormous nature dawns upon anyone who sees the slums of Lima behind the flowering face of the city. All thoughtful Peruvians are aware of this, and indeed it is not a problem only for Peru but for the benevolent forces of the western world. Something has to be done about this, and done quickly. I have tried to draw a picture of the *mestizo* or *cholo* population of Cuzco and La Paz in their brilliant dresses, but the colour of those only points the theme and does not help the problem.

There can be few landscapes more inspiring in their scale and colour than those on the high plain approaching Lake Titicaca; with elements of Castile and, one imagines, of high Tibet but adding up into Peru. Having seen Cuzco, it was a further consummation to be visiting this further region which must be one of the strangest places in the world. We were able to prolong our journey and go into Bolivia in the one direction and to Quito in the other, the latter being almost obligatory as a complement to Cuzco. In this manner although we missed seeing Arequípa owing to the earthquakes we saw to the further confines of the ancient Viceroyalty of Peru. What unexpected footnotes there are to Latin-American history! It comes as a surprise to find that Domenico Zipoli, organist of Sant' Ignazio in Rome and forerunner of Domenico Scarlatti, should have ended his days in 1726 as organist to the cathedral at Córdoba in Argentina, that city being at one end of a trajectory of Spanish civilization that stretches as far as the Colonial city of Popayán in Colombia. But that Peru is historically and aesthetically the country of all others in South America must be beyond argument. That it is also one of the most beautiful and interesting lands in the world is as demonstrable as its surpassing variety and its strangeness.

We were able further to extend our travels to Guatemala and to Yucatán. It was one of those last minute and unexpected decisions that, it may be, add a little to the freshness of one's impressions. This is the opportunity to thank Mrs. Willard Tisdal Hodgsdon of Guatemala City for her help in procuring illustrations for the Guatemalan chapters of this book. The photograph of a sculpture at Dos Pilas, near Petén, is from a very large site unknown to archaeologists until an oil company found it early in 1960. It may turn out to be even larger than Tikál, and could be even older. It shows a bound prisoner struggling violently, and is one of a series of bas-reliefs on a great stairway so arranged that they are trodden upon by those climbing the stair. The photographs of Chichén-Itzá, Uxmal, and other sites in Yucatán were obtained from Senor H. Barbachano of Mérida through the kind offices of Mrs. Swadener of Uxmal. And I owe a deep debt of gratitude to the well known writer and archaeologist Mr Victor W. van Hagen who most generously placed his archive of photographs of Peru and Ecuador at my disposal. Finally, I would express my grateful thanks to Sir James Henderson, then British Ambassador to Bolivia, and to Lady Henderson for all their kindness to us while we were their guests in La Paz; and to Mr Gerald Meade, British Ambassador to Ecuador, and Mrs Meade, who entertained us so hospitably while we were in Quito.

Not for the first time, this has been a journey of the sort that could only be realised through the help given me by my friend, Bryher. But indeed this fellow writer has encouraged all my schemes for writing. In conclusion, it is impossible for my thoughts not to go back again to Don Fernando and Claribel Berckemeyer because it was under their roof in 1946 that I first saw drawings by Pancho Fierro and admired the *tapadas* of Lima wrapped around in their shawls or mantles and with but one eye showing. Now, many years later, I have been to Peru and am able to present this sketch of Lima and of Cuzco, inadequate as it is to the immense history of the Incas, and to the earlier, even more interesting cultures of the Indians of the Andes. And in a last word I would thank my wife who came everywhere with me, and once again has read the proofs for me.

13 *February*, 1961   *SACHEVERELL SITWELL*

Chapter One

◆◆◆◆◆◆◆◆◆◆◆◆◆◆◆◆◆◆◆◆◆◆

DAY FLIGHT TO LIMA

THE START AND THE END of our journey was Miami International Airport which we flew in and out of no fewer than eight times in transit for Peru, over and across the Caribbean, to Guatemala, and via the United States and Canada on the way home. But the later destinations were, one could say, in supplement. The prime and main purpose of our journey was Peru.

However, in the course of so many sorties and returns Miami Airport became, of necessity, familiar ground and we developed a sort of affection for this unlikely place.

It is the beginning and the end of all Latin-American and Caribbean journeys. You leave it, but you have to come back to it again and again.

For this first experience we arrived three or four hours late, having dawdled and been delayed at Washington because the air was overcrowded, 'touching down' none too lightly, 'kind of bumpy', as the air-hostess called it, towards midnight, and going for this first time to a hotel down town to spend the night. It was horribly hot, even at that hour, or seemed so, coming from the snows of England and North America, and this was in the second week of January. But it was not too late to see the street was lined with funeral parlours. Is this in token that the older holidaymakers come here to die? For it is one of the sadder features of American life that you seldom, if ever, see anyone young in their holiday resorts. These have become so expensive that few can afford Nassau or Honolulu, or the Virgin Islands until old. This is not true of Miami which can almost be called the tourist centre of the entire American nation but it is a fact that there would appear to be more funeral parlours than there are sea-food joints, and signs advertising cheeseburgers and barbecue chicken, under the neon lights lining the long boulevard from the Airport down to Miami Beach.

What a place it is! With nearly a million inhabitants in Greater Miami, and a population that grows at the rate of a thousand persons a week. With over five hundred 'major hotels', and thousands of holiday-makers paying $40 or more per night just for a hotel room during the height of the season. With, of course, stores and picture-houses beyond counting. And, curiously, with chapels or places of worship for no fewer than thirty-two different denominations, to include Bahai World Faith, Calvary Fundamental and Calvary Taber-nacle, Latter-Day Saints (Mormon) and Jehovah's Witnesses. But, and it may seem to be the saving grace of Miami, Spanish-speaking personnel in all hotels, coming mostly from Cuba and Puerto Rico, Miami Airport being, we say it again, the gateway to Latin America, to all the cities of Central and South America, and for the islands of the Caribbean.

It is to the Airport that we return early next morning though the hour makes no difference since it is working day and night. Surprisingly, all the activity is upon what in England we call the first floor, the ground floor seeming to consist of little more than the elevators and the drive-in for motors and taxis. It is upstairs, though there is no apparent stair-way, that the fun begins. On a Sunday afternoon a little later in the year it was bedlam let loose, but that is because on Sundays there is all the local air traffic to and from St Petersburg (with over a million visitors every year, two hundred 'centrally located hotels', and a twenty-mile strip of beach hotels facing the Gulf of Mexico: 'try perlews and shilladas which are not encountered in restaurants but often appear at church suppers'[1]; to Tampa; to Sarasota where the Ringling Circus spends the winter; and other resorts on both coasts of Florida. But this is neither Saturday nor Sunday. The Airport is half empty, and there is an hour or more, all air-conditioned, in which to get the new taste of time.

If it is true that all buildings stand in physical and mathematical relation to the beings that made them, then Miami Airport has those anatomical defects to be expected of an electronic brain. Many things are altogether omitted, as though certain faculties are no longer work-ing. For instance, there are no facilities for left luggage. Having come

[1] *New Horizons U.S.A.*, Pan American World Airways, 1959 ed., pp. 197, 198, the sister volume to *New Horizons World Guide*.

out of the frosts and snows and being about to experience great heat, we wanted to leave behind a suitcase full of warm clothes. But there was nowhere to put it. The Airport has no left luggage office, neither has any individual airline any arrangement for storing luggage. The 'red cap' had no solution to offer. We must enquire at the Airport Hotel. But the Airport Hotel has none of the usual storerooms, which is as if the electronic brain has no stomach and no bowels. The entrance to it is a glass-walled lobby with reception and cashier's desks and a few armchairs, in the middle of the row of shops that occupies one entire side of the Airport Building. It is, indeed, quite difficult to locate with all the airline offices opposite and the 'concourses' or gates that lead down to the aeroplanes. But it is next to the Airport Bank and this is the best way to find it. The hotel desk seems to function like an organism apart. It could be—whichever one prefers—the cabin or gondola or capsule of some interplanetary missile worked, it must be said, most efficiently, through remote control. The elevators are altogether removed or disembodied from where the bell-captain has his desk out in the anything but pure air of the main building. And having set foot in the Airport Hotel we go up in the elevator some eight or nine floors to the roof-restaurant where the food is good even if dishes, over-familiar upon American menus, figure a little prominently, and only the organs of sight can tell the difference between blueberry or corn muffins, jumbo shrimps or Idaho potatoes. The restaurant is nearly, if not entirely, insulated from outside sound so that you scarcely hear the aeroplanes, and the windows looking out on the airfield are all occupied so that one gazes down on the other side upon thousands of parked cars.

The floors of bedrooms below, for we continue as if staying the night, are comfortable even if they carry the feeling that their area has been calculated inch by inch, and that every square inch must pay its way. For some reason, perhaps because there is not space enough in the dining-room, a printed notice on the breakfast menu on the dressing-table is insistent on the delights of dining in one's bedroom, and it was while studying this that we realized we were, so to speak, hermetically sealed in the apartment by windows that would not open to let in the fresh air. Meantime, and all the time, through a grating high on the wall, air-conditioning was in full play. Wherever we moved, it blew upon our necks and shoulders in confident promise of stiff necks, fibrositis, or worse, and by no exercise of ingenuity could it be turned off or diverted. As in an aeroplane, the air may have been changed for us and completely renewed every three minutes but all we wished was to turn it off and open the window. Because, as well as causing a perpetual draught, it made a buzzing, humming noise. The hotel engineer or electrician when sent for told us that if he turned off the air-conditioning we would all be suffocated, and so, loving the sea, we had to bear with it, pretending to ourselves all night long that the humming was the noise made by a liner's engines. So it is the truth that the windows will not and can not open, and that this is the price to pay in order not to hear the aeroplanes.

But indeed there is little or no choice in the matter, for sleep would be out of the question with the noise of jets and turbo-props coming down or climbing all day and night only a few hundred feet away. Instead there is this ceaseless, endless humming. The bedrooms are clean and comfortable enough but there is another and worse side to the infernal clatter. Restaurants where air-conditioning has been installed in many parts of the world are so glacially cold that one risks pneumonia in setting foot inside them. Probably this icing of the air we have to breathe is only tolerable in towns where it is *really hot*, along the Persian Gulf, let us say, at Aden or maybe in Bangkok, while the mere name of Florida proves that here are no extremes either of heat or cold.

On the other hand if it is so noisy that you cannot open a window and must be insulated from the outer world something has to be done about it, and in this change of mood the buzzing of the air-conditioner is to be preferred to the hum of a mosquito even without the mosquito's sting. And we leave the problem unanswered and come down by the elevator and out into the main building, wondering if it can be true that there are seventeen millions who are 'mentally ill' in the United States.[1] For somehow it is difficult to believe that there is the same proportion with the Russian population who have had no over-heating, no air-conditioning, no television, and no iced water. This ascending figure becomes, itself, nightmarish and haunted if it is applied to the Chinese who have about four times as many inhabitants as the United States, giving a total of some sixty-eight millions

---

[1] 'Neurotic at six, she is one of America's seventeen million mentally ill'—advertisement for *Look, the exciting story of people*, in the *New Yorker* for Jan. 30, 1960, p. 73.

'mentally ill', which is more than the entire white population of the British Commonwealth of Nations.

The main hall of Miami International Airport has the desks of all the different airlines ranged along one side with the illusion of a huge schoolroom carried still further by painted maps on the wall, coloured posters of far-away cities in unlikely juxtaposition to one another as though ready for a guessing game, and travel folders that are like an attractive form of holiday task. In front of each section of a desk is the name of its occupant as though to put relations at once on a familiar basis while the notice *Position Closed* at intervals, here and there, slows down business and makes for delay. But, at first, it is a chase from one end to the other of the Airport hall with Pan American occupying a huge space just opposite the hotel elevators, Eastern and North Eastern Airlines to the right at the far end of the building, and Air France, Sabena, S.A.S., K.L.M., Panagra, Avianca, and how many more, in long enfilade in the other direction. We were looking for Tan, one of the lesser known airlines, while all this time unseen voices announced the arrivals or departures, repeating it in Spanish, and ending with a last injunction: 'All aboard, please!'

There is a feeling that you can go almost anywhere from Miami, and it is nearly true. We have found the right desk, and weighed our luggage, and now there is nothing to do but sit and wait until they call our flight number. Time, too, to look at the shops which are more like Miami than Miami, itself. So, also, are many of the passers-by, and impossible to imagine what business they can be about in an Airport. A stout woman, fiercely and defiantly dark, wearing a pair of shorts, with such fat and ugly legs that one has to look away. What can she be doing? And a strawberry blonde—surely?—with an interesting figure, in black trousers leading a black poodle. Also, several families with children, and truth compels an Englishman to say that American children are now as curiously dressed as were French children in fashion plates of the Second Empire. Those short frilly knickerbockers, floppy bow-ties, smoothed hair à la Fauntleroy, and odd boots with blocked or cut off toes, are no stranger than this pair of twin boys with bullet heads, wearing space suits, playing at our feet. The strawberry blonde has by now found a female companion with silvered hair, and they are talking outside a shop window full of citrus fruit, which is the boast of Florida.

After a simple haircut and shampoo that costs the equivalent of thirty shillings, and a session in a tall chair for a shoeshine, there are still minutes to spare, and an empty seat next to a young woman coming from any one of the nineteen Spanish-speaking countries of Latin-America. Or she could be Brazilian, dressed in semi-tropical version of the bridesmaid at an English village wedding. But, in fact, she came with us in our aeroplane, and got out at our first stop which was Tegucigalpa, so that she was almost certainly Hondurian.

She wore a large diamond ring and coral and diamond earrings, had tiny feet in shoes with stiletto heels, and showed an inch or two of lace petticoat. Her shining black hair was elaborately curled and piled up on her head like the coiffure of a Roman Empress, while her finger-nails were iridescent and had mother-of-pearl varnish. How old was she? Anything between sixteen and forty with the emphasis on her being a good deal younger than one might think possible.

The minutes are running out. It is nearly time to go. But enquiring at the information desk for the number of our concourse it seems there is a delay which will be announced in a few moments, and it is a pause or hitch of forty minutes which passes quickly in thinking of the places one could fly to. For the lure and bait of Miami is the Spanish Main. It is not of interest that one can fly from here to Ottawa or New Orleans; nor even to New Mexico and Santa Fé. Mexico, itself, was easy and within grasp; it was but a sidestep across the Sargasso Sea. For once in my life I did not hanker after Tehuantepec or Oaxaca; for neither the golden masks of Monte Albán, nor the churches of stone that go green after it has rained. In those few moments it was not even interesting that Central America was but an hour or two away; Yucatán, Campeche, and mystery-sounding, indeed still mysterious Quintana Roo; what I would call the feathered or West Indies, as opposed to the lacquered or East Indies at the other side of the world.

Now Nicaragua was near. Nicaragua of the great lake, of old Colonial towns, Granada and León, and ill-omened Costa de Mosquitos or Mosquito Coast; Honduras, the habitat of the quetzal, and upon its borders with Guatemala, Copán of the Mayans, with huge ruins; Honduras that we did not then know we were bound for on that very flight; Guatemala to which we came back at the end of our journey and so for this moment need say nothing more. There were all the isles and cays and every choice among them; Grand Cayman of the pirates, and in that instant knowing none of them, all or any of the cays from the Bahamas down, dozens, or even hundreds of them scattered over the Sargasso and the Caribbean. Even the farthest of the cays were but an hour or two away. The quarry was more distant; half-way down the huge South American continent on the Pacific Coast. At which moment our flight number was called out, and so farewell to Miami for the time being. And with no more ado to Lima.

On board the aeroplane both crew and passengers were Spanish-speaking. There were children and babes-in-arms, mothers and grand-mothers. Two old women sitting together across the companionway, in deep black, one telling her beads, the other with eyes shut already before the take-off, and holding a large crucifix in both hands, could easily be great-grandmothers. And there was a young woman or two, almost indistinguishable from her we had already noticed, dressed for all the world like country bridesmaids; young women of the Southern matchbox lid, cigar-box label, or bull-fight poster. Coats and parcels were stowed away and safety belts fastened. We taxied along, and halted for a last trial of the engines. They stopped and then silence. Then, started once more, and we were off to Lima.

Miami International Airport was already far behind, and we had a panorama of that most extraordinary of towns, now revealed as a nightmare union of Venice, and the Lido, and Tenochtitlán, the Aztec city of Mexico, all in one. Lagoons, and straight lines of water for the canals; and causeways, and what look to be floating islands; parked cars by tens of thousands, in contradiction; and temples or teocallis for the hotels of Miami Beach; and in an instant we are over the coast and far away. Coming back though in a moment or two and flying over swamps that must be The Everglades, and diving into a mist that, maddeningly, hid the chain of islands, Florida Keys they are called, instead of cays, more than a hundred miles of them, linked by a road and railway line, and ending at Key West, deep in the Gulf of Mexico, and the only semi-tropical city in the United States. We must be over the head of the Gulf Stream where, the map tells exultant, the equivalent of 10,000 Mississippi Rivers begins its flow of warm waters to the coast of Norway.

We bump a little at cloud edges, looking down between them to

B

patches of grey sea, but are soon above land again which must be Cuba, and not far from Havana, at the western extremity of that long island. It is indeed ten times bigger in area than little Jamaica, but so narrow that we have crossed it in a few minutes, seeing nothing interesting, and now it is the blue Caribbean, just as we hoped it would be, blue, blue, or rather, blue and gold for the sun is pouring down on it from a cloudless sky. So it goes on, hour after hour, or for two or three hours, but it seemed longer, and was islandless, for in this direction there are no islands between Cuba and the mainland of Central America. It was a disappointment to see no palm-fringed coral islands, no atolls with fresh water lagoons inside them, but I suppose those are in the South Seas. There seem to be no islands, so shaped, in the West Indies. But there are, in fact, two islets hereabouts, called Swan Islands, in United States possession, with lighthouse and radio station of the United Fruit Company (the Almanach de Gotha for 1939, of all things, gives this information), but we saw no sign of them. Their fame is that they are the home of a special race of legless lizards that it would be curious to see.

We are nearing Honduras, at about the point where the map says Columbus 'saw a large canoe loaded with merchandize and manned by Indians from Yucatán'. And we are a long way from Miami, little opportunity though Miami has had for travelling in time for this is no affair only of distance. Other things beside mere mileage divide Miami from the Mayans. Now we are over Honduras having eaten a sandwich luncheon some way before this, and been told there is no alcohol on board which is something of a deprivation on a flight of fourteen hours. Having found also that we are to come down in the capital of Honduras for a little supernumerary and unexpected taste of Central America. And it has become extremely mountainous, of brown mountains, with one or two lakes in obvious volcanic craters.

We are beginning to lose height and are soon flying below the hilltops winding in and out between them, and quite plainly looking for Tegucigalpa. I can only add that, myself, I have been looking too for the capital of Honduras, if in desultory fashion, and never hoped to find it. The airport may be a little difficult to land at but leaving the tiled roofs of the town on the left hand we see the runway and the airport building which is distempered pink, and in a few moments are enjoying this first experience of a new sub-continent. It would be exaggerated praise to call the airport at Tegucigalpa spick and span, or anything but dirty and untidy in the old Mediterranean meaning of the word. That is to say, beggars, old men and women, and a small boy showing with pride a sore place on his chest. Only they are Indian, and not Latin, and this is the novelty. There are even monks, a group of them in white habits talking with animation to two young women who had spoken French to each other all the way in the aeroplane. This was one of the surprises; in fact one of the minor mysteries of the journey. What could be the link between them? For they came on with us as far as Guayaquil.

Nothing good was for sale except straw hats of Panamá type, called here *Sombreros de junco*, the first of many of their sort all down Peru, and in Ecuador where the best come from, and up again to Guatemala, and handbags and baskets of the same straw, if that is the right word for it. We went up and sat on the terrace of the airport building feeling a little apprehensive that 'they' would leave without us. For we were scarcely half-way on our long journey, a thing which would have been entirely incomprehensible only a few years ago, and to which one cannot get accustomed. Just to think of it. To be able, starting rather earlier in the morning, on one and the self same day, to call in at all the chief cities of Central America, beginning perhaps with Mérida in Yucatán, then dropping in at Guatemala for a few minutes only, and continuing to San Salvador, and here to Tegucigalpa, and on to Managua the capital of Nicaragua, thence to San José of Costa Rica, ending at Panamá City! By sea, or road, or railway it would be a journey of many weeks.

Meanwhile it was improbable, to say the least of it, to be un-expectedly at Tegucigalpa, a town which must vie in difficulty of pronunciation with Antananarivo—or is it Tananarive?—the capital of Madagascar. If dumped here without warning, where would one's guess be? Coming down again into the main building, more nervous than ever of being left behind, all conjecture was settled, once and for all by a man, noticed earlier sitting at the desk of one of the airline offices. He did not seem to have moved or stirred in half an hour, and must be the temporary occupant while his superior was away. For one could get nothing out of him. He seemed to be pure blooded Indian, not *mestizo*; wearing a white linen suit, and a peaked hat which could only be Mexican or Central American, and nothing else.

Copper-skinned and stoical, distant cousin of the Red Indian, indifferent and imperturbable. In fact his hat had taken on all his character; and now there were other little Indian men, all slight and small, with maybe just a touch of the Spaniard in them, and it could be nowhere but Central America. Though it must be someone with years of local experience behind him who could tell at sight if this was Costa Rica or El Salvador, Honduras or Nicaragua.

What time of day was it? For this was puzzling. One already knew the flight was a couple of hours longer than expected owing to a change of hour. But, of course, as we get near the Equator, even at this considerable way from it, the days are shorter than one would imagine, and after eight hours flying time from Miami it was beginning to grow dark. What a pity we could not stay in Honduras in order to see Copán! It is little more than an hour away by air. One had read as a child the old description of its stone pyramids and carved monoliths or stelae in Stephen's *Incidents of Travel in Central America, Chiapas and Yucatán* (1841), with Catherwood's wonderful and mysterious drawings of them. And Tegucigalpa, and indeed Honduras generally, with its local dishes, *nacatamales, mondongo*,—what could those be?—and *quesos blancos de Olancho y Choluteca* (white cheeses?)—and tropical singing birds with lovely names, *zorzal, jilguero, zensontle* and all its humming birds and parrots. But there was no time for these, or anything further, for we were off again.

Taxiing away to the left for the longest possible run, and airborne in a few moments up among the brown hills. With no view of Tegucigalpa, and soon out of Honduras and over Nicaragua. Now there is the sight of more than one volcano, there being some twenty odd in all in Nicaragua, and we are above a big lake over to the left which must be Lake Managua with the capital on its shore but we do not catch sight of that. The smoking volcano may be Momotomba, but the shores of the lake keep curving away and coming back again. Now it is no longer the same lake, and must be Lago de Nicaragua which is a hundred miles long and very wide, and which I thought must be the sea. The old Spanish city of Granada is on the lake, with hundreds of little islets near it called 'Diamonds' by the Granadinos, where tropical fruits are raised, papayas, pomeloes and mangoes, and there is a large island in the lake with two high volcanoes on it. But the most interesting thing about Lago de Nicaragua is that it has salt water fish, and especially tarpon, sharks and swordfish. There is deep water tarpon fishing in the Lake of Nicaragua, the theory being that the lake was once part of the Pacific Ocean, that volcanic eruptions cut it off, and that by gradual infiltration from fresh-water rivers the salt water was changed and the fish became adapted to their new surroundings. It is not so long ago that a fresh-water lake with sharks and other salt-water fish in it was discovered in New Guinea and announced as being something unique in all the world, but they had forgotten Lake Nicaragua.

The landscape was now hopelessly confusing, and impossible to know whether we were over lake or sea. We must, in fact, be flying over Costa Rica, but we saw little or nothing of it, and were soon over the Pacific Ocean. One becomes air-conditioned, so to speak, and acquiescent after eight or ten hours' flying. It seemed that we were for some hours over the Pacific, and there was a sunset with enormous long straight bars or lines of light, something not seen before, part of the human experience of cloud-viewing from an aeroplane. What an excitement and an intoxication this would have been to Ruskin who was the cloud-master among writers.

We had the whole wonderful sky to ourselves, and only the sky. There was now no sign of land or water. The dying colours persisted at this great height for longer than one would think possible for we were, I remember, at twenty-three thousand feet which is Himalayan, or indeed, Andean altitude. Somewhere hereabouts we must have crossed the Equator but there was no mention of it on the loudspeaker. It has become a commonplace to aeroplane crews who cross it two and three times in a week, and at least we were spared the tiresome and embarrassing sea ceremony of King Neptune coming aboard, a tradition which is endemic only in British-owned ships. It must be quite dark down below, and now we seemed air borne, effortlessly, as if the difficulty would be in coming down, not staying aloft. Also, time had no meaning, and was it seven, or eight, or nine o'clock at night? At about which time we were given a tasteless, timeless dinner. Or was it now, or later, after Guayaquil? But that was in fact what happened. The endless sunset seemed to prolong itself until we were over land again, and the landfall was South America.

We came into it over Ecuador while there was still light upon the mountains. Row after row of them which made one nervous because night-flying is never pleasant among mountains. But, at last, there were the lights of a town, and more lights reflected from water, and we were coming down at Guayaquil. What a huge distance we have covered already! Having flown out of Costa Rica and over the Pacific just in time, as it were, to avoid Panamá, skirted the coast of Colombia, and now arrived at Guayaquil. By sea, it is still ten days' sail from New York to Guayaquil. What a miracle to be in South America in as many hours! We had made a good landing, and in a few moments were ashore in a new continent. It is a small airfield for so large a town and the principal port of Ecuador. In fact, disappointingly colourless for a town with a tropical climate and with hyacinths, we were told, floating on its river.

But it was tropically hot, at any rate, and the more torrid for having come only the day before yesterday from the snows of Canada and Washington. So hot that we came out of the crowded building and walked up and down in the red dust outside it in a red twilight that spoke of heat although it was but January. A pair of Indians, a new kind of Indian, were selling scarves. Silent-footed, quiet moving, as alike as brothers, and to outward appearance quite dumb. Shadow-men, not, as all other hawkers and hucksters, shouting out the prices. But holding out the scarves, and trying to attract one's attention by silent per-suasiveness, like a beautifully behaved dog begging in a corner of the room by itself, and trying to catch one's eye. This said with the im-plication that dogs are often more agreeable than human beings. Both Indians were dressed alike in ponchos and white trousers, and wore their hair in a pigtail, and both had white hats. South American Indians, apart from the savage tribes of the Amazon, are as hat-bound as the older generation of Englishmen. This is true of them whatever the altitude, and it is because of the strength of the sun's rays. We shall see that they were Otavalo Indians who are great weavers. But that is for our return to Quito, we did not know this at the time, and only guessed they were a new and particular kind of Indian peculiar to Ecuador.

But for the last time we are off again with a load of new passengers who are only going from Guayaquil to Lima, local traffic compared to the distance we have come. It is some two-and-a-half to three hours' flying time, and being tired it goes by so quickly we hardly remember it. But certainly in a few minutes we are over the Pacific again, con-tinuing along or near the coast all the rest of the way. On the return journey flying from Lima to Quito we covered just the same ground in daylight, and it is the coastal desert nearly the whole time. It was wonderful enough to have set foot in Central America, at Tegucigalpa, and to think the long wished for Mayan ruins in Yucatán might perhaps materialize on the way home. But on this memorable evening we were going further afield to Lima, somewhere which had hitherto seemed entirely out of reach. Indeed, Peru must be about as far away as one can get from England. Farther in inaccessibility than New Zealand and at any rate to an Englishman much more remote. We were hoping to get to Lake Titicaca, and on reaching that had never felt so far away from home. But it is still, and must always be incredible to many of us, that Peru is within two days flight from London. It brings Peru nearer, while making it still seem just as far away.

This feeling was even magnified by the long stretch of coastal desert which one had heard about, but could not see. If you come to Peru from the other direction you have to fly over the Andes, by way either of Bolivia, or Chile. Whichever way, it is an arduous flight across the mountain ranges, and one that people warn you requires an experienced pilot. It is safer not to trust to local airlines. We must be over Peru now though there is still six hundred miles to go. It was more than exciting to be nearing Lima, just as it must always be a fascination to be approaching a tropical or semi-tropical city of a million inhabitants with a Spanish history behind them. How would Peru compare to Mexico? For there is a Mexican style in all things, that is descended from, but not a part of Spain. Mexico has taken on an individuality of her own, and grown in four centuries into little resemblance to her parent. What is interesting is how unlike, and not how like Mexico is to Spain.

It was difficult to believe we had in the same day seen the Gulf of Mexico and the Caribbean, the volcanoes of Honduras and Nicaragua, and the Pacific Ocean, and were now making down the desert coast for Lima. For how long had the golden altars of the Mexican churches seemed so remote that one would never see them? For it was not, in fact, till twenty-five years after I first wrote of them that I saw them with my own eyes. Now they were even far away behind us, and ahead lay Peru. It was a wish-fulfilment nearly impossible to believe in, that at any moment now we would be coming down at Lima.

And for Cuzco to be within reach, that had seemed as far off as Lhasa! The cyclopaean walls of the Incas apart, every lover of Spain must want to go to Cuzco.

It was late, and nearly midnight. Lima could not be far away. A city in Andalusian style, one had read, only known to this moment from descriptions in books, from some paintings to be described later, and from the caricatures of Pancho Fierro. And that it had the palace of La Périchole, and green wooden balconies, and *miradors*. And now there were thousands of lights below us, and we were manoeuvring for a landing. This was Lima.

A few moments' delay owing to a pair of matadors who must have arrived in another aeroplane and were being mobbed by their admirers, and we found the friends who had come to meet us. We were out of the airport, and driving through the warm night past the scented gardens. The flowers are a lasting memory of Lima. But in this lovely city there are other things than flowers.

'Rose-pink Camellia! The worm is on your leaf.' There are the appalling slums called the Barrieras with three hundred thousand persons living in them. They are the most urgent problem in Peru. So all is not flowers in Lima. But who could know that, talking into early morning by windows opening on another flower garden, and tired out by our long flight, going upstairs to bed!

❖❖❖❖❖❖❖❖❖❖❖❖❖❖❖❖❖❖❖❖❖❖❖

Chapter Two

LIMA

IT IS TRUE THAT COMING to Lima in January you find the tropical equivalent of May or June at home, and the quicker you get there the more dramatic the change in climate. There are even large areas in Peru where it has not rained in living memory. South of the Equator so many basic images and ideas have to be altered, and for an instance 'the dew-dropping south' of Mercutio's speech has quite lost its meaning.

> *True, I talk of dreams,*
> *Which are the children of an idle brain,*
> *Begot of nothing but vain fantasy;*
> *Which is as thin of substance as the air,*
> *And more inconstant than the wind, who woos*
> *Even now the frozen bosom of the north,*
> *And, being anger'd, puffs away from thence,*
> *Turning his face to the dew-dropping south.*

In Peru it is the south that leads down bare deserts and snowy Andes to Cape Horn, and they are Antarctic waters of Humboldt's Current that lave the guano isles and feed the penguins found there but a few miles from Lima's flower gardens. By the same token, and in the contradiction that is typical of most things South American, the north grows hotter into Ecuador, or would were it not that Quito lying almost on the Equator stands at nearly ten thousand feet.

Arriving in Lima in January we saw it at its best before the fogs came down. Even so, it is only necessary to climb a few hundred feet into the hills, and you are in the sun again. But South and Central American seasons are nearly impossible to arrange by system because of differing altitudes, those again portending something quite different in the Andes from what they do in all other mountain ranges. As an example of differing climates, in March the jacaranda trees were in full bloom in Guatemala, though they would be over and in leaf by January in Peru. The important point to remember is that it grows colder as you go south, and hotter going north. In Peru the spring begins in September, and the summer in December. With which in mind it becomes normal that one should be eating a papaya or a mango for breakfast in Lima on a January morning.

But, for the first day or two, and partly owing to the excitement of arriving, it is at times quite difficult to remember just where we are. There are beds of splendid cannas in Miraflores, the part of the town where we are staying, and they set me thinking of Lisbon where there are cannas along the road on the way to Belém. It is those red and yellow flowers that begin the train of thought for Lima has none of the hilly streets of Lisbon. Neither have any of the roofs that Chinese tilt to them; nevertheless it is the flowers and something in the architecture that give a momentary illusion. A Latin town somewhere, but where exactly can it be? It persists only for a few moments. For at the end of a bed of cannas, where there is a big road crossing, a legless beggar is sitting whom we get to know well by sight. He is obviously an Indian, his cheerfulness and quick hobbling after sols (the Peruvian currency) apart, for neither quickness of movement, nor gaiety of expression are typical of his race. Or at least he must have Indian blood.

Now some stoutly built women in bright shawls and bell-shaped crinoline-like skirts pass by who are *mestizas*, or half-castes. They form the middle class of the country, though their Indian blood is always predominant, and one sees few marks of the Spaniard in them. Or let us call them *cholas*, at once, which is a prettier name for them. They give the colour to Peruvian and Bolivian cities, and are more lively than the pure blooded Indians.

The houses in Miraflores are mostly villas in casino style, in un-inhibited dreaming of Monte Carlo. Or it is no more than a natural affinity for probably neither architects nor owners have visited the Principality in person, or seen the public buildings of the Société des Bains de Mer. But there are moments, many of them, when Monte Carlo seems the architectural ideal, however remote and distant. It continues over many sections of this part of Lima. The palm trees are magnificent. So splendid that one may feel one has never seen palms before. In particular, there are some avenues of royal palms with fifty or sixty feet of whitish stems before their crowns of fronds. It is easy enough to say they resemble some cathedral aisle, but where, and of what architecture? There is an avenue of these palms at Palm Beach in Florida, and there it is like the first taste of another land for they are, in fact, Brazilian. Even here in Lima they look exotic and an importation from the tropics. These must be mature and nearly at their full height; aloof and Amerindian, and one feels a feathered savage with his blow-pipe should be gliding between their stems and looking up into them, and not the shadow of a white man. An American-Indian, and not someone in a car, held up in a car among other cars at a traffic crossing.

But in order to see Lima one has to drive in the other direction and into the town. Past a florid building which is the Argentine Embassy, and another which must surely be the casino but is in fact the new museum. There are statues hereabouts, but alike the bronze eloquence of their gestures and their patriotic feats are lost on us. And now we are in the town among high modern buildings with a restaurant, and a panoramic view from its windows, on the top floor. Nothing old in sight unless you look for it, and no more flowers except those of the street vendors. But, quite suddenly, a barrow-boy with a stall of mangoes, something we had not seen before, or a *mestiza* woman selling exquisite and rose-like roses, that is to say, roses of rose-colour with a dewy freshness. The roses of Lima are beautiful indeed, and no wonder this is the name of the patron saint of the city. There are beginning to be churches, but we are not proposing to go into them this morning. One or two of them have most elaborate Baroque façades of the sort that seem to be carved all over with cupids and bunches of grapes, at a quick glance on passing by.

There is a right angled turn by a big church, where a new bridge is building, and we come to an equestrian statue that can be of none other than Conquistador Francisco Pizarro, in full armour with feathered helm, and the plumes are distinctly of some tropical bird—brandishing his Toledan blade. The street has been narrow, and there are one or two of the wooden balconies along or near it. But now we come out into a big open square with Lima Cathedral on one side, the Town Hall or Alcaldería on the side next to it, and the Presidential Palace opposite.

The Alcaldería, a modern building, has the big wooden balconies or casements, and the Cathedral we will find has been entirely rebuilt and so is modern, too. As to the Archbishop's Palace, next door, up to this moment it is impossible to be certain in one's mind as to how old it is. Certainly it gives rather a nice Rococo-Archiepiscopal impression. A fluttering, busy façade as though to hinder you from looking too closely into it, with elegant balconies and windows.

The Presidential Palace is gaily casino-like in architecture and now, looking round, the whole square is delightfully southern, or even subtropical in appearance. In the gateway leading to the Palace a trio of the Presidential Guard is always standing with a fourth, some sergeant, or exon, or harbinger just behind them. It is a surprise to see this *corps d'élite* on duty at the Palace for one had not known there is anything of the kind in Latin America. Distant relations of the Garde Républicaine with, it seemed, more than one dark Indian among them, in jackboots, red breeches and white tunics, gold epaulettes, and gold and silver helm with black horsetail hanging from it, with drawn sword on shoulder, their uniform is most appropriate to the richly fretted Palace. They make one more and welcome addition to the diminishing return of ornamental bodyguards, now so few of them are left in Europe. A mounted regiment, obviously, though we never chanced on them on horseback, and not to be confused with the 'Junun' hussars, 'in red and blue and gold', who formed the guard of honour when the Duchess of Kent visited Peru a year or two ago. They are clearly dragoons or lifeguards, and not hussars, and must be unique in all South America except for a Presidential Lifeguard of the same character in Brazil.

On the way back, in order to remind us where we are, we pass by more than one small shop where llama and alpaca rugs are for sale, black, or brown, but in the main of Polar whiteness. Not long ago, as we will soon know, herds of llamas were to be met with in this very square in front of the Cathedral, but nowadays llamas are as rare in Lima as giraffes or ostriches on Fifth Avenue, or strolling down the Strand. Indeed there is not a llama in the whole of Lima unless it is in a Zoo, but there are plenty of llama skins. The nearest flock of llamas may be several hundred miles away. And we get back to the house where we are staying in time to sit out in the garden and drink a refreshing 'pisco sour', something quite indigenous to Peru, and most delicious. It is a form of grape brandy, white in colour, and resembling if only in idea *Vieux Marc de Bourgogne* which is the brandy made in Burgundy, but it is less strong than that and with a quite different taste. There are many different makes of pisco from good to bad, with horrid kinds to which have been imparted cherry or other flavouring, when pisco can become like the cheap scents sprayed in cinemas. At its best, from an honest vineyard, with fresh lime added, pisco can be better than any concoction of gin or rum. It is only a pity that so little of it is made that there is none for export, and pisco is quite unknown in North America and in Europe. Or indeed, anywhere except in Peru, and to some little extent in Bolivia.

Of course, one of the fascinations of that garden was to watch out for new kinds of birds, the most common, of which it is shaming never to have found out the name, being about the size of a blackbird, and as brisk and lively as that, but with thinner legs and a long tail, no song but a kind of chattering, and with some of the run and dance of a water wagtail. This bird seems to be found all over Latin America for we met it again in Guatemala and in Yucatán. Another small bird had a comical habit of jumping straight up into the air and down again, with an almost vertical take-off, up and down and up and down, as if at a game of bouncing. As well, a bird with a fantail, but rarer, and sparse at putting in an appearance. But the great excitement in the garden was the humming birds that darted and hovered at the fuchsias outside the dining-room windows, but as though of a mind to keep themselves for a further inspection for in all the time we were there we never saw them.

A turkey on a near-by roof kept up an incessant gobbling, night and morning. Some nights, because one goes late to bed at Lima, I would wake up early and before I could remember I was in Peru, think I was hearing again the fishwife whose stentorian voice crying 'haddock' could be heard all over the seaside town where I lived as a child. But this is Lima. These are mornings of the mango and papaya. And of another fruit—a grenadilla?—lovely to look at, but starchy in texture, and with too many black pips to it. Then would be heard the flutings of the knifegrinder who, as in towns in Spain, is making his morning round and playing on his panpipe as he goes from street to street. In Spain all the knifegrinders are Gallegos and come from a couple of villages in Galicia. One supposed here in Lima they must be second or perhaps third generation emigrants. In the garden below there is a jacaranda, now in ferny leaf and with its flowers gone, and a tall tree which has clusters of yellow flowers and, we are told, is a cassia. It has the habit of flowering only towards its top so that the individual flowerheads are difficult to see. But also, there are flowering creepers one has not seen before, one of them appearing to come from no-where, but it has been planted cunningly on the far side of the loggia wall. And there is a jasmine, doubtfully named, which bears white and blue flowers upon it at the same time, one colour fading into the other by evening, but as I write this I am more certain than ever it is no jasmine.

Other, and smaller gardens were in full fortissimo of flowering. Bougainvillea can be known at its best in other places, perhaps parti-cularly in Madeira, but plumbago, inseparable companion to bougain-villea in Victorian conservatories, one is seeing for the first time, effectually, in Lima gardens. It is a Cape plant from that Mediterranean clime along the South Atlantic and Indian Ocean shores, with a flower-ing here in ideal conditions not to be recognized from its sister grown in a cold conservatory at home. Here and there is a frangipani in some small garden, in the different colours of the frangipani, yellow or white, and rising here to giant hemlock height, or taller. Hibiscuses, too, and especially a double rose variety like some pink rose growing on straight thornless boughs. But perhaps the most dazzling of all are poinsettias, their fiery scarlet bracts eight or ten feet above ground, the scarlet crowns at candelabra height and borne on candelabra stems. Such little gardens as these are in their hundreds all over this part of Lima, and all different by virtue of their flowers.

It is only necessary to go a mile or two out of the town and you are in the desert which makes more remarkable the mystery of all these gar-dens. And it is not exactly a sandy desert, but all dust and detritus, giving the feeling of powdered stone, the grain of it being even smaller and finer sifted than ordinary sand. The first dust experience may be on the road to Pachacamac, the nearest Inca ruins to Lima, and at the coming of the conquistadores a more sacred place than Cuzco. In the knowledge of this, Pachacamac is disappointing, or one could say that it returns a dusty answer. For all is dust there, dust terraces and dust escarpments, with human bones in evidence and protruding from the white-grey surface. On a tremendous scale, at least, to fit the landscape, and like one huge cemetery, step after dusty step up to the topmost terrace. With a magnificent view from that down over the Pacific, and to exceedingly odd-shaped islands. No ornament or carving of any kind at Pachacamac, and only a family of llamas and an alpaca in a pen by the custodian's cabin for the sake of the tourists, and in order to help the sale of rugs and postcards.

On the way home we pass again the long line of beach, and it is a vast landscape drawn in a few lines. The only sign of the tropics is at the wayside stalls where the lorry drivers take their choice from huge mounds of mangoes and green hills of melons. It is perhaps inevitable that this first contact with the Inca civilization should be dead and depressing. That is the fault of the coastal desert, and makes only the more welcome a return to the flowers of Lima.

But the nearer one goes to the older part of the town the fewer the gardens. Already, on the way to the Cathedral, or to the other main square the Plaza San Martín, there are a few old houses, one in particular, now the Jockey Club, showing the characteristics of what is most definitely Peruvian style. This does not, it may be added, resemble the Mexican Colonial style as shown in houses in, for instance, Cuernavaca or Querétaro. Peruvian is entirely distinct from Mexican, as anyone will know who has been to both, and tries to compare in his mind the picture of Cuzco in Peru and of Taxco, which is in Mexico. The large old house in Lima into which we are entering is post-Colonial in date, having been built in the early years of independence from Spain, probably in about 1830 or 1840 with later flavour added at long distance from the French Second Empire. It belonged, in fact, to the grandparents of our friends; and curious to think the friend accompanying us remembered going there to see his grandmother. For it came out of another age of carriages and many servants, in scale like many an old town house in Europe; what was distinctly Peruvian, or, at least, characteristic of Lima being the arabesque doorways and the dark wood panelling. Though no longer a home, it would only be necessary to put down llama skin and alpaca rugs on the floors, instal again a collection of silver stirrups and other ornaments on dark wood tables, add a retinue of *cholo* servants, and we could be nowhere but in Lima. An old city which, by now, is beginning to be the younger, 'gone overseas', sister of Seville in our minds.

Of which maternity there could be no surer proof than the Torre Tagle Palace in a narrow street in the same part of the town. It is like a

breath of Spain only to be told who built it. He was José de Tagle y
Brancho who came to Peru as a captain in a regiment of lancers, and
after campaigning in Chile against the Araucanian Indians was made
Marquis of Torre Tagle, and appointed Permanent Paymaster of the
Royal Armada of the South Seas, or, in fact, the famed silver fleet
of the Pacific. It is difficult to put a year to it for one has never before
seen anything quite like it, but the Torre Tagle dates, in fact, from 1735.
There is a splendid arabesque doorway or frontispiece, two storeys high
and to each side of that huge boxed-in wooden balconies. It is these
one has not known before, though there is some attempt at them in
Malta where the influence comes obviously from near-by North
Africa. Such wooden balconies are *the* architectural feature of Lima, and
they are evidently of Oriental inspiration. But this must be instinctive
and not copied, unless we are to imagine they are in conscious imitation
of the streets of Cairo. They are, in fact, *mudéjar*, meaning, as in Spain,
the work of craftsmen of Moslem origin, or, at least, Moorish tradition
in their workmanship. The effect of them is to raise expectation of the
ladies of Lima who were so closely guarded, and indeed, wooden
shutters in the balconies could be opened outwards to allow the ladies
to look down into the street. In no other land in Christendom was
there such outward, at any rate, seclusion of the women. They had to
walk abroad veiled from head to foot which gave rise, as we shall see,
to vagaries of fashion that put them on a par with the masqueraders of
the Venetian Carnival.

Another *mudéjar* feature of the Torre Tagle Palace are the trefoil
arches of the patio, running in arabesque fashion, large and small,
round all four sides of the upper gallery. There are patios with similar
trefoil arches, it is true, in Colonial houses at Querétaro in Mexico,[1]
but here in Lima this has the real touch of Moghul buildings and of the
Alhambra. The interior of the Torre Tagle has been well restored; the
tiles from Andalusia have been copied and are in place again, and the
precious woods, cedar and mahogany and cocobole, give a furnished
air to where there can have been but little furniture before. This house
is typical, if best of its kind, and nothing other than Peruvian, so that
it is in some sense the model of houses in Peru. But what is curious is the
strength of the *mudéjar* influence two hundred years after it had been
extinguished, or died out in Spain. It is odd indeed to look out through

[1] Marqués de Villa de Villar de Aguilar.

'Peru', from the Gobelin tapestry *Les Nouvelles Teintures des Indes* after Desportes

A late seventeenth-century portrait of a *cacique*

Street scene in Lima, showing wooden miradors. Watercolour by J. Wayne, 1835

those pierced jalousies that have their only parallel in the grilles of nuns' choirs in Spain and Portugal and Southern Italy. In Lima they are called *miradores* though this romantic name applies, also, to the look-out towers in some of the old houses. Only a few of them are left, but there is at least one *mirador* built specially so that the ladies could look into the bull-ring.

Lima must once have had balconies beyond number. Those of the Torre Tagle may always have been among the most elaborate in the town, but there were whole streets of them until not long ago. Now those remaining are nearly all of early nineteenth century date, and painted green. But the most intact part of the old town is across the river Rimac where the houses are undestroyed, if humble. There has been widespread destruction in two fearful earthquakes of 1687 and 1746, followed by wanton burning of most of the gilded woodwork in the churches by neo-classical iconoclasts, contemporaries of our church 'restorers' rather more than a hundred years ago, and the good work of destroying has continued in the guise of urban 'development' into our own time. It is a tragedy because there is reason to think Lima was in its day the most beautiful city of Latin America.

As you progress into the older part of the town, near or across the river, so the *mestizo* population increases, until it predominates. Already, there may be dwarf-like figures you have not seen before; a woman, smaller than a child of ten years old as we know them, in a little peaked hat with a babe in swaddling clothes on her back, or sitting on a doorstep with a baby at her breast. Pure-blooded Indians these, on occasion with the characteristic inverted saucer head-dress of Cuzco, or another of the interior provinces. Always to the Anglo-Saxon they are unbelievably little in stature, so puny that one wonders they survive at all. And another, a type of slinking ruffian with frayed trouser ends, barefooted, and bearded, portending more of Spanish blood for the pure Indians are imberb. This 'wretch' in the nineteenth century meaning of the term, seems to be always running from some crime, and there are, in fact, poorer parts of Lima which are full of pick-pockets. His shadowy figure out of a slum I saw again and again, but concluded there were several of them, who would have been happier in Naples of a hundred years ago.

Across the river, and out of the slums, is the Quinta da Presa of romantic association with La Périchole, more accurately, la Pérricholi,

c

compound of *chola* and female dog or bitch, as popularly known, but, in fact, the dancer and actress Micaela Villegas, mistress of the Viceroy. His name in full, for it must be written down, was Manuel Amat y Junyent Planella Aymerich y Santa Pau, Viceroy from 1761 to 1766. He was a Catalan who, for all his noble-sounding name, had trained as an architect and military engineer, and it emerges from recent research that this lover of La Périchole not only built his villa the Quinta da Presa from his own designs but, also, the church of the Nazarenas in Lima, and on returning home the Virreina Palace, correctly Louis XVI in style, and the 'most important town house of the time' in Barcelona. It is a little as though Count Almaviva had designed his own town house in Seville, or, for the Quinta da Presa, an *estancia* outside the town, and we could see the very bed and its silken curtains for which Figaro and Susannah are taking the measurements when the curtain rises, the servants' hall where they ate their meals, a bedroom said to have been Cherubino's, and the steps that led down into the garden of the 'letter' song. Or am I alone in thinking that Lima, after Seville, a city which has been the setting for four operas,[1] is ideally suited for an operatic *mise en scène*! La Périchole, at any rate, is the heroine of Offenbach's enchanting operetta of that name, and as a subject she seems to call for more serious operatic treatment. As for the Quinta da Presa, it is exceedingly pretty in its pink and white stucco, and the *mestiza* actress and dancer who never lived here but had her house near by, must often have been here and walked in the charming garden at the back. It is the place perhaps of more musical association than any other in Latin America for no very clear reason except its memories of La Périchole, and yet most certainly it seduces and inspires.

What a contrast to this haunting by popular tunes of the Second Empire—by the 'letter' song, itself transposed by Meilhac and Haléry, Offenbach's librettists, from the letter sent by Manon to Des Grieux in *Manon Lescaut*, 'Je te jure, mon cher chevalier, que tu es l'idole de mon coeur . . . je rendrai quelque jour le dernier soupir, en croyant en pousser un d'amour'—by the other songs, 'Tu n'es pas beau, tu n'es pas riche,' or the Périchole's own song:

---

[1] *Don Giovanni, Marriage of Figaro, Barber of Seville*, and *Carmen*. Offenbach's operetta *La Périchole* is based upon *La Carrosse du Saint Sacrament*, a story by Prosper Mérimée. On occasion the Viceroy Amat is supposed to have called out after the actress had left in a temper, 'Perra Chola!', 'Ce que signifie chienne d'indigène,' and hence her name La Périchole.

Oh quel diner je viens de faire!
Et quel vin extraordinaire! . . .
Si ma parole est un peu vague,
Si tout en marchant je zigzague,
Et si mon oeil est égrillard
Il ne faut s'en étonner, car . . .
Je suis un peu grise . . .
Mais chut!
Faut pas qu'on le dise! . . .

What a contrast to these never-to-be-forgotten tunes, to this immortal popular music—one would think! Yet with inexorable time they have been forgotten and, now, no one remembers them—what a contrast a visit to the Guano Islands!

The *venue* being Ancón, now a seaside resort, but with 'the great aboriginal cemetery behind it' . . . 'dug in for centuries, first by native looters and later by archaeologists, and still yielding quantities of "mummies" to the spades of government scientists.'[1] Ancón of the huge circular tower of modern apartments, shaped like a gasometer, and of the yacht club and casino! But, also, along the sea front at Ancón there are charming pillared houses of one storey, in fact villas in the classical taste of the early years of independence so that Ancón is the Cheltenham, more still, the Brighton of Peru. No four-wheeled traffic is allowed along the sea front, but on the summer nights of January all the children ride their bicycles, trick-cyclist fashion down the promenade. Our floating headquarters was a yacht lying in harbour, and the next morning we went out to the Guano Islands.

They are only a few miles, three-quarters of an hour's sail, or less, off shore; and are the odd-shaped islands we saw on the way to Pachacamac, or so exactly like those as to make no difference, being indeed in the other direction from Lima, but a newcomer could be forgiven for not knowing this. It was a big, strong sea that morning, not in the least Pacific but with a wide swell to it, as though heaving and shaking itself after thousands of miles of freedom from the other side of the world against the shores of Peru. The Guano Islands even from a distance are like no other islands one has ever seen, rising like white or sticky white chalk hundreds of feet out of the water. They

[1] *The Ancient Civilizations of Peru*, by J. Alden Mason, Penguin Books, 1957, p. 101.

are, we all know, accretions of seabirds' droppings over hundreds or even thousands of years, and are, or were, as valuable as coal-mines. No one, by law, may shoot any of the seabirds, with the result that we are back in the age of Robinson Crusoe when they were not afraid of man. Nearing the islands is sensational because of the vast numbers of birds flying in long lines up and down and across the horizon. Through a pair of glasses one sees huge townships—there is no other word for them—dormitory towns of birds standing, wing to wing, on high shelves or plateaux of guano with no room to put a foot, webbed or human, in between them.

But there is something exciting and spectacular a few hundred feet in front of us, a shower, and then a downpour, a dive-bombing, of which you only see the splashes, and not the darting bodies. A concentrated dive-bombing just on one patch of water, where a shoal of fish has come to the surface, and it is over in a moment, but begins again like a downpour out of another cloud in the sky. The Stuka dive-bombing may be going on in several places at once, and as in an air-battle the action moves rapidly this way and that. Now we are round an island and in rough seas in the open, till we anchor off some kind of guano factory or station, the only sign of human habitation, on a promontory. There we lie for some little time, fishing by the simple expedient of putting a hook and line into the water, and always, and every time taking a fish, and every now and then a *pesch'rei* which is most excellent eating. The *pesch'rei* is the gourmet's favourite among all Pacific fishes, but *ceviche*, another kind of fish, is eaten straightaway in little morsels marinated in lemon or lime juice, and is very good indeed.

The next project is to row in close to the islands and watch the penguins. It is in the meantime cold and even a little raw, outwardly, but, in fact, intensely, scorchingly hot in the sun's rays, and absolutely necessary to wear a hat and, if possible, something to protect one's neck. This peculiar mingling of the tropic and antarctic is what is unique about the Guano Islands, a contradiction due to Humboldt's Current, or Gulf Stream in reverse, for it brings the Antarctic waters that make conditions possible for the seabirds and the shoals of fish they live on, up here to almost the latitude of the Amazon. But, first, we see great quantities of cormorants sitting on the rocks, and in profile, they could almost be long-haired poets or musicians. And pelicans, but not the simple sort that have been since the time of King Charles II on the water of St James's Park. These have immense, pterodactyl beaks, and about their shaggy heads some suspicion even, could one get nearer to them, of green hair, but for all their clumsiness they are most swift and elegant upon the wing.

The penguins, too, are not of the ordinary sort seen in zoos. These are smaller and darker and sleeker, without the white shirt fronts, and the amusement is to row in near to them, so that they rush and scramble down into the water. There, at once they are in their element until they get it into their heads to climb ashore again which they must accomplish by landing on the back of a wave, and then jumping and waddling up the rocks upon their flippers. It was only sad there was not time to watch them fall asleep, which, we were told, they do, lolling first to one side and then the other, till, finally they drop down flat on the rocks and fall fast asleep.

This Antarctic experience, in torrid heat, and just off Lima, is most curious, and a thing we had not anticipated. It is one of the typical, and basic contradictions in Peru which is, indeed, a land of extremes and opposites. The Guano Islands must inspire nearly everyone who has seen them with a wish for the Galapagos, far out in the cold sea-current, but not more than two-and-a-half to three hours distant to a million-aire with a private aeroplane. The Guano Isles are just the landscape for giant lizards of the race that live upon the Galàpagos except, that, on second thought, here is no vegetation, and there are no plants growing of any description. What does that huge lizard population feed upon for one has seen photographs of the rocks as thick with them as any seal colony? But this is as nothing to the mystery of Easter Island, two thousand miles away from us almost in a straight line, and with literally nothing in between, the nearest land beyond it in the farther direction being Pitcairn Island with its Seventh Day Adventist inhabitants descended from women of Tahiti and the mutineers of H.M.S. *Bounty*. At thought of which the clime seems to become warmer and no longer chilled by waters from the Antarctic, and it is no surprise that the next landfall could be the Marquesas where dwell the *vahines* whom Gauguin painted, and where Gauguin died. It was with such thoughts in mind that we rowed back to the ship from watching the penguins, to be met half-way there by what seemed a primitive human form, cat-faced, for as much as a cat has human physiognomy, and with military whiskers, seen on the instant it cleaved the wave. This was a big seal on its fishing ground, and it went under and was seen no more.

Another time we went in the opposite direction from Lima, passing again on the desert way Pachacamac, like one huge ossuary, half-dug up and bones flung down and left there, for that is what time has done to the stepped pyramid. Or is it that the bones in the end work themselves to the surface as a thorn in the flesh? Where we are bound for is La Onda, a little landlocked bay. But, first, we stop at La Maddalena where a seaside resort has been made out of the desert, trees planted, and a salt-water swimming pool made, the size of a lagoon. Beyond it, and on the same property, we were taken to see a private house, built out on the rock, and, in fact, only joined by a bridge to the mainland. The lighthouse-style residence has a marvellous view from it, amid the splashing and roaring of the waves for, once again, they are Pacific breakers. This is no Mediterranean, but one of the coasts of the world. The seas come in, unbroken and unchallenged. Crabs, of evil appearance, crawl, or scuttle at racing speed upon the rocks. They are of lurid colours never seen before, an electric scarlet were that possible, and a darker purple, and viridian green, but it is the scarlet ones, brighter than sealing-wax, that make rushes at each other and grab each other's tentacles, and give evidence of being cannibal. One can imagine a minor painter being absorbed by them and devoting many years of his life to their study.

After all this La Onda is in another world where there is not much more one wants to do than talk and look at the incredible colours of the sky. A huge rock opposite, across the water, shuts in the bay, and in this clear light is as big as a mountain. The scale of things is altered, and exists according to a canon of its own, just within the limits of what we can see, and no farther. It is a village of flat-roofed houses with stairs down to the water. A terrace for liberal conversation, here on the South Pacific, with a persistent reader of the *New Statesman*. The children go down to the shore to pick shell fish from the rocks, and we have *chupe de mariscos*, a fish soup, in beautiful green-hued mother-of-pearl seashells, and *ceviche* mentioned a little way back, and next evening, *corvina* which only becomes less interesting when we call it sea-bass. The season for *camarones* (big prawns) is over. We sit talking of everything under the sun, and watching the sun go down. In the morning it is marvellous to look out at the mist hiding the rock opposite, and above that the purest colours one has ever seen in any sky.

But it was time to begin looking at Lima in detail, and to visit the museums. The Archaeological, but it is called perhaps mistakenly the Anthropological Museum, is one of those institutions in which, according to taste, you can spend an hour or the greater part of a lifetime. Being no archaeologist by training it is only possible to write of it in very general terms, and to remark on its contents from an aesthetic and not a historical point of view. Their quantity is quite astounding, but we remember that it is as though we had the cooking utensils and domestic articles of a large population over many hundreds of years. We must presume that the dead were buried with nearly everything that they possessed. There is room after room of pots (*huacas*). It is as though all Greek tombs, and the contents of every Etruscan tomb are gathered here. All are present, and only line and aesthetic sense are lacking. To quote from a leading authority: 'Pottery is the consuming interest of the archaeologist—at least of the archaeologist working in America. This interest, however, is only in slight degree aesthetic; in fact, a bit of a broken plain unpainted vessel of unusual provenence is of more importance to him than an artistic creation from a better known region.'[1] But how few of the ceramics are 'aesthetic creations', or anything approaching that! On the other hand they display a high degree of skill, and are of absorbing interest as illustrations of pre-Incaic life. Perhaps it is just because they could have been specially commissioned to illustrate archaeological or medical treatises, or other specialized scientific interests, that they are not works of art. Whole shelves of pots portraying physical deformations, or illustrations of recognizable diseases welcomed by the medical profession, do not add up to works of art. Or there are the Mochica portrait vases which are no better nor worse than Toby jugs, excepting only that they are a thousand, or even fifteen hundred years old.

Other cultures, Chimú, for instance show the same ingenuity in their ceramics, and are more aesthetically satisfying when they are confined to black-ware vessels; but the Nazca polychrome pottery is of another standard, though the epithet 'lovely' applied to it by the same authority hardly fits the case. His suggested classification of the designs on the pottery as Monumental Cat-Demon developing into Cursive or Man-

[1] J. Alden Mason, *op. cit.*, p. 258.

Cactus well describes their character. The Cat-Demon is much in evidence with pin-point pupils to its eyes, and alarming whiskers; but, as well, there are ingenious and delightful birds, that are clearly pelicans, cleverly stylized, and flat saucers each with a springing dolphin that fits its circle. Coming out of these rooms filled with pots from floor to ceiling, and preferring by far the Nazca, we find ourselves in a dark room given over to trephined skulls—skulls that have had the operation of trepanning performed upon them—of surgical interest, mainly, and also, artificially deformed skulls.

This latter must have been the most curious of all sights in the pre-Columbian world. It is something to which no person alive has seen the living parallel. We are all, in order to start the theme, familiar from portraits with the Habsburg and Bourbon physiognomy, a trait which was produced over the centuries through intermarriage, or, in fact, by selective breeding. Something of the same sort must have occurred among the Incas who, to strengthen its probability, married their own sisters.[1] This practice of skull deformation by binding the infant's head was common all over the American continent. Very curious instances of it are to be found in the engravings to Catlin's *North American Indians* (1841), and particularly among the tribe of Flatheads whose foreheads were compressed with wooden boards from childhood. The practice prevailed, also, to an extreme degree among the Maya where it is a conspicuous feature in nearly all their sculptures and their rarer paintings. We may be certain that among the Inca, and pre-Incaic priests and rulers, the physiognomy was of extreme type from the combined results of skull-binding and incestuous marriage. Something missing from the world is the live study of these living specimens of heredity. Here it is to be seen, dead, and in the form of immensely high, elongated and slanting foreheads. How much we would like to see them clothed in flesh, and walking! There could be a gallery from all over pre-Columbian America of the most extraordinary looking human individuals there have ever been.

An idea of the sartorial appearance of one portion, at least, of the

---

[1] 'The last several emperors married their full sisters, and nobles were allowed to wed their half-sisters. . . . In the earlier years of the empire, the emperor married the daughter of a neighbouring ruler, as among recent European royalty, but in the last three or four generations before the Conquest his person had become so exalted that none but his own sister could be considered a fit consort. Here was the *ne plus ultra* of the idea of aristocracy, of blue blood; none but a replica could be an equal'. J. Alden Mason, op. cit., pp. 151, 182.

mysterious American Indian nation may be gained from the dresses and textiles on view in the circular sub-Albert Hall in this Anthropological Museum, but it is a depressing background for them. The hall is dark and gloomy. The glass cases are of the dusty kind used for natural history specimens. Also, the prevailing tones of dark reds and browns in the textiles only serve still further to darken their own setting. If only this difficulty could be overcome the Lima Anthropological Museum would have one of the most rewarding and interesting exhibits in the world. The textiles and dresses are chiefly from Nazca and Paracas, the latter being one of the great and lasting mysteries of human history for nothing whatever is known about the weavers of Paracas, not even their tribal name. Their date, which is somewhere in the eight centuries between 400 B.C. and 400 A.D., is practically the only ascertained fact in their history, and this has been done by carbon-dating. The rest is all mystery—Paracas is a desert peninsula in the south of Peru, described as consisting of red sand, red sand and nothing more. There is not a human being within miles. But the bones of the early inhabitants are protruding from the sand. And bundles of rags are blown about in the wind. But, as recently as between 1925 and 1930, discovery was made of the Paracas Cavernas and the Paracas Necropolis, two different forms of burial. In the first, the bodies were found in bottle-shaped chambers in the rock, as many as fifty-five together. Their heads were artificially deformed, and many had been trepanned. In the Necropolis were found no fewer than four hundred and twenty-nine mummy bundles, the bodies sitting, knees drawn up, in baskets, and wearing magnificent woven and embroidered cotton shrouds. Such, then, are the clothes of Paracas. All this elaborate work was done purely for mortuary use, never to be seen again, though it is clear that the wrapping was not accomplished at one session, but that the tomb-chambers were opened and new clothes added perhaps at intervals of years. That whole area is one huge graveyard and I was told, whether correctly or not I do not know, that an estimated twenty-six thousand burials remain to be unearthed.

The textiles on view at Lima should be among the finest so far found, but they are seen by few persons compared to that public which has the opportunity of visiting the National Gallery in Washington where the Robert Woods Bliss pre-Columbian collection is shown. There, too, compact in number, they are seen to better advantage. They can, also, be studied in magnificent colour plates,[1] the introduction to which tells that the Peruvian textiles are woven either of spun cotton or of vicuña hair, which is the finest of any known animal, with a count of about two thousand five hundred hairs to the inch, adding that the animal is entirely wild, cannot be domesticated, and that as many as forty of them must be killed in order to make a coat. Under the Incas, vicuña hunts only took place once in every four years. It is especially the mantles of Paracas that are magnificent. The patterns are excessively, indeed inexplicably curious, being really and authentically something from another, or new world. But all that has to do with Paracas is odd and cannot be explained. Why, for instance, had a 'large proportion' of those fifty-five corpses been trepanned? Were they all, quite simply, warriors who had suffered head injury in battle, the favourite weapon being a mace or club? It seems too coincidental an explanation. Or were they operated on to let evil spirits out of their heads? Or for the direct opposite, to let in wisdom.[2]

If the technique is marvellous, the woven or embroidered patterns are no less far fetched and extraordinary. A mantle border in the collection at Washington has a design of little demon-like figures doing some kind of dance, a staff in one hand and a fan in the other, and leaning over backwards in order to leer straight at us from their masked faces, from which hang fringes of false beard. Their colouring seems arbitrary and according to no rule, and alternately to right or left of each figure is its own tiny facsimile in exactly the same posture. What is it all about? Does it mean anything? Or is it mere ornament? If that, why devote so inordinate an amount of time to it, only to put it away in darkness. But the mantles of Paracas of which Peru, given the opportunity, could put on a magnificent display and always with the hope that more of them may be found, are in their turn almost simple in design beside the ponchos of the coastal Tiahuanaco culture. This is a little later in date than Paracas, from A.D. 500 to A.D. 1000, deriving from Tiahuanaco which is in Bolivia on the far side of Lake Titicaca, but having migrated to the coast of the Pacific. They are at any rate to a personal taste, of a simple complexity beyond parallel,

---

[1] In the Phaidon publication, London, 1957. The section dealing with the textiles, from which we quote, is by Joy Mahler.

[2] Medical opinion suggests that there is very little bony growth round the hole in the skull, which is generally about an inch in diameter, and that the 'patient' could seldom have lived for more than ten days to a fortnight after the operation. This makes one more curious than ever as to why they were operated upon.

and utterly and entirely inexplicable as pattern units for the reason that they are so far removed from the norm of ordinary experience. Each unit could be a hieroglyph meaning everything or nothing. The field of the ponchos is usually made up of bands of blocks that may, or may not repeat themselves. All over patterns of 'eye-mouth', 'weeping eye and mouth', or stepped grec, with perpetual feline or puma hintings are identifiable, but hopeless of interpretation. In fact, no one has any idea what they are about, and all one can say of them is that no master of naivetés, no Paul Klee or Joan Miró could do better. The coastal Tiahuanaco, even more than the Paracas while wholly different from those, may be the most original and effective textiles ever made. It is only sad in thinking of them that the extravagant claims put forward for the antiquity of Tiahuanaco by Posnansky,[1] and others, should now be discounted, together with the theory that this mysterious place that we were lucky enough to visit was once the centre of a great and forgotten Megalithic Empire. Would it were true, and that the marvellous caps and shrouds and ponchos were ten or fifteen or twenty thousand years old, instead of merely a few hundred years older than the Bayeux tapestry! They could not give a more thrilling mental picture of a Megalithic reign. This is disproved, but all said and done these fabrics keep their mystery.

That various of the Peruvian pre-Inca cultures had an astonishing genius in their textiles is beyond dispute and it is, therefore, the more curious that their ceramics should be at pedestrian or jog-trot level, however interesting the information that can be deduced from them. There is a private collection in Lima devoted wholly to the pottery found upon the owner's estate. A large building has been erected only to house it. No fewer than forty-five thousand objects are assembled there, all from this one *estancia*, which gives an idea of what is still to be found in Peru, the richest archaeological terrain in the known world. Here, the *huacas* are arranged according to subject, so that it is like working in a library from the subject, and not the author's index, a more sensible system than to have to run through culture after culture. Nazca, Mochica, Chimú and so forth, though, of course, within those limits the different cultures are arranged together. If the aesthetic level is not high, the historical interest is so entire in all its aspects that this private museum has the attributes of a historical information bureau.

[1] *Tiahuanaco, The Cradle of American Man*, 2 Vols.: Arthur Posnansky, New York, 1946.

That is to say, every conceivable topic from the mutilation of limbs for criminal offences in one culture to the prevalence of eye disease and ophthalmia in another, can be studied here. There are even Mochica portrait vases of Toby jug type showing the same individual person at different ages, including a rogues' gallery series of a one-eyed man. There is a 'dwarfs and freaks' section, a medical department with no detail omitted of every disease under the sun, and an erotic sidewing which is not at all appetizing owing to the physical ugliness of the participants and partners in so varied a hand-list of sexual commitments. The effect of it all is pre-Inca Peru presented in sections from one enormous strip cartoon, but the compendium of information of all descriptions is staggering, merely in bulk and from accumulation. Here is book illustration on every conceivable topic, ready-made.

In a darkened room, skilfully lit, are the real works of art in this collection. Here are the legendary golden *caciques* of the Andes in all their splendour, a marvellous and an inspiring spectacle. Who can have been these golden princes? For the names given to their cultures by the archaeologists would mean no more to them than to tell the *condor real* of the high cordilleras of its Latin name. No Chimú, or Charín, or Nazca, would answer to his name. A golden breastplate is one of the loveliest objects shown, beautiful alike in texture, in design, and in poetical association. Golden crowns and sceptres there are, as well, and other golden objects that would have awoken the cruel instincts of the *conquistadores*.

Another and smaller private collection in Lima has beautiful golden masks and diadems. If we ask ourselves if they would be as lovely in another metal, in iron, or copper, it is to beg the question, unless we are to concede that a rose petal is as pretty as a leaf of laurel. The Indians liked gold for its glitter, not for its intrinsic value. It bought nothing, and was of no use for barter. Therefore, it must have had for them some of the poetical association of imagery that it has for ourselves, and as goldsmiths, and as *caciques* and owners of the golden masks, they responded in something of the same way to its invitation. The coruscation of such golden artifacts at the end of a long room is so remarkable that one may think its value in their eyes was its glitter, even though muted, in the darkness of the burial chamber, the only principle of light in eternal darkness. A golden mask, then, has reason and purpose whether found in the Peruvian desert or in Agamemnon's Tomb. Ear plugs, and golden pins and ear-rings, are in supplement to this golden collection which is neither too big, nor too small. It allows the golden objects to be seen in something of the dignity of isolation that was intended for them.

An attribute that attaches in our minds to the American Indian is his robe of feathers. This is true of all of them, from the Red Indian chieftain with his crest of war eagle's quills falling from the back of his forehead down to his feet, to Montezuma's green robe which was formed of quetzal tail feathers. In Peru it was especially the Chimú who excelled in featherwork, and at a later date the Chosen Women or Virgins of the Sun wove the vicuña shirts and feather tunics worn by the Incas. But so far, one had not come across any sensational pieces of this featherwork, and might even begin to question the eulogies by Jesuit, and other early chroniclers describing it. However, in a little and beautifully arranged museum a short way from Lima, on a site just in the foothills where an ancient fort has been restored, and where there is an Indian burial ground, are two marvellously prepared and set up mummy-bundles, if that is the correct term for them. This pair of *caciques* or chieftains are shown sitting or squatting in glass cases, the effect being that they are reigning in state in an enthroned posture which is most solemn and impressive. Their feather mantles have been cleaned and should be very nearly in their pristine colours. In particular, one feather mantle has pale blue feathers as bright as a jay's wing. One would like to know from what bird it comes. These figures, owing to the skilful arrangement, are more marvellously, more authentically 'Indian' than anything in the Anthropological Museum. A few, and only a few, chosen pieces of ceramics enhance the effect of it all by their underplaying and their reticence.

It is a wonderful experience to behold the feathered 'Indians' of legend even in the dust and decrepitude of time. For they are just as one imagined them and hoped that they would be. If China was pre-eminently the silken land, Amerindia was the feathered continent, not one kingdom only, but many. The feather robes of the Peruvians and Mexicans made so strong an impression upon the early voyagers that up to the time of Louis XIV, and later, 'Indians' in paintings and in tapestries are to be known and recognized by their feathers. Perhaps, then there was a much larger bird population, in the sense in which parts of South Africa were one vast game preserve, roamed over by herds in their hundreds of thousands, within the memory of persons still alive. Certainly, to-day, from all Honduras and Guatemala it would not be possible to remake Montezuma's robe of quetzal feathers. The quetzal, though rare and precious, must have inhabited a much larger area than now. Probably all birds were commoner, or there could not have been this impression that the distinguishing mark of the 'Indians' was their plumed head-dresses and tunics. At long last in an ancient fort outside Lima one had seen evidence that the old reports as to the beauty of this featherwork were true.

A museum of quite different sort remained still to be seen. For we had not yet been round the churches of Lima, and only the Torre Tagle Palace had established itself as epitome of the Colonial style. But, in the meantime, there was that large and brand new museum, referred to earlier as looking like a municipal casino, still too big for the works of art it contains, and likely to remain so, for where pictures are concerned it is easy to exaggerate the merits of Colonial painting. It has some four or five beautifully coloured rugs hung upon the walls, proving that the native Indian genius for textiles descended in some part into the *mestizo* population of two hundred years ago, and it has one or two most delightful paintings of archangels as musketeers. They are in a category by themselves, and coming from remote regions of Peru and Bolivia, to which they are indigenous, are as unique in their own way as the wooden balconies or *miradores* of Lima. But let us wait to describe them in their proper place, only here and now admiring their Court dress, embroidered surcoats, elegant shoes and breeches, great pair of wings, and plumed Cavalier hats. One of them is loading his arquebuse. Another of the musketeers is even taking aim and shooting as we go by. What curious fairy-tale figures from the Court of King Florestan XXIV, strayed from some Royal shooting-party on to the Altiplano, the high plain of Bolivia and Peru. Lost, one opines, but keeping here because of the alpacas and vicuñas, and the good shooting, as a shot seems to ring out in the—aesthetically— empty halls, and we move away.

There are often old paintings, though not of this degree of fantasy, in private houses in Lima, and always they are attributed to the school of Cuzco and called Cuzqueñan. Usually they are in association with the Cuzqueñan mirrors that one notices, almost in spite of oneself, immediately on reaching Lima. Impossible not to be aware of them for they have much individuality, and are not like anything one has seen before. They are, generally, very deep and stand out a long way from the wall. One does not know, at first, whether they must have come from churches or private houses, and in the end one is still uncertain, but leaning to the opinion that they come from sacristies and from convents, certainly. This, after seeing the convent churches in Cuzco, for the interiors of one or two of those have whole areas of looking-glass. The quality of the Cuzqueñan mirrors is their gilding, done with the gold of Peru, and their variety of design, which is indeed amazing, and one would think it scarcely possible to work so many changes out of gilt wood and looking-glass. Star patterns are numerous, and there are octagons, dodecagons, and so forth, always with little surrounding strips or panes of mirror. No two Cuzqueñan mirrors, it would seem, are ever the same. The patterns must be as many in number as there are abstract mathematical designs in Moorish tilework, and an amateur painter who has nothing better to do could make a book of them.

The private museum we had still to see was the huge collection of Cuzqueñan art belonging to Señor Pedro de Osma. So varied is it in scope, and so full in presentation, that before going to Cuzco one wonders how much can be left there. It must house the contents of how many sacristies and *parlatorios* of convents! A feminine art, and it would come as no surprise to be told most of the carving and gilding was done in a convent workshop. One can imagine the *mestiza* nuns with their skirts tucked up, sawing away and planing, except that there is no level or flat surface anywhere, everything is on the move, and not coming forward but convoluting and contorting, taking the longest possible time to get there, and in fact advancing by the most circuitous route, and sprinkling itself with gold dust on the way. A museum, for that it certainly is, and withal, something of a *boutique fantasque* and a Dr Coppelius' workroom or laboratory in one. In room after room are paintings in gilded frames and golden mirrors hung from floor to ceiling, with statues, and shrines that open and shut, and statuettes, and whole collections of silver laid out to view on tables. There are the silver pins, huge in size, which the *mestiza* women use to fasten the front of their dresses and that at other times do duty as a spoon. There are silver ladies' stirrups, that are one of the hallmarks of Peru. For contrast, there are one or two small sculpture groups of the school of Quito, which one can see at a glance to be quite different in style. They have more of what antique dealers in Italy call *epoca* about them, meaning that they have more 'period', and are nearer to the fountain head. One begins to feel already some rivalry between Quito and Cuzco. Did one but know more about it, doubtless one would be able to tell things made in Arequipa, or in Ayacucho, from those of Cuzco, for distances are so great in Peru that there are strong local differences in style. However that may be, an hour or two here goes by happily in seeing things, important or unimportant, the like of which one has not seen before.

We had now, one hopes, begun to get the measure of Lima. Perhaps no other city has so many small gardens with such lovely flowers in them. One had grown to understand that iconoclasts had ruined most of the churches that had not already been destroyed in numerous earthquakes, leaving only one or two of the smallest and humblest of all unscathed. One has not to expect too much, then, of the churches of Lima. To do so, is to be disappointed. On the other hand, it is a city of enormous character, bearing every sign that for many hundreds of years it was the capital of South America. There are legendary stories of its riches; of how when the Viceroy, the Duke of Palata, made his entry into the city in 1682, the street of La Merced for the length of two town-quarters was paved with silver ingots;[1] and of how there were four thousand mule-drawn calèches in Lima in the early eighteenth century, probably a greater number than there were hackney-carriages in London or Paris. If there are not many of its antiquities left, there is all of its character to explore, and not less of that than there is in Spanish cities like Barcelona or Valencia.

But now it was time to go away from Lima, and we had been upon the point of starting for Arequipa when there was the disastrous earthquake of January, 1960, with luckily not many lives lost, but the city was laid in ruins. Moreover, the earthquake shocks were continuing day after day, the initial one, we were told, having been a vertical earthlift of ten feet, in view of which, and of the breakdown of water and electricity and all other services, and the roads and railways broken,

---

[1] *Baroque and Rococo in Latin America*, by Pál Kelemen, Macmillan & Co., New York, 1951, pp. 7, 8.

Cathedral square, Lima, with group of *Tapadas*, by Johann Montz Rugendas (1802-1858)

Tapadas at Lima by J. M. Rugendas (1802–1858)

it was decided we should miss Arequipa, and go instead to Cuzco, seeing Machu Picchu on the way. This we did; while for the sake of a continuous narrative, appearing in our next chapter never to have been away. But in fact, we had left Lima and come back to it.

D

◆◆◆◆◆◆◆◆◆◆◆◆◆◆◆◆◆◆◆◆◆◆◆◆◆◆◆◆

LIMA *(continued)*

RETURNED, AND AS WE WILL explain when the time comes, relieved to be able to breathe again after the rigours of the Altiplano, we were now guests of the city of Lima and staying in the Country Club in San Isidro, another of the flowering suburbs. Here it was beautifully quiet at night and after the late diners had left, for dinner is *à l'heure Espagnole*, one could look out on the lights of Lima. But it was no less beautiful in the early morning when the flowers had all the garden to themselves. One could look down on the park of palm trees, while the bougainvillaea at the window was gently trembling in the morning wind. There were scarlet and yellow hibiscus only a foot or two below, and that paragon the double-rose hibiscus not far away. But, quite early, children invaded the near swimming pool and the babel of voices started that was to last all day. This would die down a little during the 'sacred hour' of siesta, and by six o'clock all would be quiet again. Sunset comes early and the exquisite scented evening follows, or so it is at least out here among the flowers, if for most of the population it is the evening rush hour. And now in midsummer February it is the pleasantest hour of the day perhaps even in the Barrieras. So far we had only seen the pleasant aspects of Lima, going to visit the shops and churches, and delighted by the avenues of palm trees and the flowering suburbs of the town.

How lovely it was to be here again in Lima! Just to think of the fantastic improbability of being here at all! Here at the other side of the world with the Pacific Ocean only a mile or two away. How unbelievable that the Spanish *Conquistadores* should have got here more than four hundred years ago, the more incredible for having seen with one's own eyes Trujillo where Pizarro came from, in Estremadura which is the remotest and most backward part of Spain. No wonder he left Trujillo, a town where in 1947 we saw thin and famished persons in the streets, and children who looked hungry. In the Plaza Mayor at Trujillo is the 'House of Pizarro', so called, a little roofless cyclopaean hovel with a large round arched doorway; and in the church of Santa María Concepción, which was boarded up and in total darkness, we struck a light and found the kneeling figure of a knight in stone. This is the effigy of Pizarro, whose father was a swineherd in the acorn woods of Estremadura, and to whose lot fell some of the most extreme hazards and adventures that have ever befallen mortal man. His body, or what passes for his body, is entombed in Lima Cathedral, and the skull is fastened to the skeleton with silver wire. His descendant, the Marquesa de la Conquista, still has a 'palace' in the town, with a corner balcony of Renaissance times, and a splendid coat-of-arms. At Cáceres, the other town of the conquerors of Peru and Mexico, not far away, are the granite-built town houses, or *casas solariegas* of the *Conquistadores*, with huge doors and coats-of-arms. On the front of one old house is the escutcheon of the Moctezuma family, with the sun in the middle of the field of arms. Little wonder these men of violence left Cáceres and Trujillo! And impossible here in Lima not to remember their birthplace, and think of them!

In Lima, once more, and what shall we do this fine February morning? Shall we call upon the Lord Mayor of Lima, the Señor Alcalde Hector García Ribeyro, in the Town Hall or Alcaldería, which is in the square opposite the Presidential Palace, and next door to the Cathedral? A fine building with floors and walls of native wood and marble, and in the library, which has huge mahogany bookcases, we will be shown the first charter of the city of Lima, signed by Pizarro with his mark because he could not write his name. Also, the first book printed in Peru; but no document with the mark of any Indian, or, indeed, relic of Atahuallpa, or other of the Incas. They went like ghosts, and are now but shadows. That is all long ago. But if it had not been Pizarro and Cortés it would only have been some other Spaniard who put an end to the Incas and the Aztecs; and if not a Spaniard, a Portuguese, a Dutchman, or an Englishman. Our own colonization of Canada and Australia and New Zealand took place largely, if not entirely in the nineteenth century during the steamship era. But the Spaniards set up the city of Lima thousands of miles away from Spain, and a civilization like that in Seville or in Salamanca, long before Bath became a focus of fashion, and a generation or two earlier than the Plague and Fire of London. And we walk up the stair that could be the staircase of an opera house, and past the ballroom and through the marble halls of the Alcaldería in order to tell the Alcalde of our journey to Cuzco and to Lake Titicaca, and to thank him for having had it all arranged for us. He is a fervent Anglophile, despite having been taken away from his home in Lima and sent to school in England at an early age. Here and now is the place to say that but for his forethought and kindness we would have seen much less of Peru, and that little in less propitious circumstances. We had come to thank the Alcalde, and also to make the final arrangements for the speech I was to deliver at the Town Hall in honour of El Greco and Velázquez on which occasion, too, I was given the Freedom of the City.

During the next day or two we busied ourselves with seeing the churches which it would be idle to pretend are not rather disappointing. Perhaps the prettiest of them all, and one of the most humble, is the little chapel in the square beyond the Anthropological Museum. It has gilded woodwork in plenty, but leaves little behind it but a pleasing memory. Thence, once more, to the Cathedral to be disillusioned by the choir stalls though they are proclaimed by recent authority to be superior in their figure work to any Baroque stalls in Spain excepting those at Málaga.[1] One or two churches, La Merced and San Agustín, have richly carved façades, of richness without distinction, and invariably it is a disappointment to go inside. Jesú y María, with some remnants of Rococo elegance, is perhaps the most rewarding. Always, of course, being a Spanish city there is good woodcarving, and at Santo Domingo and San Agustín are sacristies with superb vestment cupboards in some dark hard wood like mahogany. Or there are the wooden sanctuary grilles carved in the technique of cast iron gates at Las Nazarenas, the church built by the Viceroy Amat, lover of La Périchole; or the pair of Rococo opera-box tribunes in San Carlos, together with one of the carved pulpits that are often to a point of monotony the main interest in churches in Peru. This, it is only fair to remark, is one of the most graceful of them all with its bombé, closed balcony and steepled or tiered canopy.

Much of the social life of seventeenth- and eighteenth-century Lima

[1] *Art and Architecture in Spain and Portugal and their American Dominions*, by George Kubler and Martin Soria, Penguin Books, London, 1959, p. 177.

centred round the nunneries, as in all Latin cities. They were conducted upon the same scale of lavishness as the monasteries, that of San Francisco having more than two hundred monks in it by the middle of the seventeenth century, while another monastery, La Merced, had no fewer than five cloisters. The monks taught in schools and ran hospitals, while the nuns were similarly employed and worked, also, with their needles. And, as well, they were expert at making all kinds of sweets and cordials. The nuns of one convent in Lima make a sweetmeat resembling the Yemas de San Isidro of Seville that must be of like Andalusian-Moorish origin. A lot of research work on this delightfully unimportant topic which yet is part of the history of Lima and of other old towns in Peru remains to be done, and the daughter of a Peruvian friend is engaged upon it and had already got the permission of the Archbishop to enter the convents in Lima and in the north of Peru in order to take down the secret recipes of the nuns, which work completed she has the intention of working through the southern half of Peru and publishing the results. It would be a pity were this feminine lore which has accrued through four centuries to be lost, for it will never come again.

At about this time the friend who had instigated and encouraged our whole journey arrived in Lima from his post at Washington, and we spent several afternoons with him in the old parts of the town. We admired the *miradores*, whether wooden balconies or conning towers to catch the evening cool, and went to the Torre Tagle Palace, and to anything else that savoured of old Lima. We visited the dealers in llama and alpaca rugs, in a street of shops where no motors are allowed, learning in the course of it a trade secret which is that they are brought down in bales from the mountains, largely from the region of Ayacucho, and if good ones are not in evidence you must wait for the next consignment to come in. Only poor specimens were visible on this occasion, but better ones had arrived by the following week. Besides this, there was the jeweller's shop of Laffi, an Italian woman artist, who makes the flexible copper fishes with wings and tail of silver and glass which again form one of the hallmarks of Peru, and, as well, designs jewellery of Tiahuanaca and other pre-Columbian patterns. This excursion into arts and crafts is not complete without mention of the objects in the workshop of Mr Truman Bailey who had lately died, but we saw the crafts revived by him, typical of which are certain wooden figures of birds (pigeons?) with silver heads and wings for table ornaments; and adaptations of the Pucará bulls, pottery figures in their origin that we were to see later on exposed for sale at the railway station of Pucará; but these are again of that same dark wood, with silver horns and dewlaps, or all silver, when they make a decidedly characterful impression with their curled hair and stalwart attitudes. Finally, in a shop run by the wife of Victor von Hagen, the archaeologist, there are the Sylvania prints, textiles with designs by her taken from Inca and other pre-Columbian motifs.

In a house across the river in the old part of Lima our friend has installed his collection of bullfight paintings and engravings. A pink-washed building with green shutters and a pleasant atmosphere of summer or, at least, siesta time. It is a museum of tauromachy, and probably the most complete one in existence. There are paintings of bull-fights by J. D. Becquer (1810-41) who was poet as well as artist, and leading spirit in the Romantic movement in Madrid round about 1830. Pictures, also, by M. R. de Guzmán, an amateur painter of the same family as the Empress Eugénie, but the best artist of the group. In paintings of this school which is little known, if at all, either in England or the United States, are to be noted the brown and white or dappled bulls of a strain rarely to be seen now in the bull-ring. There are portraits of Montes, the famous matador, admired by Theóphile Gautier who calls him 'the first swordsman of Spain', whiskered, of heavy build more like a picador, and wearing a vivid blue *traje de luces* or 'suit of lights'. The old bull-ring of Seville appears in a lithograph by 'Spanish' Lewis with the president's box towering up like a theatre proscenium at the bull-fight on Easter Sunday, *Domingo da Gloria*. A bull of the dappled breed charges a picador, and the shadow of the Giralda falls across the bloodstained arena. That or another shade, making the division of the public into the classical *sol y sombre*, extends into our own time with the bull-fight subjects of Picasso. This is but one of many bull-fight lithographs, some of rare excellence being by obscure artists as, for instance, those in illustration of an improbable annual of the eighteen-forties called *The Andalusian Album*. It is to be presumed that both this ephemeral and *The Sketches in Spain* of J. F. Lewis circulated among veterans of the Peninsular War which had ended only some twenty years before. All in all, this is an unique opportunity of seeing pictures and drawings of the bull-fight. They are, it may be, even more violently Spanish through being seen here in Lima, in an ancient Spanish city thousands of miles removed from Spain.

That evening, or it may have been the next, we were given a typically Peruvian dinner in an old-fashioned hotel in the old part of the town. *Chupe de mariscos*, which is just what its name would suggest, soup of shellfish like a semi-tropical *boullabaisse*, appeared on the table; there was *ceviche* and *corvina* and *anticuchos*, and we drank *chicha morada*, a pink-coloured liquid made from purple corn. This was consumed in the time of the Incas and of many another and earlier pre-Columbian dynasty, though nowadays it is prepared by more modern methods and no longer by the chewing or mastication process that in the old days was their native parallel to the treading of the grape. Later on, our friend and host ventured into the bar where the *aficionados* of Lima fore-gather of an evening, and seldom has one seen such a welcome. More is known about bullfighting, and there is a higher level of intelligent talk about it and other kindred subjects, in Lima than in any other town of Latin America. Certainly it is a heartening experience to be in the company of someone who on that evening seemed to be the most popular person in his native city. Here, and in the summer night in the street outside, no one had any intention of stopping talking for several hours. It transported one to the streets of Madrid or Seville, and there were all the noises of a Spanish town.

But the time had come for our one unpleasant experience, and we started on the following afternoon on an inspection of the Barrieras. The hour fixed was five o'clock, and the reason given that at that hour the smell would be less. The Barrieras, as said earlier, are one huge slum or series of slums lived in, if that is the word for it, by three hundred thousand persons. The approach, or rather, descent to them, although there is no hill to come down, is gradual and just takes you to poorer and poorer quarters of the town. At last you seem to be driving almost outside the city along some kind of embankment that at times stands in the way and prevents you looking over it to what lies below. But, eventually, it flattens as though no longer caring, or unable any more to keep up the pretence, and reveals the Barrieras, first indicated by some smoking hills or slag heaps of sinister darkness that I take to be the method of disposing of the night soil of three hundred thousand persons where there is no sewerage of any sort.

Now row after row of grey adobe hovels all huddled together lie just below us, most of them roofless because it never rains. Many are not even made of adobe, but are merely screen walls of some kind of rush or reed. From above the owners appear to keep turkeys and chickens who share the hovels with them. It may even be a less poor quarter of the giant slum. And now the driver turns directly into the Barrieras, and we are advancing at about five miles an hour, the maximum speed possible, down an enormous perspective of adobe hovels, a straight avenue some hundred and fifty feet wide, perhaps two or three miles long, and floored with huge round pebbles as big, or bigger than, your hand. They must be painful to tread upon.

Every two or three hundred yards there is a water tank in the middle of the roadway, and always a queue waiting at it. This is the only supply of water. It is an ugly scene of desolation with the one-storey houses bordering the long, endless and empty road for as far as the eyes can see, and only an occasional store of humble sort. One begins to think those huge cobbles have been put down on purpose to prevent people collecting together, or moving far away from their houses. The intersecting avenues are no less cheerless. How far do they have to walk in order to get to their work? How much of each day do they spend in transit? For that matter, how many are working, and how many unemployed? It is no use to be hypocritical and deny that there are, or were, dreadful slums in England. A mining village, Arkwright Town, a few miles from my old home in Derbyshire, is an appalling, heart-chilling horror in its dirty red brick, with the squalid rows of outside lavatories. Doubtless there were worse village slums in Durham. It is the scale of the Barrieras which is the nightmare. We entered two or three houses which were part of a new building scheme. The floors were earthen, there was no water, no lighting, and no sanitation. But within those limitations it was scrupulously clean, in spite of the chickens running about even onto the flat roof, and sharing the accommodation with the family. However, this was one of the better houses. After about a mile or two we came back to the older part of the Barrieras where the hovels are made just of sticks and straw lattice, and we went into one of them where there was a woman with a large family. That is to say, the man had gone off, having married her. It is one of the most serious problems. A woman has no rights at all, and the man can then return and claim her money, if she has any. It was an appalling habitation for a family of human beings, and utterly degrading. They are Indians, who have not the standard of living of the very poorest Europeans, and the villages they came from would be no better in respect of light or heat or sanitation. But, at least, those would be small agglomerates of population, and not a huge slum town in the capital city of Peru. They must be ready victims to any form of political agitation, and the riches and delights of Lima are but an hour's march away.

This is the worst national problem that confronts Peru. It is quite beyond the resources of Lima to rehouse more than ten or fifteen thousand persons in a year. And during that time perhaps as many, or it may be even double the number, have come down from the mountains into the Barrieras. There is this tendency all over the world for people from the country to flock into the towns. It would seem there is no solution except to build up local industries that might keep people in their home localities. But this would mean higher wages than a new industry could afford. The population of the Barrieras is a torrent that might burst its banks and carry all away with it. In ten years' time the catastrophe could only be worse than now, unless something is done, and done quickly. All wise Peruvians are aware of this, but there is very little they can do.

The hideous and aching monotony of the human labyrinth is in a sense almost relieved where it becomes worse still, which is nearer the town proper, and indeed nearly in the shadow of those smoking dunghills. Here is the stupendous and hellish vision of a river, probably that on which Lima stands, but metamorphosed, and like a river in Tartarus, flowing in a deep worn channel half below ground. The effect is nearly indescribable, and one of the worst things one has ever seen. The walls of this gully must be fifty or sixty feet deep, or more, and the soil or rock is of grey substance as though puddletrenched. There are human habitations on both sides or edges of it. What the view from it must be on a soiled morning, or the stained evening! Perhaps the painter has never lived who could do it justice. I must add that all sensible Peruvians are acutely conscious of the Barrieras. Far from putting obstacles in one's way, they urge one to go and see it for oneself, knowing it is a most urgent problem. The Alcalde arranged our visit, and we only missed by a day attending the ceremony when the wife of the President of Peru was to turn on the lights of a district of the

Barrieras where electricity had been installed. One must be glad to have been shown the Barrieras and to know the seriousness of the situation is appreciated.

After this experience it may be a little while before one can stomach the more conventional delights of life which one may feel one has no right to enjoy while other human beings are living in that way. It is a mood in which even the flowers of Lima lose their loveliness. The only remedy for this is to contrast the past and present in the knowledge that in so many countries of the world life is now worth living for millions who could never have enjoyed it before. If we narrow the subject down to the historical past of Lima it is to acknowledge there is but little visual evidence of that life in the matter of paintings and drawings. This is where the name of Pancho Fierro must come in, the half-caste or mulatto who made a large number of drawings of life in Lima during the third and fourth decades of the last century. He is not a good artist, he is hardly an artist at all, but he tells us what we want to know. If indeed he is little more than a satirical draughtsman of amateur status who had to live by selling his drawings we must remember how many other, more famous cities of that day went unrecorded. What contemporary draughtsman was there who gives us the picture of popular life of the time in Dublin, or Liverpool, or in New York? Lima was lucky in having even a minor artist like Pancho Fierro to record its daily life. He was born in 1803; and died in 1879; and some two hundred and thirty-eight of his water colours bound in two albums are the property of the municipality of Lima. Countless more drawings by him are in private collections. Pancho Fierro was especially fond of masqued processions, street dancers, and musicians playing uncouth instruments. Had he come to London he would have drawn the organ-grinders, or the acrobats and the man playing the bones to a theatre queue. But he had more than enough to interest him in the street life of Lima. There is about Pancho Fierro at his best the touch, if no more than that, of Goya in his weaker moments when he is off guard, or thinking about something else. If it is true that he painted frescoes or popular scenes on the patio walls of one or two private houses, and on the walls of various quintas, all of which have now disappeared, we may have lost something that had a little hint in it of Goya's tapestries. It is sad to think that the contribution of Lima to those scenes of popular life in Spain could have been the *tapadas*.

There are a number of albums of bound drawings, not from the hand of Pancho Fierro, and entitled, in at least one instance known to me, *The Ladies of Lima*. Another album, on rice paper, would seem to be by a Chinaman. Invariably, their theme is the *tapadas*. The drawings could be by almost anyone who could draw, and had been to Lima. Also, of course, Pancho Fierro drew them, but he is not the only witness to their charms. *Tapadas* were the women of Lima of all classes who affected a peculiar form of dress. It may have begun among the lower orders, and then become fashionable, and at last faded until only a few old women showed some traces of it. The peculiarity of it lay in so completely veiling the face that only one eye was left visible. The streets of Lima were thronged with cyclop women. It is easy to say that this custom is the carrying of something instinctive among Spaniards to ridiculous lengths, and that it bears all the signs of Moslem influence. Even to-day, at Vejer de la Frontera, near Cape Trafalgar, in sight of Africa, the women go veiled from head to foot, like nuns. They shroud their heads and faces, leaving but an eye visible, and maybe a hand. The analogy is obvious between them and the *tapadas*, except that at Vejer de la Frontera only black is worn, while the *tapadas* wore bright colours when they walked abroad. But certainly the custom was of Andalusian origin. In a water colour of a group of four *tapadas* by Pancho Fierro, all wear the black shawl or *saya*; but one lady has a bright blue skirt and has light brown sleeves, another a green skirt and vivid red cloak or *manta*, while a third wears a white *manta* with a scarlet double stripe upon it. As they are unaccompanied by servants these must be women of the poorer classes for the rich were preceded generally by a negro footman. Fulminations were hurled at the *tapadas* on the score of immorality. One author, writing as late as 1865 talks of the beautifully graceful garb of the ladies of Lima in olden times, but describes the *saya y manta* as a thing invented only for immoral purposes. He describes the *tapada*, its successor and ultimate development, as a 'garb of equal, if not greater foulness of design, and as a device of Paris civilization'. Charles Darwin, visiting Lima in 1833 on his famous voyage on H.M.S. *Beagle*, comments in his diary on the *tapadas*, remarking how inordinately proud they were of their small and elegant feet, and of the wealth of expression they contrived to get into the one eye showing from their headshawls.

In fact it is difficult to see how the *tapadas* can have been anything but charming. They were purely a Peruvian invention to be met with only in Lima in all the world, or perhaps at Trujillo further up the coast. Of Spanish descent, decidedly, and it is only a pity that Goya never saw them. They are in the key of his tapestries precisely, although those antedate the *tapadas* by nearly a generation; for the time this dress was at its most fanciful was in the eighteen-thirties when Darwin saw it, and it was seen by another and final witness whom we now bring forward.

This is Johann Moritz Rugendas (1802-1858), a painter of German nationality and member of a well-known family of Stuttgart artists. At an exhibition of 'bull fighting' held in a Bond Street gallery some years ago, two pictures by him were on view which were obviously of Spanish towns until it was noticed that in one of them a herd of llamas is advancing into the square, and Lima Cathedral was recognized in the companion painting. In this first of the two pictures what is probably the figure of Rugendas himself is seen, sketch book under arm, behind a portly white clad monk. The herd of llamas is just at the back of him. Two handsome young women are riding past, *en Amazone*, one of them looking back at us so that we see her pretty face framed in her straw hat. The rest of the scene is all bustle in the market place, with a church at the back and a house next to it with one of the characteristic wooden balconies. But what draws our attention in this picture is a group of *tapadas*, three of them, talking to a soldier. They are posed so that we get the full force of them, one of them with her back turned showing her slim figure looking as if it would pull easily through a napkin ring, and the other two close together and making a pair, as though the artist was telling us this is no lone apparition but that the *tapadas* of Lima were really like this. Each holds her shawl tight with one hand and looks at us with her one eye showing. A curious feature in the painting is that the five or six Indian or *mestiza* women wear the high peaked hat not worn in Lima any more but still a characteristic of Cochabamba in Bolivia.

The other painting is an animated scene in the cathedral square. To one side of it a performance of *Romeo y Julieta* is advertised in a theatre bill on a pillar below a wooden balcony; and the long arcade at the other side above a poster of *toros* has a mirador from which a spectacled gentleman and child are looking down. Under the arcade a man in a tall hat, thin-faced and with fair hair, has been identified as an 'eccentric

Tapadas of Lima, drawing by Pancho Fierro, *c.* 1840

Englishman' who lived in Lima. Probably there are several other portraits in the picture, for instance the man looking down from the *mirador*, and in it all there is a very slight element of caricature. Almost certainly there are portraits among the top-hatted gentlemen grouped to both sides of the painting under the two arches. The cavalier on the white horse may be a portrait, perhaps also the priest in his shovel hat, the hat of Don Basilio in *Il Barbiere*. There is not the same, but a different burly monk in white habit, and a native woman creeping away, load on back, wearing another of the Cochabamba hats. But the central interest of the painting is the group of three *tapadas* in the foreground. The shovel-hatted priest is escorting them, and the top-hatted small Indian boy in front of them is their page or footman.

This pair of paintings by Rugendas form the most important pictorial document of life in Lima. It may be doubted indeed if there are comparable paintings of any other city of Latin America. Another picture by him of *La Feria de Amancas* or the *Day of San Juan* is rather more of a caricature and therefore less of a good painting. There are galloping horses all over the picture, and a picnic and comic incidents. The picnickers are a party of *élégants*, one of them smoking a cigar, and with a top-hatted negro footman in attendance on them. They are watching the antics of the lower orders, some of whom are dancing to the harp and guitar, probably dancing the *cueca*, while a woman in a white Cochabamba hat, a true 'Cochabambina' is being made love to, drunkenly. In fact, and evidently, it is time to ride home.

The discovery of the two paintings by Rugendas encouraged our friend who purchased them to try and locate other pictures and drawings by this nearly forgotten artist, who is known, if at all, by his album of Brazilian views. With the exception of the Dutchman Frans Post (1612-1680) he is by far the most interesting European painter who has ever worked in Latin America. Frans Post painted views of Brazil, and the only other competition is from Debret, a pupil of David, who published a book on Rio de Janeiro which fetches high prices in the auction room. But both Frans Post and Debret worked on the Atlantic seaboard of South America, only Rugendas penetrated as far as the Pacific. He first arrived in Brazil, going thence to the Argentine. He made his way across Bolivia, worked in La Paz, and came the arduous way to Peru, via Lake Titicaca, taking sketches en route at Pucará where the pottery figures of bulls are made. He stayed some two years in Lima (1832-4), and seems to have painted there more than anywhere else in South America. Later on he went to Mexico, and there are paintings by him in the palace at Chapultepec. Eventually he returned to Germany where he may have worked up his sketches into finished paintings. A number of drawings and some paintings by him are in the State collection of drawings at Munich, and there are others in the gallery at Augsburg.

It is among the collection at Munich that, among much else of lesser interest, these two further oil sketches by Rugendas that we illustrate came to light. That their subject should be the *tapadas* bespeaks Lima, and no other city. In the first of them a group of four young women is sitting on a wall with the domes and towers of Lima behind them in the near distance. The scene is a garden just outside the city. But it is getting on for a hundred and fifty years ago, let us remember, long before the flowers of our time were growing in the gardens. Alike, bougainvillaea and plumbago, hibiscus and frangipani, are importations from abroad. It is an ordinary garden with no hint of the tropics, and only the buildings of some Spanish town for background. But for many persons the *tapadas* present a phenomenon they have never seen before, and many of us might be enquiring of ourselves where on earth we are. In some fantastic prolongation of Andalusia might be the answer, a lost sister of Seville that is unknown to the geographers. For the dress of *tapadas*, of Andalusian provenance and inspiration, is an extreme of female coquetry not known before. Remark the fascination of the four bare hands and arms holding the shawls tight underneath their chins! The cyclop heads with something of a seal-shape to them—the heads and necks of two or three of them together, leaving their one eye out of the argument for the moment— move and turn about rather like a sleek family of seals. Not now, though, for all four of them are looking at us. Note, too, the white frills of their sleeves, not having known the attraction of a sleeve before! The middle *tapada* of the four dangling her shoes in front of us, knowing, as we may do, that Spanish women are proud of their small feet, and she shows as well the hem of her petticoat like an edge of white foam. What a beautiful warm evening with the four young girls sitting there just in front of us! But they seem silent to me. I do not hear their chattering voices. Only a muffled word or two coming from what we might think to be the waistline of their shawls. It could be that there was not much talk about, and that they are sitting still to have their portraits painted. And in any event how much of a portrait can be done of a young woman who only lets us see her one eye!

The painter, if charmed but a little baffled on this one occasion, delivers the final word on the *tapadas* in his other oil sketch. It is a full concourse of *tapadas* on their knees in Lima Cathedral, an unexpected and most peculiar spectacle. There may be as many as a hundred of them, all kneeling. The interior of the cathedral is rendered simply and boldly with shafts of light flashing through it, and a blaze of lights is indicated at the high altar. But, in fact, it could be any one of the big churches of Lima. The scene, wisely, is not particularized. It is just a large church with a lot of *tapadas* kneeling in it. The painter has so far simplified their kneeling forms that each of them is put in almost with a single stroke of the brush. They have nearly the outline of insects, on their knees with their backs turned. Something of an ant-waist, not a wasp-waist, for they are in sombre black, with the huge cowls that resemble an insect; one knows not which, but it is not the praying mantis, for that has a little triangular head and toothed legs, thinner than matchsticks, but as sharp as saws. St John's Cathedral at Valetta, with a whole concourse of kneeling women in *faldettas*, the old costume of Malta, was no comparable sight. For the *faldetta* has been described as looking like a boat in full sail. It has nothing attractively feminine to it. Here, with the *tapadas*, the accent in more feminine fashion is on the waistline. It is a costume that uses concealment for purposes of coquetry, or that has converted an ordinance of sobriety to its own purposes. As in a dream, one finds oneself going from each to each to find her for whom one is looking, and choosing the way carefully so as not to tread upon the dresses of the others. Once I was given a peacock to take home to the garden, and for convenience of transport the peacock was put into a sack. I had to carry it on my knee inside the car, and remember the slightly creepy feeling of its neck and head darting to and fro, blindly, inside the sack. The sight of so many *tapadas* kneeling in the church has a little of this effect upon one. If only they would turn round and look in our direction. When Mass is over, and they rise from their knees, so many of them with only the one eye showing will seem like one corporate body, and the image of them in my mind suggests some kind of octopus, all part of the same animal. They break off, and disperse from that, and now the only mark of identification will be the depth of expression or of recognition in one eye and an eyebrow and a small white hand.

It was perhaps appropriate that we should go direct to the bull-fight from thinking of Rugendas. In the old bull-ring of Lima, on the other bank of the river, and overlooked by more than one of the *miradores*. Here, too, as in the bar of the Hotel Maury it was something of a triumphal progress as our friend was recognized by the *aficionados*. Sadly, there were no *tapadas* among the spectators, as there should have been. As there most certainly were not far back in the long history of bull-fighting. One is to suppose they looked more than ever like Cretan, like Minoan women, more even than the young women of Seville with their high tortoiseshell combs and white mantillas. It is only a pity there is no picture by Rugendas of *tapadas* at the bull-fight. He is not a great painter of Latin America, but there is no other. Colonial painters of the schools of Cuzco and of Quito in their religious pictures are of little use as human or social documents. There are only a few mouldering canvases of some interest in one or two of the Cuzco churches, but skied so high that you can hardly see them. And now in fact we were about to start for Cuzco.

In our last few days at Lima there was the purchase of guanaco and alpaca rugs to be completed. Not of the horrid sort that have a wretched llama in relief, in wool *répoussé*, worked into them. But the proper and true guanaco or alpaca skins, sewn together, some of them snow-white, but more exactly a snowy-cream, others a beige colour, and a very few of them pure black. Vicuña is now almost impossible to procure, though woven vicuña cloth is to be found in Cuzco, and imported and woven into cloth, here in England. The expense is great; excessively but understandably so if, as reputed, a vicuña coat is made entirely from vicuña ears—the sale of vicuña is forbidden entirely in Bolivia, but the other wools or furs can be bought cheaper than in Peru, though it is a truism to say that in order to effect that you have to get there, for Bolivia seems to be the most distant and inaccessible country one has ever been to. The rugs, in any case, are to be had much cheaper in Ayacucho and other inland Peruvian mountain towns than in the capital.

There were the farewells to Peruvian friends whom it is not likely one will ever see again, for Lima is at the other side of the world. It made the last few days of our stay in Lima a little melancholy. The journey may only take a day and a half by air, but it costs a great deal of money. So far as we were concerned it was a marvellous experience to have been here at all, and an ambition which had taken many years to fulfil. Peru is so huge and vast, and so extraordinary withal from its triple nature of desert plain, Andean mountain and Amazonian jungle, that the writer must despair of how to leave his mark on it. Most of the only unexplored country left in the world is shared by Peru, Bolivia, and Brazil. We were to see none of this, not the Peruvian province of Madre de Dios which has space and excuse for a score of Colonel Fawcetts to disappear in it, not more than a momentary sighting of the tropical jungle down in the river gorge below Machu Picchu. But, at least, we had a draught of the steep winds of the Altiplano and crossed Lake Titicaca, to which the only comparable experience must be to travel in Tibet. Till now, for contrast, the theme has been Lima and its Andalusian airs and graces. Or Andalusian, at any rate, until the Garua and the months of mists and fog come down.

It is impossible for the writer not to develop a nostalgic feeling for a city of which he has such happy memories, where, too, he was accorded a welcome of a sort that is unfamiliar at home. But it is to be noticed that most accounts of Lima are uncomplaining. Limeñans look on it as the most beautiful city of South America, and quite a number of them in their satisfaction have not tempted providence by climbing to the Altiplano, or even venturing as far as Cuzco. There is no difficulty in breathing down among the flowers of Lima. Not a few persons expressed their distaste and horror at the heights. Some had been there, but would not go again. But, also, we met mining engineers who had come down from camps at sixteen and seventeen thousand feet, and in consequence felt ill in Lima. In no other country in the world can you climb so quickly from sea-level to such heights as that, or come down so fast. In everything it is a land of contrasts. Peru, in itself, has three different climates like as many separate worlds apart. In face of which immensity the writer can but reflect what little he has seen.

This had been confined so far to Lima, and was only the beginning of a long journey. We were to go to Bolivia and Ecuador and Colombia, and to end in Guatemala and Yucatán. We went to Cuzco, Quito, and Antigua, three of the oldest cities of Latin America. Lima is a gentler place than any of these, in spite of earthquakes. And, as is the case

E

everywhere, too much of it has been torn down to make room for office buildings.

There is but little left of Lima except wooden balconies. But on one of our last evenings we dined in a house which could only be Peruvian, and nothing else; in a large house which was modern, but had echoes in it of the Torre Tagle Palace. It had a collection of silver and of inlaid tortoiseshell and mother-of-pearl cabinets brought all the way by galleon from Manila; it had an open court with wooden balconies in argument that it never rained, and a big tropical garden. Dinner was in the garden; but in fact it was more of a banquet, ending with ices made of *loucoumi*, a fruit that we were told, and would like to believe, only grows in Lima. It can not be eaten raw, but makes excellent ices of faintly scented taste. With this were served little packages wrapped up in gold paper, that contained a kind of nut, or the kernel of some sort of fruit, reduced by magical process into a delicious sweet. Nuns have made these for longer than anyone can recall, and they are something peculiar to Lima. Our friend the Alcalde, who was at the dinner, remembered that they were sent to him when he was an unhappy child at school near London; that a large box of them arrived, and that the English schoolboys refused to eat them. As the result of which, and of the banquet, I dreamed I was back at school myself, but woke up knowing it was only a nightmare, that the holidays were here again and we were going in a day or two to Machu Picchu and to Cuzco.

Chapter Four

◆◆◆◆◆◆◆◆◆◆◆◆◆◆◆◆◆◆◆◆◆◆◆◆

MACHU PICCHU

THE JOURNEY TO CUZCO is preluded in mock-serious fashion by a visit from the doctor. Though, in fact, it is serious enough and there is no farce about it. The doctor sounds your heart with his stethoscope, omitting nowadays to ask for the missing formula 'Say ninety-nine', and takes your blood-pressure. He warns you to be careful what you eat and drink, advises against smoking, and tells you immediately on arrival to spend a couple of hours in bed. Above all, one must walk slowly and not attempt to rush about. One is to eat a light dinner and go early to sleep, with a final injunction always to take the lift and never to walk upstairs. For medicine he prescribes cardamine with glucose added, something one has never been told of before but is to cling to as close as the pre-Revolutionary Chinaman to his opium. Precautions that sound a little absurd at the time, and rather as though one was warned to take swimming lessons before going to Venice, but one is to find they are not ridiculous at all but very necessary. Quite a number of persons with abnormal blood pressure or weak hearts are warned off from going, and wisely. Particularly if they intend, as we did, travelling beyond Cuzco, and therefore higher still.

For the trip to Cuzco is an air-lift if ever there was one. It is an early start, the take-off being at six-thirty in the morning. This is in order that the return journey to Lima should be over by the time the clouds gather on the mountains. There was more than enough mist already that morning, and we looked with apprehension at the half-hidden hills and down the runway. The local airline, however, has a good record, and if conditions are at all bad at either end the flight is cancelled. So we fasten our safety-belts and in a minute or two are over the sea, making a wide arc in order to gain height and go 'straight at' the Andes. By the time one is drinking a cup of coffee we are

67

already thousands of feet up, and the steward comes round to instruct us in the use of the oxygen-tubes. Each has its sterilized mouthpiece, and the sensation is half-way between attending a wartime gas-course and smoking a hookah or hubble-bubble. For so short and so high a flight it seems a much more sensible method than the customary pressurization. You do get immediate and instant relief from sucking at your oxygen-tube, and there is the feeling that it is giving you individual care and nursing. By which time we are at a huge height, but seem to be almost near enough to touch the mountains. Forbidding little lakes are on the tops of many of them; one can see for what could be hundreds of miles into other mountain ranges and there is not a sign of a human being in all of them.

Looking down at the Andes the extent of corrugation, if that be the correct word to apply to it, is quite fantastic. Down there all looks entirely impossible for human habitation, and even the valleys are so high up that no animal could live in them. This continues for an hour or more with range after range of mountains that are one vast solitude. Without their becoming perceptibly lower in height there are now green sides to some of the hills, and now and then a circle or ring of stones that means human beings. We are flying the shortest way to Cuzco, straight over the mountains more or less, but how did the Spaniards come through the Andes four hundred years ago? For that matter how did travellers get to Cuzco only a hundred years ago, before the railway? Compared to this even the wildest of the Spanish *sierras* are lands of milk and honey. No other land, not even Tibet, can have more bony ramparts.

It is an eternity up here at thirty thousand feet, and one is beginning to enjoy it and not wanting to come down. Also, the clouds are stupendous, when one can lift one's eyes to them off the hills. Every time we go into a cloud there is slight shaking and shuddering of the aeroplane, and a momentary misgiving because we are flying blind, and tilting straight into their dissolving forms. Not the least extraordinary feature of the air-lift being to look round at the other passengers and watch them, nursery fashion, sucking at their oxygen-tubes. But at last, after two hours of this, we are losing height, though it is not like the ordinary problem of coming down from twenty or twenty-five thousand feet, for Cuzco, one could say, is already half-way up there, lying at ten thousand four hundred feet above the sea. And we come down at a steep angle, a little nervous at having been told that the aerodrome only just satisfies the minimum requirements for length of runway, and so forth, and we make a perfect landing.

There, at the airport, the mayor of Cuzco is waiting to tell us in fluent English learnt in Canada that we must drive straight to the hotel and go to bed for two hours at least. And either the mayor, or the prefetto, tells us in warning the story of the young man described as 'like a Viking', who had come to Cuzco only a week or two before us and had collapsed on getting out of the aeroplane. He had to lie down at the airport, and they sent him back in the same aeroplane to Lima. And an ambassador—the Netherlands, or the Belgian, or the Danish—which was it?—from one of the flat countries in the north of Europe, had come staggering and gasping down the tarmac, and had to be put to bed and given oxygen in the hotel. The effect of the horror-tales being that one realised, suddenly, how tired one was after the early start and the late night in Lima prolonged by last minute packing, but found oneself breathing fairly well. Perhaps just that little bit too well? And we climbed into the mayor's car, and started off for the railway station.

In that manner we drove through just one corner of Cuzco on the way to Machu Picchu. But it was long enough to get a little of its character, driving under a triumphal arch, and noticing the prodigious number of *mestiza* women wearing brilliant coloured skirts and peculiar hats. A sensation of being in a big town with a population entirely new to one's experience, and that one was too tired for once in one's life to take it in. At the station we were kept waiting for some time, and it was then that we knew just how tired we were. There was nowhere to sit down, and it was nearly impossible to breathe standing up. If one dropped anything, it was a dizzying and terrible effort to stoop to the railway platform and pick it up again. But in the end a little one-coach train backed itself towards us from a siding and we got into it, letting everything, even our coats and hats, be carried for us, for by this time we had gone far beyond lifting anything for ourselves. It was but the first, as we shall see, of a whole series of journeys made in little private trains. Just now, and for a while longer, one was too exhausted to take in the novelty of the experience.

The point of going immediately to Machu Picchu instead of staying in Cuzco was that Machu Picchu is some two thousand feet lower in altitude. We were told that on returning to Cuzco after a couple of nights in Machu Picchu one would be acclimatized. But, also, we knew that in order to leave Cuzco we had to climb higher still, and the knowledge of this had become an urgent and pressing dread. By now we had begun to crawl very slowly upwards through the suburbs where women wearing petticoats of flaring colours were washing or beating out laundry, or carrying heavy burdens, but always and everywhere in their *mestiza* hats. Never without their hats, so that we wonder, do they sleep in them, and the answer could be, not improbably, 'Yes!' Groves of eucalyptus trees now appear, and we are high enough to look out over the tiled roofs of Cuzco which give a particular character to this old and famous town. That character is Spanish to this moment, so that it could be some town in Spain with as many churches as there are in Compostela. No Inca remains are visible from here, but there is this new and unfamiliar *mestizo* population, and now we can see three or four huge monasteries or convents and what must be the Cathedral Square.

Soon we come to a stop altogether, and have to start again backwards up an even steeper gradient with the driver looking over his shoulder for a hundred yards or so. Then, another halt and we go on again but once more in the forward direction. It reminds me of going up in the tram from Florence to Fiesole when I was a child, a kind of monkey-walk progress that seemed designed to please both small boy and tram driver. Can it really have been as steep as that with trellises of wisteria overhanging the long white walls? There was another parallel between Cuzco and Fiesole, for at both places there are mysterious cyclopaean walls; and by now we had another and higher view of Cuzco far down below, vanishing for long intervals behind a bank of earth, and then visible again but much lower as we climbed. It was becoming not so much difficult to breathe as that there was a horrid unpressurized feeling that made one stupid, and too uncomprehending to do more than look down on the roofs of Cuzco, hoping one might be less doltish on the return journey when we came this way again.

It was a coach about the size of the waggonette I was driven to church in when staying with a grandmother away from my irreligious, or at any rate non-Sunday-observing home, but with perhaps a little more room between the rows of seats. I sat across the gangway next to the driver, luggage was piled in the racks and all round us, and the rest of the carriage was occupied by three or four railway officials, all *mestizos*, who were coming with us, it seemed, just for the fun of the journey. The coach ran on a petrol engine and the maximum speed, we were told, was forty kilometres per hour. Perhaps it was not so much like a waggonette as an electric brougham, of the sort that would turn left out of Berkeley Square and climb Hay Hill, but making of that a feat as though it was a Himalayan, or, at the least, an Alpine crossing, and in a few seconds one was in Dover Street.

Only once do I remember driving in an electric brougham in London. A unique experience, but many times less extraordinary than this 'ride' from Cuzco to Machu Picchu, and a memory that was of nostalgic inspiration for we had never felt so far away from home, though this was as nothing compared to how one feels in Bolivia and on the Altiplano of Peru.

By now this first of altitude tests was over and we were coming down the slopes in great wide arcs onto a gigantic and far stretching table-land. The whole morning in this little one-car train was an adventure on its own 'out into the blue', in an isolation as complete as in the 'gondola' of a balloon, or, progressing from Jules Verne into our own age, in the capsule of an interplanetary rocket. So it seemed, though in fact we were anything but by ourselves; but that feeling comes from the extraordinary loneliness and desolation of that landscape which is on a huger scale than anything one has ever seen, yet this is but a little taste of it, equivalent to being taken to the edge of it, allowed a quick look at it, and immediately whisked away. Immediately in this extended sense meaning an hour, or an hour and a half of it, during which time we stopped at several stations, but only for long enough for a man in our car to dash into the station master's office and ask if the line was clear. No sign of another train had we seen yet. It could have been a private railway line.

Even so, one was in no mood that morning for the mystique of railway management. All our senses were engaged upon the brilliant groups of Indians squatting upon the station platform. It is their social centre. They gather from miles round to spend the day there, waiting. It is nothing unusual for them to arrive at early morning and stay till after dark. They are the same race after all who spend a day or two, either way, trudging, or rather trotting, to the weekly market, and who will pass a whole day and night dancing, marathon-wise, on a saint's day fiesta. Have they come here to catch a train, themselves, or to meet someone, with just a few hours in hand? There is no means of knowing; and only the probability that they have never heard of a platform ticket, and get all the entertainment for nothing.

It is another and new crowd brilliance with the 'shocking pink' of the Peruvian Indian here and there, so bright that it does really exclaim aloud out of all the other dresses or rather petticoats. No more perhaps than one or two of them in twenty times that number, but the rest are bright enough, all sitting about like gypsy women at the campfire, and nearly every one of the women with a baby slung on her back, and wearing the white Quechua felt hat. They wear their hair in a couple of short pigtails looped together with a strand of llama wool. They have a picturesque way of sitting or standing as though posing naturally for the camera, now that no conscientious painter would any longer address himself to such a theme. In spite of which, every time one sees a railway platform in Peru swarming with Indians one's first wish is that a good artist would come along and paint it. I realise now that their resemblance is to the Navajo Indians of New Mexico to whom they are as closely akin in physical appearance as are Siamese to Burmese, and can see a group of them in my mind's eye, as I write this, in their white hats and multi-coloured petticoats. The Quechua men in their knee breeches are less interesting. It is the women who catch and keep the eye.

Already this early part of the morning had seemed to last for ever, and it was impossible to realize we had been in Lima still earlier on this same day. There was the sensation of crawling on the edge of an immensity, on the rim of a huge Indian continent, as we travelled for what seemed miles at a time out into the blue distance, and then came to another wayside station where usually there was no village, but the Indians came walking to it over the horizon. But we were not to continue in this way for the whole morning. After a wait of three-quarters of an hour at one station, and the passing at last of a severely crowded train, we reached the beginning of a valley and began descending among low stony hills at first, and then coming to a turbulent and swirling river which is none other than the Urubamba, the interest of this being that its waters flow into and join the Amazon. In theory, at least, you could float a message on this, and it might reach the

Tapadas in church, by J. M. Rugendas (1802-1858)

Panorama of Machu-Picchu

Church near Cuzco

Atlantic, two thousand miles away for some bird with a straight flight, not the soaring, chasm-drinking condor of the Andes; for some bird flying over huge distances, and migrant by the shortest route. It is an extraordinary moment to feel that almost the only unexplored regions of the world lie between oneself and these waters rushing down through them towards the distant Atlantic.

Presently there are stone terraces that are the signs of Inca cultivation, and the stone foundation towers of an Inca suspension bridge, smaller counterpart of the great cable bridge across the Apurimac which Thornton Wilder made famous as *The Bridge of San Luis Rey*. The river was, in fact, dashing and swirling in horrible, almost frightening fashion, for there had been torrential rain accompanying the Arequipa earthquake and connected, no doubt, with the chain of seismic disturbances that had their culmination in the earthquakes in Chile early in 1960. It was a torrent that no swimmer could possibly have survived in, falling and dashing against huge rocks. The relief was in looking away from it and trying to follow the flight of some biggish, yellow and black birds. There were not many of them and they flew faster than our rail-car with short jerky motion, a stone's throw at a time.

We came deeper and deeper down the gorge, stopping at last at the station of Ollontay-Tambo, being even now nine thousand feet above sea-level, and here we got down from our train, for it was intended that we should visit the Inca ruins, but we were too tired and breathless to attempt this. It would have meant further climbing and scrambling up stone steps from terrace to terrace, and into the ancient fortress, and we would have seen the six red porphyry monoliths, slabs twelve feet high by five feet wide, quarried the other side of the river and brought by some means or other across the torrent and pushed or hauled up the mountainside. Also, and near where the precipice is steepest, the five buildings one above the other with steep roofs, once grass-thatched, where the ñustas or virgins of the sun may, or may not, have had their schools or dwellings. But, in fact, even the photographs of Ollontay-Tambo in a pamphlet we were given caused slight vertigo. And as for the Inca bridge across the Urubamba, in two spans, and made of twisted rope-cable, with a 'cat-walk' four foot wide, that swayed and rocked as you crawled along it, this was a little too much in the same morning as our flight from Lima, even if the rope cables which were still in position until the 1880's are now gone, and the bridge is modern.

So, with regret we decided against Ollontay-Tambo. The station-building had accommodation above it, consisting of a large bare room with bed and chair, and clean enough. But we thought it better to go on the other hour, or hour and a half, to Machu Picchu, first for purposes of convenience taking a short walk in the station-backyard where proof of our extreme fatigue, if any were needed, was there waiting. In the chicken-run in that backyard was a large bird, and I was so utterly tired that I have never been able to think since then what kind of bird it can have been. It was neither duck, nor goose, its feet were not webbed nor was it any sort of gallinaceous bird, not turkey nor guinea-fowl. It was large and black, as big as a goose, with a bright red beak and, I think, red legs and feet. Obviously domesticated, but more of capercailzie or *coq de bruyère* type; and at a loss to think what it could be I remembered reading of lunatics or weak-minded persons who were shut up and certified on the strength of not being able to tell the difference between a horse and cow, or sheep and pig. And looking at it once more with misgiving, and none the wiser, we got back into the train.

The Urubamba raged more furiously than ever but we were coming down into another climate. At the bottom of this river gorge is the beginning of the Amazonian jungle. There were trees about the size of holm-oaks, and as we came down further they had epiphytes like hanging baskets swaying from their branches. None were in flower, but there were long straggling blossoms near the rock face that we recognized as begonias, and low bushes with splashes or drops of fire upon them in dark corners, as we came in or out of tunnels, that were fuchsias. There was a landslide ahead, we had been told, due to the abnormal rains, and in fact one felt a little nervous of finding a tunnel blocked at one, or even at both ends, and being imprisoned in it. The waters were yellow and more yellow from the mud, and at last we came to the landslide, where the line was broken, and got out and clambered through thick yellow mud and fallen rocks and boulders with the roar of the river loud in our ears, and in a heavy mist or drizzle. This porterage, reminiscent of when explorers meet the rapids and have to haul their canoes and stores along the river bank, continued for some two hundred yards or more, beyond which another train with an empty coach was waiting.

It was but a half-hour's descent from here to Machu Picchu, and becoming more tropical it really seemed, at every quarter of a mile, until at last we saw a white orchid, and another, and orchids galore growing now to both sides of the line. It was a white odontoglossum, and probably not at all an interesting one for experts, but to see orchids and begonias and fuchsias growing is an experience to set beside that first moment of seeing oranges upon their trees. The fuchsia hedges of Connemara are another matter, even after we are told that the Erse-speaking peasant women get the dye from them for their red petticoats. The fuchsia, like the montbretia growing there, is a foreign importation into Ireland. But this is fuchsia, begonia, orchid country, and the long tubular calyx of the flower calls for the humming-bird to pollinate one blossom with another and sip their nectar. Fuchsia species, in particular, seem designed for this.

All this time one could look out for flowers, and watch the river, but owing to the roof of the car one could not crane one's neck and look upward. It would mean staring up, vertically, from where we were sitting. We only knew we were deep down in a valley and that there must be steep heights above us. Very soon we were at Machu Picchu station, where we transferred to a car and crossed the river on a steel girder bridge through which one could look down ominously upon the foaming waters. It was only then that the stupendous scene unrolled itself, for in fact the only landscapes like it are those of the great Chinese landscape painters. The road up to the ruins is quite new, and only a year or two ago one had to make the climb on foot, or ride on muleback. The ascent is violently zigzag, with little or no parapet, and one dreads meeting another car upon it, but the road in fact only goes from the railway station to the ruins, so that a couple of hotel buses are the only vehicles, and their start and arrival are reported on the telephone at either end. Collision is, or should be, impossible in these conditions.

What a curious day it had been! Only a few days after seeing the pelicans and penguins of the Guano Islands, to pass the gardens of Lima that morning with their frangipanis and their scarlet poinsettias, be given oxygen in the dawn aeroplane, be driven half-dazed through that corner of old Cuzco among the *mestizas*, then shunted up above the town to where we looked down on the tiled roofs, and after that the illimitable hour or two upon the high plain with its gypsy and *flamenco* gatherings and encampments at every wayside station! Then, the descent down beside the tearing waters to Ollontay-Tambo, along waters hurrying to join the Amazon, and now this little taste, this inkling, if no more than this, of the Amazon jungle. What could be more fantastic, looking at it from the other direction, than that you can sail on a regular steamship service (the Booth Line) from Liverpool up the Amazon to Manaos, and thence by small steamer to Iquitos which is in Peru; and that there should be government hotels at Iquitos and at Tingó Maria, both Amazon cities of the river jungle! Or is it odder still to be able to sail on a river-steamer and then an ocean-going liner from Iquitos to Liverpool?

Such were our thoughts while zigzagging from corner to corner of that breath-taking precipice, and now at some considerable height above the river and the lilliputian railway line. At every twisting of the road the view grew more terrific until it reached a pitch of magnificent wildness never known before. Most fortunately there was no mist that morning and the huge mountains rose unencumbered to their full height to which, I say, none but the greatest of Chinese landscape painters of nearly a thousand years ago could have done justice. The mountains group themselves, miraculously, into tiers of an enormous amphitheatre, not in haphazard fashion, posing one of their number which is cone-shaped and covered with vegetation from top to bottom, right forward in order, as it were, to focus the perspective. It is but necessary to look at that mountain for a moment, and then move your eyes to take in the whole scene. We are now on the top of it, not gazing open-mouthed from below, but looking down on it from the 'gods', in the gallery close under the roof with the proscenium arch in front of us just across the valley.

This is the most stupendous approach there has ever been, to something which in its own right is perhaps the most startlingly dramatic archaeological site in either the Old or the New World. For the setting is enough, is almost too much in itself. It is nearly too good to be believed that there should be something more to see here; the Valley of the Kings at Luxor in its apocalyptic setting, where the mummy of Tutankhamen lay among his tumbled and disturbed treasures in a tomb-chamber not much larger than a bathroom, but the Pharaohs Seti I and Rameses III were put in excavated galleries the size of the tube stations at Piccadilly Circus or Leicester Square—the Valley of the

Kings is a necropolis, a city of the dead. When we were shown Tutank-hamen's newly discovered tomb by Howard Carter, we were told it had not rained in the Valley of the Kings since 1912, and that the nearest cultivated ground in a straight line towards the west was in Jamaica. It is a marvellously appropriate setting for remains which are invisible in any case for the tombs are cut into the rock.

There is only Petra that can be compared to Machu Picchu; com-parable in drama and for the excitement of getting to it. First the aeroplane flight to Ma'an, as there is to Cuzco, and then the journey by car to Ain Musa, the Well of Moses, whence one rides on horseback in single file down the Siq, the rocky passage which in places is barely ten feet wide, between cliffs that tower eighty to a hundred feet to either side. Then, suddenly, when the tunnel is at its narrowest and darkest, there is the vision of the Khazné Faraóun right in front of you, the façade of a temple cut into the rock, a rock the colour of rose petals, in a chasm that runs at right angles to the Siq, put of course at that exact spot in order to be opposite to us as we ride towards it out of the darkness. The siting of the Khazné Faraóun at Petra is no less than a stroke of genius. The most imaginative of architects could not better this.

But the gorge of Machu Picchu is on a greater scale. The discoverer of the ruined city, Hiram Bingham who died only in 1950, must have experienced sensations not less exciting than those of Dr Schliemann when he went into the beehive tomb at Mycenae and held in his hand the golden mask that hid the face of Agamemnon. Or so he thought, at least; and Hiram Bingham for his part thought he had found the lost city of the Incas. It was no longer ago than 1911 that he came to the valley of the Urubamba, and on the hint from his Indian guide that there were old ruins high on the mountainside, climbed the canyon and, it could be said, took possession of Machu Picchu on behalf of archae-ology. But all is mystery to this day, and even the true name of the city is unknown. What indeed could there be in the matter of ruins at such a height as this? There would seem not to be space enough for a ruin of any kind. But the zigzag road levels out a bit, and there on a little plateau under the overhanging rock, convenient but prosaic, stands the government hotel. It could be a hotel on a high mountain pass in Switzerland, and is as comfortable as that, standing in spite of its apparent extreme altitude at only seven thousand feet, which is only about half the height of Puno, or La Paz, and other towns we were to visit. Indeed we came to look on nine thousand feet as the maximum height that could be endured without discomfort.

On arrival, after one of the most exhausting days I have ever had in my life, a day charged with so many and varied impressions, for in the space of a single morning we had tasted the coastal plain, the high Andes, and the beginning of the forests of Amazon, or, indeed, all three of the triple zones, we broke a long fast, had luncheon, and then obedient to the advice of all and sundry lay down for two hours, after which, we set off to see the ruins. They begin only a few yards from the hotel beyond a curtain wall which is one of the outer walls of the town. It entails skirting a minor precipice and squeezing oneself against one of the many terraces. Then, all of a sudden, the whole of the extraordinary Inca city springs itself upon one at aeroplane height above the river. It is clear that the inhabitants had all they needed for their frugal wants up here, half-way into the sky, and did not have to come down into the valley. That is the purpose of all the *andenes* or hanging terraces, laboriously banked up with stones, with soil laid upon them, and fed by stone watercourses. On these they grew corn or maize, other vegetables, and some of their many varieties of potato. They were, in fact, self-provisioned and could maintain themselves in almost complete isolation for an unlimited stretch of time. There seems indeed little reason why Machu Picchu should not still have been inhabited when Hiram Bingham got there. Perhaps its inbred population might have become dwarfed by perpetual intercrossing and a little more than semi-cretinous in the course of ages. It would appear that something of this sort happened with the Viking settlements in Western Greenland in the thirteenth century, after they were cut off from all communication with the outer world. Bodies found in the burial grounds are of stunted growth and show other signs of abnormality. The isolation of Machu Picchu is so entire and haunting that fantasies of this sort come easily to mind, and one could even think the inhabitants are away for the day and will be back by night.

It is not known when Machu Picchu was built or when it was deserted. But the probable answers to both questions are not long before and not long after the Spanish conquest. Above all it is this kind of *Marie-Céleste* mystery of sudden and unexplained desertion that is so fascinating. There are certain clues as to its date, for fragments of blue

beads found in the houses are of European origin and were probably
traded by the Spaniards and may have reached here after many changes
of hands. Also, it is known that the fortress of Ollontay-Tambo
guarding this same Urubamba river was still in process of building
when the Spaniards got there in 1534. Machu Picchu is one of a chain
of such *pucarás* or fortresses, its peculiarity being that the Spaniards
never came to it, and the Incas remained here besieged, but with no
besieging force, for a generation, or maybe a couple of generations
longer. But they must have evacuated Machu Picchu and gone elsewhere, considerably before 1600.

Perhaps the ideal conditions for seeing Machu Picchu are that it
should be fine and clear down in the river gorge as one climbs the road
and the tremendous mountain panorama unrolls itself before one, and
then misty with cloud upon the mountain tops as one starts off to see
the ruins. This is certainly as the Chinese landscape painters would
have had it be, and only they have ever painted such a scene. This is
now we saw the ruins on that afternoon, having come now to some
sort of fountain stairway wet with rain, with rills of falling water
collecting at each stage or landing into stone troughs that are called
'baths' in the guide books. There are sixteen of these fountains all
flowing from an aqueduct higher on the mountain side, but the wet
water stair, all dripping, was entirely in the mood of that misty afternoon. Now the slope is steeper still, and after a good deal of scrambling
over slippery and loose stones we are shown a building that the guide,
an Indian boy of about fourteen, says was an Inca mausoleum where
mummies of the dead rulers were kept, covered up or wrapped in gold,
a doubtful story because Machu Picchu was probably never more than
a fortress or outpost, and there is no evidence that Hiram Bingham was
correct in thinking an Inca, Pachacuti VI was buried here. He was
obsessed with his discovery, and no wonder, but it worked on his
imagination in the same way that Schliemann was affected by his
discovery of the royal burials at Mycenae. Just this one *pucará* out of
many has survived intact, but for its roofs of grass thatch which have
perished, and for the small personal belongings of its inhabitants.
Yet it is not so simple as that, for there is a mystery here which is
absent from Pachacamac or Sacsahuamán, and what is mysterious is
the number of stone houses which are so entire, but for their roofs,
that many of them could bear the notice 'to be let unfurnished'.

If the roofs were put back they could be occupied tomorrow.

Nothing whatever happened at Machu Picchu from the date at which it was deserted, probably in some year between 1560 and 1580, and 1911, the year of its discovery. That is for three hundred and fifty years, more or less. Its existence was known to a few Indians but no use was made even of its building stone. A concerted effort on the part of many hundreds of Indians was needed to build Machu Picchu, but after it was deserted there were not enough Indians left to pull it down. Its purpose was gone, and there was not sufficient labour force to roll the huge stones down the hill. Originally a fortress, it had become a place of refuge, and now no one wanted to be hidden there. Most of the graves that have been opened were found to contain women's bodies from which it has been deduced that it was a sanctuary for the *ñustas* or virgins of the sun, but again there is no reason for thinking this was so. It could be true that most of the men were killed in battle and buried elsewhere. If they took refuge here from fighting the Spaniards they would have lost many of the male population anyway. Nevertheless, it is more than likely that *caciques* and other persons of importance, and even members of the Inca family, may have fled here, and this would explain why it was strongly garrisoned. For Machu Picchu is more than a mere fortress. It must have had some fifteen hundred inhabitants, two or three hundreds of whom perhaps were soldiers.

After being taken to a building with underground cells which may well have been a prison we climb still higher, and it is only now we know the full extent of Machu Picchu. For it continues to the ridge or saddleback between two mountain walls, and it is here that on a flat space of ground they made their square or plaza which was the centre of the city. Even at the first glance it is the forum or assembling place of Machu Picchu, and a site which has still an important air about it. Indeed it seems inhabited and only momentarily deserted, as though an excitement of some sort or other is going on elsewhere and has drawn the population. They may come back at any moment. The buildings are roofless and in bad repair, but one feels some other part of Machu Picchu must have people living in it. The town can be no more than half-deserted.

There is a steep stair running up along a wall, and buildings which seen from below may well have roofs upon them. It is only when you climb higher still that you know they, too, are roofless, and that the whole town has no life in it. Not that the isolation of Machu Picchu was ever as complete as one would like to think, for at least eight such terraces or staged villages have been traced in the neighbourhood, one of them only three miles from Machu Picchu and connected to it by a paved road.[1] The only analogy in Europe is with mountain villages in the Abruzzi, or in the hills above Amalfi and Positano, but in the supposition that such villages were built of solid stone with the determination and energy of the ancient Romans. If the quantity of ruins in this area proves it to have been 'one of the most densely populated of the Andean valleys' we are left in our minds with the need for mountaineer inhabitants inured to running and hopping among these crags with the agility of chamois or mouflon, and with astonishment at the extraordinary character of the Inca Empire, a sensation of awe and wonder that only increases as we climb higher into the Altiplano.

There is, of course, a temple at Machu Picchu and—*sine qua non*— a number of huge Inca monoliths. It seems to have been a point of honour with them to have these immense stones for which there was certainly no need. It was a form of signature for their most curious civilization. The stone slabs are set up, side by side, and their very size and flatness made one think, incongruously, of the card houses one built as a child. How easily they collapsed and fell! And the challenge was to put up an immensely long card house and build a second storey on it. Such a Versailles of a card house would stand for a while just from the internal pressure of its long wings until one attempted some repair or alteration at one end. Then the whole edifice, like the ancient French monarchy, would fall in on itself and collapse from end to end. What vivid memories of a projecting wing of clubs and diamonds, or of a wall of hearts and spades! Harlequin houses made gay with red or black on white, bringing the realization that here at Machu Picchu there is no ornament of any kind at all. We had spent the afternoon and early evening in ruins as devoid of ornament as the stones of Carnac or Stonehenge, and where the only patterning had come in the last few moments, with the long lines of rain.

Yet these are houses and human habitations. They are not only shrines and monoliths. A total of some thousands of persons must have lived here down the generations. But there is no more ornament than

[1] *A Guide to Cuzco and Machu Picchu*, by Victor W. van Hagen, 1957, p. 25.

F

at Sing-Sing or Dartmoor. All is stern and spartan, the product of an ant-world or welfare state where every hour is organized and there is no time for pleasure. How, otherwise, could the huge monoliths have been dragged here? And in what other manner could they have continued here without the Spaniards hearing of them? Perfect and uncomplaining discipline must have been the rule. It is difficult to think of another civilization where there could be a stone-built village or small town without any carved or painted ornament of any description. A Quaker or Moravian settlement makes some concessions, however slight, if no more than a flowering window-box. At Machu Picchu there are fuchsias in flower among the ruins. I was given a fuchsia from Machu Picchu years before I came here, and grew it in a cold greenhouse. But they are accidents and have crept into the ruins. The only ornaments of Machu Picchu are fuchsias and the slanting lines of rain.

Back in the hotel on that rainy evening the only other guest was an American lady who had been here for a fortnight after experiencing the earthquake at Arequipa. She gave a lively, if horror-stricken, account of that, repeating it again word for word the next morning. How did she spend her days at Machu Picchu? She went out sketching early, at dawn if she woke up in time, wrote up her notes in the afternoon, and went out to sketch again in the evening. Later on we were to meet her in a strange sun-hat, sketch-book in hand, scrambling about the steep lanes of Cuzco. But she was no water-colour artist. She was an abstract painter, however vague and absent-minded, and an admirer of Piet Mondrian, whose acidulous, austere ground plans of paintings may have been affected by his being born a Dutchman among canals that run straight, or turn at an angle, but are never curving. Machu Picchu is a groundplan in high relief, it is like a relief map, but I did not want to spend a fortnight here. It would be most terribly depressing, going out to the ruins and coming back again. But neither would one want to be at Petra for a fortnight. So long a sojourn would only spoil the first impression.

There are certain places, among them some of the most impressive and beautiful in the world, that call for only a single dose, repeated perhaps the next morning. If nothing else, it is a tribute to their potency. Even the Parthenon, even the paintings in the Prado, are not to be seen each day, and every day. Machu Picchu, which is certainly among the wonders of both Americas, and a dual artifact of nature and of man, has hidden itself away, and it is not in its intention that we should spend too long a time in looking at it. We should come to it, preferably from far away, admire it, and move on. It would be to attribute human reactions to mountains and monoliths to suggest that the *zeitgeist* of Machu Picchu welcomes the hotel built near to it, but would have it not so comfortable that the tourist wants to stay there longer than two nights. The hotel manager at another Peruvian town in which we stayed, an Andalusian from Málaga, had spent some months at Machu Picchu where there is not a single other house, and only the station building and the huts surrounding it two thousand feet below, and one could not but sympathize with his sufferings. He had, he told us, grown to hate the ruins. Let us put it another way! Would the most ardent music-lover appreciate the performance of Beethoven's *Leonora No.* 2, and nothing else, all night and day? The greatest achievements of the human spirit are not for perpetual repetition. If they stale, they stale badly, and it is only after long silence or absence that they become fresh again. Machu Picchu, sited in one of the most astounding landscapes in the world is not, and never was, a work of art. It is a historical relic in marvellous and unaccountable preservation and, once seen, curiosity is satisfied and one can go away.

The morning was clear and fine with only a little mist upon the higher walls. We went out once more early to the ruins and looked at them again. More fuchsia buds had opened, and their long corollas were the colour of kniphofias ('red hot pokers'). Machu Picchu looked not a living, but a fossil town with no more of humanity than attaches to a primaeval skeleton found in a stalagmite cavern or a coal-mine. And hardly the skeleton itself, but the impression of it left in the soil. But an imprint of order and regularity with nothing haphazard up here on the mountain top. Shells or coils left behind by man with no other traces of him; only his handiwork in stone, and none of his possessions.

The hotel bus was waiting, and we started on the hair pin bends. With a driver who enlivened the road with songs in Quechua, that sounded much like folk songs from anywhere else, varying it with popular tunes from Mexico. Then, more Quechua in translation, of a lover comparing his sweetheart to a flower. At which he stopped and, scrambling down the bank, climbed back a moment later with a spray of white orchid, vanilla scented, in his hand. We were coming down into the hothouses of the forest, and it was only sad we could not continue further to Quillabamba, in the jungle, where the railway ends. But at the railway station we were given bunches of the same white orchid, and had, at least, seen Machu Picchu and held in our hands the orchids of the great Amazon.

Chapter Five

❖◆❖◆❖◆❖◆❖◆❖◆❖◆❖◆❖◆❖◆❖◆❖

CUZCO

WHAT LUXURY AND DELIGHT TO be starting at last for Cuzco in a private railcar which we could ask to have halted whenever we liked if we saw more orchids growing by the railway line! It made even the station of Machu Picchu seem more interesting. There was a long row of wooden shanties on both sides that plunged one in to an unknown world of Indians. Mothers, who could not have been more than twelve or fourteen years old, feeding their babies at the breast; and however ragged their skirts nearly everyone of them would be wearing a more or less clean and new white hat. Always barefoot, indeterminate of waistline owing to their many petticoats and sturdy hips. Sometimes with quite pretty youthful faces of Mongol cast, but always with the white hats. Looking up and down the high banks where the shanties stood just above the line, there were the white hats everywhere. And starting from this one thing in common, what liveliness of movement and clash of dirtying, if brilliant colours! All, or any kind of sanitation conspicuously absent, the hunt for fleas and lice in progress all the time, and pigs become domestic pets to judge from the actions of a small boy who kept on taking up a piglet in his arms to stop it from running across the railway line. Lifting it and putting it back in his shanty home, while the piglet played a game with him and ran out again.

The shanties are jumbled together and in terrible want of repair. It would make one nervous to strike a match, so quickly would fire spread through them. No electric light, that one was aware of at any rate, and the stifling darkness of their equatorial, nearly twelve-hour darkness.

How curious in the dawn to see them come out of their houses, shaking themselves, for of course they sleep in their clothes, even

the child mothers in their white hats, one supposes! There were hungry
looking turkeys and chickens, and a duck and her ducklings walking
along the line. None of the 'shocking pink' skirts here at Machu
Picchu, but bright greens and turquoise blues, and the softer coquettish
white hats. No one had told us of the Indian crowd scenes which
are to become more lively and brilliant as we go deeper into the
Altiplano, always centreing around the chola women in their multi-
coloured petticoats and altering types of hat, that ended, so far as this
part of our journey is concerned, with the brown 'bowlers' of La Paz.
At any wayside station they are more colourful than an Oriental crowd,
where the women are veiled, having maybe just one dash of the gypsy
or *flamenco* in the Spanish drop of blood. But not here at Machu
Picchu where they are pure Indian and not *mestiza*.

Three Franciscan monks whom we had seen the day before toiling up
the road on foot, now came to ask if we could give them a lift to Cuzco.
They were missionaries from deep in the Amazon forest, living among
naked savages, and had spent the night in the, to them, comparative
luxury of the railway station, all three of them in one bare room like
that we had been offered at Ollontay-Tambo. Once we had started they
were able to tell us the Indian names of many of the trees and flowers.
So we set off, finding the return journey even more fascinating because
we were not so tired. We passed the fuchsias and begonias, and ex-
ercised our privilege of stopping the rail-car when we saw a scarlet
orchid, for a change, on a rock above the line. As we climbed higher
than the five thousand feet at the bottom of the valley there were wild
gladioli growing. When we emerged from the canyon of the Urubamba and came to the plateau one could begin to realize the wonder
of being en route for Cuzco, and there was time to take it in for there
were several delays. We were running nearly two hours late owing
to the landslide, stopping sometimes when the points were against us
in the middle of nowhere till a train from the opposite direction came
by. And, as well, there were one or two delays at wayside stations
where the groups of Indians who had come to spend the day were quite
sparkling in their picturesqueness. I remember a woman in a new
hat, white of course, and a skirt of brilliant sapphire blue, but she
had gone in a moment behind a corner of wall, having only flashed
before our vision like a kingfisher. And now a new shape of hat
began to appear, like a straw bowl or a lampshade, but solid at the

top, a form of hat which is very distinctly upland Peruvian, probably dating from Inca times, and which is worn in masculine pattern more particularly around Pisac, a mountain village that we intended to see.

Now, at long last, we were on the hills above Cuzco where the line climbs in wide arcs and must reach to twelve thousand feet or more. Whence we begin coming slowly down with a grinding of the wheels till we are where we must halt and have to proceed backwards for a little, and get the first view of the roofs of Cuzco. By which time, for one is only human, we are famished with hunger, having breakfasted at seven a.m., and wondering mutely, if there is any possibility of luncheon. For it grows later and later, and our little one-coach train is wandering, no more than that, through a eucalyptus grove, with more and more enticing views of Cuzco down below. With the Cathedral Square and the churches and convents laid out before us, losing them as we go behind a bank of earth and getting them in view again. Coming down and down nearer to roof-level, and now even with some of the roofs of the town above us, but the train appearing to be heading in an entirely wrong direction with an agonizing slowness that only whets the appetite, obstinate and stubborn-headed, intent only on shunting itself into a suburb, until at a last bend of the line we can see the station and crawl into it, and have stopped at last. Thence in a taxi heaped with luggage, and once more too tired to take anything in, through siesta-emptied streets to the hotel, which is far larger and grander than we had imagined, and where in spite of the late hour, long after three p.m., we get something to eat, and obedient to the advice given us, go upstairs to bed.

After two hours' rest, and a first dose of cardamine tablets for breathlessness, it was about six o'clock and time to open the shutters. They had been closed when we took the room so that we did not see the view. When they were open we had the whole Cathedral Square in front of us, at about half an hour before sunset when there was a golden light on everything. The long and tiring journey was indeed worthwhile. Directly under our room, as though above the engine-room, there was what later proved to be a printing-works, which had kept up a maddening thudding and humming during all the time we had tried to rest. Now, mercifully, it had stopped and we looked out of our window over a row of intervening buildings straight onto the Square. I think the first sensation it gives one is of the extraordinary

tenacity of the Spaniards. This, more than the beauty of the architecture; it is not the art, but the character of the Spaniards, whether
you think of cities as far from here as Mexico, or of how far you are
from Spain. Where, in fact, are we, if you shut your eyes and open
them again? It could be Cuenca or Astorga, or Lugo or Plasencia;
some indeterminate town in Spain, but somewhere of importance
for the *plaza* has four churches looking out on it. No sign as yet of
Inca masonry, and all we can see from the window speaks of Spain.

There was just time for a drive in the town before it was dark,
and in a few moments we were in the Square. As in a Spanish town,
there are two-storeyed houses with arcades and balconies round two
sides of it, and the churches occupy the rest. This was La Compañía,
the church of the Jesuits, with a ground plan in the form of a Latin
cross, a shape particularly suited to brilliant lighting because of the
depth and space of the transepts, giving the effect of illumination
from the theatre wings. All we were in search of that evening of our
arrival was a quick impression so we only looked into La Compañía
and came out again. After which we drove to the high part of the town
behind the plaza, and in the fading light had our first sight of the Inca
walls.

A sunset walk or drive is always the way to get an impression of
a town, and from what we had seen by now Cuzco had none of the
exuberant Churrigueresque of Mexico. But, rather, it has been said
that 'the weather-beaten andesite façade' of the Cathedral 'presents an
aspect of unaffected nobility.'[1] The interior gaiety of La Compañía,
notwithstanding, and this was due to electric lighting which the
Jesuits missed—and how they would have loved it!—this remark is
certainly true, in general, of the churches of Cuzco, and it is indeed
Peru, and not Mexico. It was a reflection that gathered strength the
more we saw of Cuzco. But, next, there was our first night in this
extraordinary town.

The month of January in Lima had been as May or June, but Cuzco
was not like this. The central heating was still on, and welcome. At
the souvenir shop in the hall of the hotel one could rally oneself and
realize where one had got to. There were little *balsa* rafts for sale,
emblems of Lake Titicaca, though that is, in fact, two hundred miles

[1] Pál Kelemen, *op. cit.*, p.33.

A Spanish doorway in Cuzco

Church near Cuzco

Cathedral square at Cuzco, showing the Cathedral and
the Jesuit church of La Compañia

Street scene in Cuzco

away, but two hundred miles is nothing in South America. It had been
interesting enough only this same morning to know the waters of the
Urubamba joined the Amazon, it is true with more than one change of
name, and reached the Atlantic Ocean some two thousand miles away.
So what is a couple of hundred miles? There were postcards of Tiahuanaco for sale which is on the far side of Lake Titicaca, and in Bolivia,
not even in Peru. There were the flat red mitre hats of Pisac as worn
by the village mayors or alcaldes at the processions on Sundays, and
embroidered coats and skirts. But all these we could buy in Lima.
What we could neither sell nor exchange was the rarefied air of Cuzco
which already made it difficult to light a match, and was but a first
inkling of the Altiplano. And we went into a large dining-room for
dinner, and were given trout from Lake Titicaca, a recent scientific
experiment in those chill waters, which has resulted in fish that
are more the size and colour of salmon, and then were only too pleased
to find a log-fire burning in a sitting-room.

The first night at Cuzco was another matter altogether. I did not
get one wink of sleep. It was one of those nights that last for centuries.
But neither is it possible to lie still and rest. Instead, one spins round
like a top in bed and cannot lie still. This has the effect that it becomes
impossible to set oneself something pleasant to think about, for all
thinking is broken off by bouts of breathlessness. I did not find the
cardamine tablet made much difference, if any at all, and in any case
the dose is only one tablet 'to be dissolved under the tongue' every
three hours, which, by then, is once in three hundred years. I never
suffered from *soroche*, mountain sickness, which can be serious, all the
time we were on the Altiplano, but I was breathless nearly continually,
and got to hate the semi-dreaming state every night which did one no
good at all and ended every few moments, not so much with panting,
as with the last few seconds of held breath. Just as though one was
holding one's breath for some reason, and had held it just that much
too long.

The height of Cuzco is given as 11,007 feet above sea level, though
another authority says 10,400 feet, so let us call it somewhere nearer
eleven than ten thousand, and consider what this means. Two great
cities, Johannesburg and Mexico City, lie at seven thousand five
hundred feet, but neither city is in Europe. To live at this height in
Europe you would have to find some shepherd's hut or chamois

hunter's lair. St Moritz at just over six thousand feet is exceptionally high for Europe. As for the mountain railway up the Jungfrau, in Switzerland, Jungfraujoch, the highest railway station in Europe is at almost twelve thousand feet, while the summit of Mont Blanc is 15,780 feet.

As against this, and bearing those last two heights in mind, La Paz, the capital of Bolivia, is 12,200 feet, and the strange and nearly incredible Potosí, once a city with a hundred and sixty thousand inhabitants and a bigger population than London or Paris, lies at 13,600 feet. The highest recorded human habitation in the Peruvian highlands is at 17,400 feet.[1] So, here in Cuzco, we are nearing eleven thousand feet in altitude, and already finding it quite difficult to breathe.

One cannot sleep, and by the same token does not need so much sleep. In the space of a fortnight I had three entirely sleepless nights, and averaged no more than an hour to an hour and a half upon the other nights. In most other countries in the world this would spell illness and delirium but it does not seem to matter in Bolivia or Peru.

A match either will not strike at all, or goes out at once, because up to a half or more of the oxygen is missing compared to its ratio at sea level. It has the cautionary effect of discouraging one from smoking. But, also, eating and drinking have to be curtailed, and one must walk slowly and go upstairs one step at a time. Life is, in fact, constricted within limits that must resemble living in an airship or a submarine. Cuzco is comparatively low lying contrasted to Puno or La Paz for after ten thousand feet every few hundred feet of altitude makes a great difference and is quickly felt. Cuzco should be supportable to most persons, and I might not have felt it so much myself if I had gone there when younger but, as we have seen, there are some who cannot take Cuzco at all, and they would be well advised not to attempt Lake Titicaca. Personally, I enjoyed Cuzco so much, and was so pleased and excited at getting there, that I did not mind the lack of sleep and breathlessness. It is true that one is given very little warning, and that many of the Peruvians themselves have not dared the Altiplano, or have been there once and will not go again.

After a sleepless night in Cuzco one is a little lightheaded, and

[1] J. Alden Mason, *op. cit.*, 1957, p. 7.

at the same time deafened by a concatenation of the church bells in all 'fifty churches' of the town, beginning their first salvoes at the unearthly hour of four-thirty, with renewed and louder broadsides in unison at five and six o'clock—though they are as nothing to the church bells of Quito. But after a sleepless night it is better to get up early and be out of one's room, before the room gets upon one's nerves; so after coffee and papaya with the slice of fresh lime that gives to it the authentic taste of the warm tropics, I started off on a brilliant morning that despite the clear air was, yet, pullover weather. None the less, within an hour, if you put your hand for a few instants on the bonnet of a car, so strong are the sun rays that you nearly scorch your fingers. Such is the equatorial climate, the altitude in spite of the apparent cold of the air only accentuating the strength of the sun rays, so that it is quickly understandable why the Indians, men and women alike, always wear a hat. Or is it something in the Amerindian temperament, all over both Americas, from the war-eagle head-dresses of the Red Indian braves, as we can admire those in George Catlin's line-engravings to the head-dresses of quetzal plumes on the Mayan monoliths of Tikal and Copán, by way of the white hats of the *mestizas* of Cuzco, and ending in our own time with the brown derbys of the *chola* women of La Paz?

One has not been walking in daylight on the streets of Cuzco for more than a few moments before one realizes it is a city of *mestizos*. Nine out of every ten persons is a *mestizo* and the language they speak is Quechua and not Spanish. This city of Inca origin, which was rebuilt by the Spaniards upon Inca foundations, is inhabited by a population with only a diluted drop of Spanish blood in their veins and who still talk Quechua which was the speech of the Incas. They form the middle class of the Peruvian and Bolivian highlands; in which capacity an authority says of them that 'through the creation of a virile and growing *mestizo* class, the influence of the Indians upon their countries has been greater than the influence of the white man's civilization upon them.'[1] They have filled, and are filling still more, the emptiness left by the decline and near extinction of the original Indian population after the Conquest, the same authority telling us that 'in the first forty years between half and three-quarters of the

[1] *Indians of the Andes. Aymaras and Quechuas*, by Harold Osborne, Routledge & Kegan Paul Ltd., London, 1952, pp. xiii, 175, 235, 236.

native population disappeared and during the ensuing two centuries it was more than halved again.' This would mean the survival of only about one-eighth of the original inhabitants. To quote further from the same source: 'There are in fact two *cholo* peoples, that which arose from Spanish admixture with the Quechuas and that which arose from admixture with the Aymaras', the latter being the race inhabiting the shores of Titicaca and the region of La Paz; and the same writer remarks elsewhere in the same book the fact, which one quickly notices, that the *cholo* class is physically more close to the Indian than to the Spaniard, the native blood seeming to predominate up to at least the third or fifth generation, but that there is now 'no increase of mestization' for this mingling of Spaniard and Indian in the early days of the colonial epoch 'has long ceased'. In fact, as time goes on the *mestizos* will become less Indian, and less and less Spanish, but more *cholo*. From the visual and merchandising aspects they are already in full possession of Cuzco.

Owing to the predominance of their costume one remembers Cuzco as a city of *chola* women in white hats. This again, like the exigencies of altitude, is something one was scarcely warned of and did not expect. The population is neither Spanish, nor Indian, but *mestizo*, and to deny this is to say there are no Turks in Istanbul. Cuzco is a city of *cholos* who speak Quechua, just as, we shall find later, La Paz has a *cholo* population who talk Aymara. The 'Indian' markets, almost more than the churches, are the magnets that draw our attention in *cholo* cities like Cuzco or La Paz, but this again differentiates them from the purely Indian markets of Huancayo or Pisac. The Quechua-speaking *cholos* are a little less colourful than the Aymara, and the market women of Cuzco less flaunting than their sisters of La Paz who have evolved a kind of fish-wife, costermonger vitality and character of their own, which must wait till we get there, while, in the meantime, this brilliant morning we are admiring a whole market-stall or even a shop-window full of nothing but their new white hats.

Our footsteps lead us, of course, once more to the plaza or main square with its four churches. An incongruous '1880' fountain in the middle of the square, inspired by some silver *épergne*, has Indians spouting water from conch-shells into its basin, while, above this, a Red Indian on the war-path in full war-paint with bow and arrows— the Inca Atahuallpa?—keeps the look-out over a lower basin where a couple of storks—or are they flamingoes?—clap their wings. The sculptor was obviously not clear in his mind as to the difference between a Red Indian and an Inca. But, at least, this fountain does not distract attention; it is not vociferous enough to be seen and heard. Its reticence is in the category of good manners. One can look at the façades of the four churches without knowing it is there at all. There is, at once, a similarity of idiom between the façades of La Compañía and the Cathedral, implying that both are nearly of the same date. It would be quite wrong, however, to agree that either façade is in the Herreran style for neither has the remotest suggestion of either the Escorial or the Cathedral of Valladolid, both of which are by Herrera. Rather, they are of medium Northern Spanish style, like any of a dozen or more cathedrals to be seen in Spain. What is remarkable is not that they should be Spanish, intrinsically and *per se*, but that they should be of all towns in the world in Cuzco. Perhaps, if dropped in the square at Cuzco by helicopter, a little reflection would make us guess at somewhere in the New World for all four churches have façades which must have been built within a hundred years of one another, and nowhere is there a trace of Gothic or Romanesque. It is Spanish allright, but could be in no town in Spain one has ever heard of, and must be, therefore, in Latin America. Not in Mexico, for not one of the four churches has any sign of the Churrigueresque which is the national style of Mexico, and in view of that it must be either Quito or Cuzco. Not Quito, however, if one knows the renown of her golden or scarlet lacquered interiors, and so the choice narrows down to Cuzco.

These are the buildings in the plaza; La Compañía of the Jesuits into which we entered last night attracted by the bright lights,[1] and next to it a much lower façade which, in fact, looks like a fifth church in the square, and was the college of the Jesuits but is now the University. The Cathedral stands at an angle to La Compañía with a building touching it to either side; El Templo de Jesú y María to the left which is plainly of the eighteenth century, and on the right El Templo de Triunfo which is another sober eighteenth-century building. After which it is only necessary to add that all these façades were rebuilt after the disastrous earthquake of 1650, and that the great

[1] and the side altars: 'a witch's cauldron of forms crowned by an attic suggesting sea horses and disassembled dinosaur bones.' George Kubler and Martin Soria, *op. cit.*, p. 181. How well that is phrased!

patron of the rebuilding was Manuel de Mollinedo, who was Bishop of Cuzco from 1673 to 1699.[1] If it is a little ridiculous to compare him, as has been done, with Julius II or Lorenzo de' Medici, who were patrons of the greatest artists of the Western world, he does seem to have been largely responsible for the Cuzqueñan style as that is manifest in painting and gilding. Four silver altar frontals in Cuzco churches still bear his coat-of-arms, he paid for most of the carved pulpits which are the pride of Cuzco, and it may have been his instigation that undammed the tide of gilt Cuzqueñan mirrors in such profusion to load collections such as that of Señor Pedro de Osma in Lima. All in all, with its Herreran interior for that *is* Herreran; and its choir-stalls and its other treasures, the Cathedral of Cuzco is perhaps 'the finest church of the Western hemisphere', that it to say, of both Americas.

If one looks for anything dashing and Mexican in Cuzco, or, indeed, anywhere in Peru, one will be disappointed. There are very curious local developments ahead round Lake Titicaca, but those are Indian or *mestizo* delayed effects. Their polychrome decorations of a very local iconology stem from the sixteenth century even if they were worked two hundred years later. There is no Taxco in Peru; or anything at all that compares to the Santuario de Ocotlán which is the quintessence of the Mexican style. Not, indeed, that those would suit the landscape of Peru; anymore than one could imagine the tiled Pueblan churches of Mexico in this bitter cold for we are seeing Cuzco, the chill night notwithstanding, in the height of summer. In all such questions the *genius loci* has its part to play. It is even arguable that tiled fronts would be cracked by frost; and although they are in the same sub-continent two thousand miles away, one must not expect the *azulejos* of Río and Bahia. They are of another world altogether, Brazil being even further removed from Peru in temperament than distant Mexico.

Leaving the church interiors for the moment, for there is plenty of time on hand, we drive a little way out of the town in order to look back at Cuzco. It lies in rather a funnel-shaped valley, the thin point of which ends at the hills we climbed in order to go to Machu Picchu.

[1] 'The most munificent patrons of the arts in the history of Spanish colonies, a virtual Medici of the seventeenth century. At the time of his death it was said that he had donated fourteen churches of brick, thirty-six of adobe, fourteen pulpits, eighty-two *custodias*, and twenty frontals of silver.' *Colonial Architecture and Sculpture in Peru*, by Harold E. Wethey, Harvard University Press, 1949, p. 67.

nd now it broadens out and is quite green and fertile. We have
come out through a suburb of mean houses, past the other railway
station where we are to embark in a day or two for Puno and Lake
Titicaca, and leaving on our left a church with a fine late seventeenth-
century façade of Cathedral and La Compañía pattern. There are groves
of eucalyptus trees and we meet a herd of llamas, once a common sight
in Cuzco, but now so much of a rarity that one stops to watch them.
Seventeenth-century churches apart, this can be like no other country
but Tibet, and yaks and llamas are interchangeable and would adapt
themselves in either land. In Inca times the principal fuel in the Peruvian highlands was dried llama dung, just as in Tibet they use yak
dung; and there are districts where each llama in a herd will wander
along with its inquisitive, disdainful air, and with its droppings tied
in a little package on its back. As in Tibet, there are no woods or
forests at this height, hence the planting of eucalyptus which one
had thought of as being a swamp-tree from Australia, useful for
draining marshes and planted, therefore, in malarial districts. But
in Peru, eucalyptus will grow at higher than thirteen thousand feet and
here are large plantings of it.

From where we are now the roofs of Cuzco give no such sensation
as when climbing above them on the way to Machu Picchu. There
no hurrying in or out of Cuzco; the Cuzqueñans live inside, and not
outside the town. One forgets, and is thinking it is some ordinary
town in Spain or Italy, when more llamas pass by in charge of a woman
wearing one of the flat hats of Pisac. A pure-blooded Quechua Indian,
but we are returning to the *mestizo* town and now go up, above and
behind the Cathedral, to the oldest part of Cuzco which has an entire
individuality of its own and can be like nowhere else in the world
but itself. The flavour is so strong that almost it is its own caricature.
As we get out of the car, sure enough a smallish herd of llamas straggles
down the stone steps. The lanes are too narrow to drive along, not
that this will stop the driver from attempting it, and it is here that
the bonnet of the car scorches the fingers after it has only been there
for a few minutes. What we see is picturesque, emphatically, and
notorious sketching-ground, but of another kind. Nothing in Asia
or Africa bears the slightest resemblance to it, and one realizes with a
little of a shock that there is no word for it. Decidedly it is not American,
though in America, and South American has too many connotations.

It is something you could see only in Peru, or Bolivia, or in Ecuador, with local differences, but adding up to the same thing. I would call it Pacific South American, which is too clumsy, and in fact by and large it is the Altiplano of Peru, with regional alternations at either end which means in Bolivia and Ecuador. In a phrase, this is a Spanish balcony or upper storey on Inca foundations with *cholo* men and women walking by.

This is a famous corner of old Cuzco with green-painted wooden balcony or jalousie jutting out, and a doorway set across the angle with a view of a flowered court within. But all the lower part of the wall and the wall opposite, making of it a cyclopaean lane, is of huge Inca stonework. It is here, lower down the lane, that there is the twelve-sided stone of which one does not perhaps get the full technical significance at the first glance. It seems just to be a most enormous, odd shaped stone. But it has been fitted into its place as if with precision instruments, and one cannot but think the Inca builders put it there as something of a technical triumph. They permitted themselves little or no ornament at all, being in this respect as parsimonious of high spirits as the architects of the Steuben glass or the Seagram Building in New York, and perhaps this was the only way in which they could express themselves outside the dull uniformity of stone on stone. More than one authority has suggested that the Incas must have had a body of workers with inherited skill in cyclopaean building to draw upon. 'Without a long practical development in stone masonry . . . the experience and ability could not have been suddenly achieved in the time of Pachacuti' (the ninth Inca 1438-1471), 'before whom the Incas ruled only a small territory around Cuzco. It is impossible to escape the assumption that Pachacuti and subsequent Incas must have been able to draw upon the services of a large body of skilled and experienced stoneworkers who had generations of tradition behind them. . . . The Incas must certainly have followed up a tradition of stone building which was widely spread long before they extended their empire.'[1]

This is argued in order to counteract another theory which is that the enormous stone walls at Machu Picchu, Ollontay-Tambo, Sacsahuamán (which we have not yet seen), and here in Cuzco, are

[1] Harold Osborne, *op. cit.*, pp. 129, 130.

pre-Inca. The fantasy of a great Megalithic kingdom or empire with
its capital at Tiahuanaco at the far side of Lake Titicaca, and its fascinating visual possibilities owing to their expert skill in textile weaving
which would have made of it one of the most wonderful human
spectacles ever to be seen, now receives some kind of shadowy support.
For there must be some kind of connection, however remote, with the
cyclopaean builders, although there is this prime difference between
them, that the builders of Tihuanaco, though they worked with
monoliths and vast squared blocks, did not know the polygonal technique of fitting together stones with a number of angles to them, in
fact a species of giant jigsaw mosaic. But, equally, as the same authority
points out, 'the Incas had inherited no tradition of architectural sculpture', so there is no direct technical inheritance from one age to the
other, and yet there must be some connection.

Never having seen before stone walls like these, composed of such
enormous units in the form of gigantic single stones, made one think,
however fortuitously, of the 'brick painter', Jan van der Heyden who
rendered every brick with microscopic accuracy in his views of
seventeenth-century Amsterdam and Haarlem. What would he have
made of Cuzco, had he come here as Frans Post, his contemporary,
went to Brazil, and painted that? Stone walls with it may be a hundredth
of the bricks to which he was accustomed. It is curious, and not quite
irrelevant to think of that, for this is the most typical, the archetypal
scene of Cuzco which has been sketched and photographed ten thousand
times, and something that is entirely of the old New World though
there is no name to call it by. It is in South America, but that does
not describe it any more than does the term 'Peruvian', which is in
diminishment of what it meant originally when it included Bolivia
and Ecuador. The painted balcony is part, in fact, of the Bishop's
palace, and leading off the flowered court are episcopal apartments
with a sort of throne room for audiences and receptions and a number
of episcopal portraits.

When we came out again through the flowers into that rarefied
sunlight, it was in time to see an exceptionally brilliant group of
chola women walking by, and another still, before the first was gone
from sight. Stonehenge apart, one has never seen so large an area
of stone construction without any ornament or carving, and it is this
that puts Cuzco and other Inca buildings in a category by themselves.

G

It may, also, be a reason for the bright *chola* dresses for which there could be no more telling background. Aniline dyes are used for them nowadays, and their colours are no longer the result of processes that may have come down from ancient times, but both here and when admiring the bell-shaped skirts (*polleras*) of La Paz, one may be inclined to think that for once the aniline dyes are better. Their shriller tones are a little muted in the unnaturally clear air, and perhaps emerge from it with the sort of force that would be lacking in the softer, more harmonious colours.

From here we went on through the high lying part of the town in order to see the carved pulpit in San Blas. This is one of the sights of Cuzco and the guide books go into ecstasies over it. But it is not, in fact, very exciting, and only one of a number of such pulpits, not only in Peru but all over South and Central America. Woodcarving was a craft that caught on quickly with the Indians, for it required patience and unlimited time. We are not far from regions where an Indian would spend months and even years making a single one of the famous Montecristi panama hats, the straw of which has to be specially treated under water for weeks at a time.[1] Furthermore, they are only made of the most chosen part of the grass which yields the fibre, and are only woven at a certain time of year during which a special temperature exists, and the finest quality of them can be folded up and put into a matchbox. Such is the kind of criterion to be applied to the carved pulpit in San Blas. It must have taken months and years to carve and put together. But it must certainly be true that the number of elaborately carved pulpits 'from Columbia to Argentina shows the importance of preaching in the evangelization of the New World'.[2] This is a prize piece of carving by a Cuzqueñan Indian, and it is only equalled by some of the pulpits to be seen at Quito but, curiously, if you look into it, the ornament is exactly that of carved oak in England, although the date is 1680-95. It is nearly a hundred years later, more or less, than its detail would imply, but served up in Baroque shape, worked to an exquisite finish, and then gilded; and if it took a long time in the carving we may be certain that the orations delivered from it were, proportionately, no shorter.

---

[1] *The Andes and the Amazon: Life and Travel in Peru*, by C. Reginald Enoch, T. Fisher Unwin, London, 1907, p. 60.
[2] George Kubler and Martin Soria, *op. cit.*, p. 177.

It is always to be noticed that the churches of Cuzco are rich in painfully realistic sculpture; figures of Christ wearing wigs of dark, dark hair, agonizing virgins, and saints with bleeding wounds and cicatrices. Such are to be seen in village churches in Castile for it is in the temperament of Spain, but at the hands of Indian craftsmen the catalogue of saints comes darker still. The golden hair that haunted the angelically-minded, of whom Fra Angelico so aptly named is prime example, seems never to have penetrated to Peru, and it is the darkness of the statues that imposes and on occasion even frightens. In San Blas of Cuzco are sculptures belonging to this category, and what with one thing and another it is a relief to come out into the air. But spirits revive on going a little way further to admire the doorway of Las Nazarenas, all Inca masonry on its lower storey with the stones re-cut, it may be, in order to make them a little smaller, and a pair of fishtailed monsters carved, one would guess, by an Indian who had never seen the sea. The doorway is very typical of Cuzco with its 'minced up' Inca stonework as high as the reduced stones would go, and above that whitewash.

By this time we had friends in the town, who had begun by calling ceremoniously at the hotel, and we went in return to see them at the club. This was something of an anomaly. One had not anticipated a club in Cuzco. It was a new building, freshly painted, with a res- taurant on one of the upper floors. But we sat downstairs and drank 'pisco sours', which never taste so good as they do in Lima, and talked of life in Cuzco. It seems to have more than a superficial resemblance to what life in Lhasa may have been till not so long ago, though no doubt the inhabitants would deny this. The truth is that Cuzco is ordinary at one moment, as in this instant sitting in the club, but becomes unique and extraordinary at a second's notice. Suddenly there comes a bout of breathlessness, and it is time for another cardamine tablet which, we were told consolingly, or at any rate the glucose part of it, is given to boxers before they climb into the ring, and to dancers before they go onto the stage. They never seemed to make any difference to me and I got to hate the taste of them.

If just this one thing were done, that motors were taken off the streets, then the analogy with Lhasa would be evident. Not that they are identical in any respect, but resemblances are as strong as

in two matching tones of red and green. Or one could say that it is
as though, not Communist China had occupied Lhasa but Catholic
Spain, and not long after the reign of Ferdinand and Isabella; that
there are Spanish superstructures upon the Tibetan buildings, that
miscegenation has taken place and there is a half-breed population of
Mongol with Iberian; at which point we may not bother ourselves as to
whether the draught animals—except that neither draws a vehicle
and both are beasts of burden—are yaks or llamas. Both are interchangeable as are the *mestizo* inhabitants. Certainly the Inca walls, and
the walls the Spaniards built out of the Inca stonework, make as much
of an impression as must the Potala of Lhasa. And that entirely on the
cyclopaean scale for all the rest of them have perished. Where they
relaxed and allowed themselves the luxury of sculpture or ornament its
effect must have been all the greater from contrast with the bare walls.
The impression of ancient Cuzco must have been of stark austerity lit
up with gold; not gilding as that is painted on to carved ornaments
but sheet gold. The stones of Cuzco, some few of them, wore gold
breastplates or cuirasses. The loot of the *Conquistadores* included golden
plates, polygonal sheets they probably were, to fit over the stones:
'these had been taken from the walls . . . they had holes in them
showing that they had been secured by nails.' They were 'golden
spangled' walls.[1] The Spaniards saw a 'quadrangular building . . .
measuring three hundred and fifty paces from corner to corner, entirely
plated with gold; of these gold plates they took down seven hundred
which weighed five hundred pesos of gold.' Perhaps seven hundred is
an unconvincing number for a building which was three hundred and
fifty yards long. One feels for once the Spaniards have underestimated.
Perhaps the number of gold plates is correct but the dimensions wrong.

And having reached the gold of Cuzco we will continue with it.
The Temple of the Sun was the golden climax. It had a roof of grass-
thatch with—a beautiful image!—golden straws set in the thatch, and
the walls had massy sheet gold upon them. It had six courts with lesser
temples, and the Temple of the Moon was walled with silver. 'On both
sides of a picture of the moon—a woman's face painted on a silver
plaque—were the bodies of the dead queens, Mama Oello, mother of
Huayna Capac in front, cheek to cheek with her, more honoured than

---

[1] The phrase is not mine. cf. *The Realm of the Incas*, by Victor W. van Hagen, The New
American Library, Mentor Books, New York, 1957, p. 142.

the others, as having been the mother of such a son': thus Garcilaso
Inca de la Vega. A golden fountain with the image of the Sun upon
it is our second intimation of any ornament. Up to this point the account
is of sheet gold which must have glittered, and by ten o'clock in the
morning in this curious climate been as hot as fire.

But now we come to the ceremonial part of the Temple of the Sun
which cannot but remind one of rites, themselves thousands of years
old in origin, performed in the Temple of Heaven in Peking. Inside
the Forbidden City; but here it is the Coricancha, the Golden Enclosure,
or Court of Gold, with the Intipampa or Field or Garden of the Sun
leading from it. Here, in the planting season the Inca and his retinue
mimicked the reaping and gathering of the harvest. According to Cieza
de León: 'there were clods and pieces of fine gold and it was artificially sown with corn plants which were of gold, as well the stems
as the leaves and the corncobs.' Among the loot listed were 'straws
of solid gold, with their spikes just as they grow in the fields'. If it is
altogether likely that certain elements of Oriental origin were introduced from time to time over a long period into America'[1], one
needs, in corroboration, some evidence as to the antiquity of very
similar rites in Oriental kingdoms which certainly read as though
there was some parallel between them. 'Besides all this they had
more than twenty llamas of gold with their young, and the shepherds
lifesize, with their slings and crooks to watch them . . . all made of
gold.'

This account reads as though it is not exaggerated. The golden
straws or wires woven into the thatch are beautiful in imagery, as is
the silvered Temple of the Moon in simulance of moonlight, poetical
touches which have hitherto been lacking in the sternness of the
cyclopaean walls, even with their golden coats or cuirasses burning in
the thin air at this altitude. But, also, the golden maize cobs are a
beautiful idea. As for the golden llamas 'with their young' they were
lifesize, we are told, which means as tall, or taller than an Indian,
so that one would have found oneself moving among figures of
a man's height and their shadows in that golden herd. The shepherds
'and their slings and crooks to watch them . . . all made of gold' are
only made the more interesting when enquiry about their slings reveals
those as being of braided wool or fibre, and up to six feet in length.

[1] J. Alden Mason, *op. cit.*, p. 23.

They were used by doubling them, with both ends held in one hand, whirling them round the head, and then releasing the stone. A sling was always carried by countrymen in the highlands of Peru, and 'was often worn as a fillet to bind the hair. It was always used to drive domestic animals,'[1] this being confined to the llama, and not even the other llamoids, alpaca, vicuña, and guanaco, which are wild or semi-wild animals, though, even so, the Peruvian Indian was more lucky than either the Aztecs or the Mayans who had no domestic animals excepting guinea-pigs and small edible dogs.

The golden splendours just described stood on the site of the present church of Santo Domingo where in comparison there is little or nothing to see. It is perhaps strange that the Spanish Conquerors did not build the Cathedral of Cuzco on the foundations of this great Indian temple, yet Santo Domingo is but one of many Cuzqueñan churches and has no exceptional or distinguishing features to it. Are there no links with the Inca city excepting for the few accounts by eye-witnesses? Among whom, one must remember, are Juan de Betanzos, a Spaniard who came to South America with Pizarro, and who married a sister, or some say the daughter, of the last Inca King Atahuallpa; while the more famous historian Garcilaso Inca de la Vega was a first generation *mestizo* of Peru, his mother being a niece of the Inca Huayna Capac, and grand daughter of the great Inca King Tupac Yupanqui. He was born in Cuzco, passed his childhood there largely with his Inca relations, left Peru when twenty years old and retired in his old age to Córdoba where he wrote his *Comentarios Reales*.

But there are indeed some strange and peculiar links with ancient Cuzco in the form of paintings, and in order to see the more important of these we go again to La Compañía, the Jesuit church in the main square, where the pictures in question are to both sides of the main door. They are proofs of the policy of the Spanish kings towards their Indian subjects and their attempts to, as it were, legalize the conquest, in pursuance of which they encouraged marriages between Spaniards of noble lineage and Indian women of royal birth, thus hoping, it seems, to set up a form of *mestizo* aristocracy. One of the paintings, that on the left of the door, depicts the wedding of a nephew of St Ignatius Loyola, founder of the Jesuit order, with an Inca princess. The inscription reads: 'Don Martín de Loyola, Governor of

[1] Op. cit., p. 191.

Chile, nephew of our Father Saint Ignatius, being son of his elder brother, Don Beltrán de Loyola, married Doña Beatriz Ñusta, heiress and princess of Peru, being daughter of its last king, Don Diego Inga. Of the union of Don Martín and Doña Beatriz was born Doña Lorenza Ñusta de Loyola, who went to Spain by order of our Catholic Monarchs. And she married in Madrid the most excellent Sr Don Juan de Borja, son of St Francis Borja and Ambassador of the Señor King Philip II in Portugal and the Holy Roman Empire. With this marriage the two houses of Loyola and Borja are related with the royal house of the Inca Kings of Peru, whose succession is now in the most excellent Señors and Marquesses of Alcañices, Grandees of Spain of the first class.' From which inscription, which it is exceedingly difficult to decipher, it emerges that the Inca princess is allowed the title of Ñusta which is that applied to the Holy Women or Virgins of the Sun. There must be families still flourishing in Spain with this mingling of the blood of Inca, Borja, and Loyola running in their veins. Not only is the inscription difficult to read, but the two paintings are nearly invisible in the darkness, and unfortunately they are by so poor a painter that he hardly deserves the name of artist. Nevertheless, if willing to believe what we are told, the princess is wearing traditional Inca dress of vicuña cloth, a sash decorated with heraldic patterns repeated in the tunic, and a large mantle worn over the dress, held in place with a golden *tupu* ornament,[1] a *tupu* being the large, spoon-shaped pin still worn by the Quechua women to hold their shawls together.

The companion painting to the right of the door is of another wedding, that of Don Beltrán García de Loyola to Doña Lorenza Idiaquez of Cuzco, and could this be seen properly it is full of detail. But both pictures are little more than the work of journeymen painters and to anyone interested it is almost torturing that they should not be better. Coming out again into the shrill sunlight of the plaza what would one not give for paintings, even as bad as these, of Cuzco only a generation earlier in time. Of scenes, for instance, in this same plaza before it was degraded by the Spaniards and turned into an execution ground. Atahuallpa, the last reigning Inca, was not killed here—he was garrotted at the last moment, instead of being burned alive,

[1] Victor W. van Hagen, *op. cit.*, p. 11. There are later versions of these wedding pictures at Lima, in the church of N.S. de Copacabana, with the protagonists wearing Louis XIV dress.

because he accepted to become a Christian as the wood was about to be ignited—he was executed at Cajamarca, although he had filled his cell with gold and paid his ransom. That was in 1533. But Tupac Amaru, last Inca claimant to the throne, was beheaded here in 1572 after his wife and followers had been tortured and killed before his eyes. And the melancholy history of the Incas ends with another Tupac Amaru, a direct descendant of the Incas, who was responsible for a serious Indian uprising, and after his wife and sons had been tortured and killed before his eyes was torn to pieces by four wild horses in the main plaza of Cuzco on 11th November, 1782, a late date for the perpetration of such barbarisms.

If only the painter of the wedding pictures, or his like, could have left painted records of the Inca ceremony to the Sun in this same square. Garcilaso describes the gathering of the Indians from all the different provinces; some 'looking exactly like the paintings of Hercules, clothed in lion's skin and with their heads enclosed in the lion's head, because these pride themselves on being descended from a lion,' only for 'lions' we should read 'pumas'. 'Others came, garbed like the paintings of angels, with great wings of a bird which they call *cuntur*, i.e. condor—these birds are white and black and so large that many killed by the Spanish have measured fourteen or fifteen feet from wingtip to wing-tip—for they boast that they are descended and derive their origin from this bird. . . . Other *curacas* i.e. *caciques* entered the festival with gestures and grimaces of madmen, fools and half-wits . . . they brought pictures of the deeds they had done in the service of the Sun and of the Incas; they brought large drums and trumpets and many servants to play them. . . . The following day, which was the day of the festival, at dawn the Inca came forth accompanied by all his family . . . to the great square of the city. There they waited for the Sun to appear, and all were barefoot and with great reverence, looking towards the east, when the Sun first began to appear all squatted on their heels (which with these Indians is the same as falling to their knees) to adore him and opening their arms with the hands raised one to each side of the face, giving kisses in the air (which is the same as kissing one's hand or the robe of the King of Spain).'

'Then the King rose, and raising two golden vessels invited the Sun to drink, and from the jar in his right hand it came out through a pipe of very beautiful workmanship which ran from the great square to the house of the Sun. So it was indeed as if the Sun had drunk. And from the vessel in his left hand he himself drank and gave the rest to the other Incas, who each one held ready a drinking-cup of gold or silver.' Then came the offering of gifts. 'The priests came out to the door to receive the vessels of the *curacas* . . . who gave their vessels and other objects of gold and silver which they had brought from their lands to present to the Sun, such as sheep (llamas), lambs, lizards, toads, snakes, foxes, tigers, lions, and a great variety of birds; in a word all that most abounded in their country counterfeited in silver and gold with great naturalness, though each thing in miniature.' After which came the sacrifice of a black llama lamb, and the fore-telling of future events from its entrails.[1]

Next came the kindling of the ritual fire, 'which had to be new, given by the hand of the Sun, as they said. For the which they took a large bracelet which they call *chipana* (similar to others which the Incas habitually wore on the left wrist), which the chief priest wore; it was larger than most; it had as a medallion a concave stone like half an orange, very highly burnished; they held it against the Sun and at a certain spot where the rays, which came out of the stone, joined they placed a little cotton very finely teased, as they did not know how to make tinder, which caught fire in a short time, for this is a natural thing. With the fire thus given by the hand of the Sun they burnt the sacrifice and cooked all the meat for that day.' And there followed a great banquet, with the Inca seated on his chair of solid gold. The Ñustas or Virgins of the Sun, served the feast, dressed in white robes, and after that was over, brought the cloth of vicuña wool they had woven during the year and presented it to the Inca and his family.

But there are no paintings, or anything but the narratives of Gar-cilaso and other chroniclers, to help in reconstructing the scene[2]. However, there are paintings, though not even as good as those in the

[1] Garcilaso says that the Indians preferred a black lamb to all other colours, for they held it to be of great divinity because they said that the black beast was completely black, and that the white, though white in all its body, always had a swart muzzle, which was a defect, and was therefore regarded as inferior to the black. And for this reason the Kings dressed in black most of the time and their colour for mourning was undyed wool which they called dun colour. This may even explain the dun colour of the Paracas dresses and textiles in the museum at Lima, though those were all so much earlier in date.

[2] A curious panoramic painting of 'Cuzco in 1650', with naïve perspective, and presenting a kind of x-ray picture of the town as though you could see inside the houses, is in El Templo de Triunfo in Cuzco, but owing to the recent earthquake, was not on view at the time of my visit. It is reproduced in Harold E. Wethey, *op. cit.*, plate 21.

church of La Compañía which go a little, if only a very little way towards telling us of what we want to know. They are the series of twelve canvases in the church of Santa Ana, and their subject is the pagan-Christian procession of Corpus Christi. Their date is, maddeningly, perhaps as late as 1680, more than a hundred and fifty years after the conquest, but one would hardly think this at a first inspection. The church of Santa Ana is outside and a little above the town, on the road by which Pizarro entered Cuzco in 1534, but we remembered it for being close to the railway line to Machu Picchu, and near that first view of the tiled roofs of Cuzco.

It is a little of an experience to get to Santa Ana, and having arrived there, more of an adventure still to go inside. The writer would claim to have visited more churches and mosques in many different lands than most other persons, but Santa Ana in Cuzco stands out in his memory as being unique in many respects. There was a wait of half an hour, no less, while the sacristan was found and, when identified, he had mislaid the key. Upon a broilingly hot morning with glacial undercurrents in the air of dangerous, pneumonic impact, and by far the dirtiest dust blowing about and getting into one's eyes and down one's throat. The open space at the side of the church like a gipsy encampment in everything except the actual tents, and at least a score of women in their brightly coloured petticoats, magenta or viridian green uppermost, and white felt hats with black pigtails of hair hanging down their necks, squatting there in Slade School attitudes, only disproved when they stood or walked about by the shortness and sturdiness of their legs, when they become fishwives, but without their creels of fish. There is always, though, the Indian predominant in the *mestiza* women, for each of them has a baby slung on her back, or more often feeding at the breast. When, at last, the key was found we had to pick our way between them, followed by a horde of children. Then came the opening of wooden shutters, and a great pulling and unfurling of blinds and curtains which did not let in enough light to see the paintings, and those hanging on both walls near the altar are, in fact, too dark to make out the detail.

We had to climb a rickety ladder to the organ-loft at the far end of the church where the nearest painting was only a few feet away. At least a dozen children followed us up the ladder. But they are large canvases, and the end of the near picture being flat against the wall was invisible, more or less. The processions of Corpus Christi at Cuzco must have been an Indian or semi-pagan mingling of the Semana Santa and the Feria of Seville. It was a kind of 'visiting week' for the statues of saints from villages all around. The much venerated Virgen de Belén was 'at home' to them all in this church of Santa Ana, and then on the feast day they were taken in solemn procession to Cuzco Cathedral where they stayed for the eight days of the octave. For the purpose of the procession the different *cofradías* or religious brotherhoods of the town made decorated floats on which to carry the images; there were embroidered robes for the statues, and decorated arches, and so forth, were put in front of the different churches. But the interest is the Indian, or even Inca character and detail in the proceedings.

Each *cofradía* had an Indian leading its procession in the ancient royal dress of the Incas, and wearing a most curious emblematic head-dress which embodied the coat-of-arms of the *cofradía* but was of Indian interpretation. These Inca personages wear a *poncho* or shirt of Indian pattern with a large sun worked on the breast, a detail which leaves no doubt open as to its Inca origin and tradition, wide lace sleeves, and Spanish knee-breeches. Their emblem head-dresses rather resemble the coats-of-arms of guilds or city companies; but it is in fact most curious to see an 'Inca' parading in this manner in front of each float or car, and that they were Indian nobles of this late date towards the end of the seventeenth century is manifest in the word 'Ynga' inscribed among the names of personages at the foot of several of the paintings.

The float of San Cristóbal with Inca or 'Ynga' drum-major walking in front of it carries the saint's image, but directly above the Indian's head a big green parrot perches on a corner of a wall, and birds 'often shown over the head of Indian personalities may have special, possibly magic meaning.'[1] If this, and the other pictures were the work of Indian or *mestizo* artists what does this portend? Some superstition of which the Spaniards were not fully aware? It is reminiscent of the Arabic inscriptions sometimes embodied into their designs by *mudejar* craftsmen working for their Spanish masters. Another float, that of the *cofradía* of San Sebastián, goes further still for it has live parrots perching above the saint's head on the branches of the tree behind

[1] Kubler and Soria, *op. cit.*, p. 397, footnote 101 to p. 324.

him. The crowded balconies of the houses in the background have tapestries and rugs thrown over them as at a Spanish *fiesta*, and in the doorway below is a gentleman in a tricorn and full Louis XIV dress. But, needless to say, on a corner of a balcony not quite directly over the 'Inca's' head perches a bird with a long tail, and now warned of this, one wonders what is its meaning.

Most of the paintings are so dark and hung so high upon the walls that it is nearly impossible to make out their detail. But the pictures are in such bad condition that even with the help of a pair of glasses it would be no better. In one of them a procession is passing in front of a temporary altar put up in the street; a silver altar which has large oblong mirrors in heavy silver frames standing upon it. But the interest here is in the angels standing on the three tiers of the altar, and they look like living children, but this could not be owing to the heat and danger of the candles. They wear lace *tutus* or ballet skirts; have big wide, most inflammable sleeves; and are carrying lit tapers. But also, their feather head-dresses are pure 'Indian'; they could be 'Indian' princesses in a Court ballet at Versailles; and in this setting female cupids masquerading as little 'Indians'. Much time could be spent in examining the paintings and trying to make out the inscriptions. But this would be a hopeless task in present conditions at Santa Ana, even with a ladder and an electric torch. It would have to be a private ladder made to order which alone might take time to achieve in Cuzco. Yet it is certainly true that these dilapidated paintings are, 'by all measure, the most important' in the old Inca capital, and it seems strange indeed that no steps are taken to save them. A competent picture restorer, of whom perhaps there are but few in the whole of South America, should be set to work for some months upon them. Or, and in addition to this, copies could be made, which should not be above the abilities of many art students. The paintings cannot be allowed just to fade away and perish. They are quite unique in their suggestion of seventeenth-century Cuzco. It is one of the more curious of historical anomalies to feel sure in one's own mind that all of the Incas are gone and vanished, and then to see in one of the paintings in Santa Ana of Cuzco, 'D. Carlos Suaynacap Ynga' which is as much as I could make out of the inscription, leading the procession, in his patterned *poncho* with the sun upon his breast and the parrot over his head, and surely an esoteric or enigmatic meaning.

Chapter Six

‡ ◆ ‡

CUZCO *(continued)*

AFTER VISITING THE CHURCH OF Santa Ana one may feel in the mood for seeing something else that is typically Cuzqueñan as opposed to experiences that would be of a higher order in their motherland of Spain. And nothing could be more appropriate to this idea than the nuns' church of Santa Clara. It is idle to deny that a part of the pleasure is in the difficulty of finding it. Never, except when sightseeing in the labyrinth of slums at Naples, have enquiries proved so fruitless, even though the guide spoke fluent Quechua. Again and again we were on a false trail, or were kept waiting. And having found the front of what was indubitably Santa Clara there was the new difficulty of discovering the back of it which was the only access. It is approached through a courtyard of a nearly indescribable, Andean isolation and remoteness, a dilapidation in which nothing had happened, and to which no news of the outer world had come, for how long? Just how long was it since this courtyard had received its last mark or signature of time? In the empty sunlight of one corner of it sat an old Indian spinning. He was less than half-witted, with an idiotic grin, and one did not like to walk near enough to be sure if it was a man or a woman. Again there was the sensation that grows on one in every town in Peru except at Lima that this is another and different population who are stoically waiting. Waiting for what to happen? For the parrot on the balcony rail to speak out a word and give the signal? For the parrot, despite its loquacity, is mute or dumb, and may one day speak its mind. And when that comes to pass?

But a door opens, and two old women servitors come out who are dark Indians. One of them has the key on a chain, and lets us into the oldest church in Cuzco. This is how architectural historians would have it, but in fact the interior of Santa Clara is both newer, and far older.

For an instant as the shutters are opened up the interior appears to be one mass of dirtied mother-of-pearl set in small panes, which then reveal themselves as panes of mirror. The high altar and the side altars, as well, are all treated in this manner, but in technique it is mother-of-pearl inlay made of panes of glass about six inches square. They form flat arches or volutes that project wherever possible so as to catch the light. Their purpose is to flash and glitter, not to reflect, but long ago they have become misted over, like old mirrors that have gone dead with the quick-silver, one supposes, run out of them or become so that it cannot move and has lost its volubility. In fact the mirrors are dumb, too, for it is not true to say they are utterly and completely blind from old age. One can still look into them from an inch or two away, or hold up one's hand to a pane of glass and see some reflection in it. But the mists and cobwebs of old age are on them all, and they have lost their reason. As a form of decoration covering the whole interior of a church, Santa Clara is said to be unique in all South America, though one can see individual altars in other places treated in this manner. Something of the sort is found in Persia, as, for instance, the cut-glass archway of the Shrine of Fatima a Qum, and the staircase and several entire rooms at the Golestan Palace in Tehran. But the refulgence and scintillation are far greater there. The cut-glass is strident and anything but dumb or blind.

In Santa Clara the high altar is three storeys high, but the glass panes are too big and the architectural design is rough and clumsy. An altar of looking-glass rising up to the roof of the church, and flanked with other altars of looking-glass, may not be an invention of a high order but it should at least have glitter and sparkle. And now perhaps the truth is beginning to declare itself that this is not a church of the white races. It is *mestizo* or half-caste decoration. The date must be the end of the seventeenth century, just the time of the paintings of the Corpus Christi processions and of the Inca weddings that we have been discussing. What far reflection is this of the Hall of Mirrors at Versailles! Seldom has one seen anything that looks older than the interior of this church of a *mestizo* nunnery. It is frayed and old like some old article of clothing; a second-hand clothes-shop of a church and with a little of the horror and distaste of that about it. The nuns are cloistered, *in clausura*, and we saw no sign of them. When we came out into the court again the shadows had moved

Mestizas at a street market in Cuzco

but the old half-wit Indian, man or woman, still sat spinning.

A convent in Cuzco with its nuns, the daughters of Cuzqueñan families, leads one on to enquire about the old houses. For the ancient families of the town had their enclosed lives, perhaps making no more than two or three visits to Lima in a lifetime, if at all, for two hundred years, till after the opening of the railway line to Cuzco in 1870. It was perhaps the deepest isolation of any city of Europeans, leaving out of account for the moment the *mestizo* population. Other far away settlements, Goa or Macao, both Portuguese, the one in India and the other in China, were sea-ports. However long the voyage took, vessels came and went. Both cities were, alike, on the ocean, and on the borders of a sub-continent. But Cuzco could only be reached on mule or horseback from Lima through mountains rising to many thousands of feet with every threat of *soroche* or mountain sickness; or after a fearful overland journey through what are now the Argentine and Bolivia, by way of Titicaca. Cuzco once attained, the tendency for many persons would be to stay there. It must, in fact, have been a small hermetic kingdom or enclave of its own with the churches and houses and the amenities of a Spanish town of considerable size, and a historical and local capital.

It had, as could be expected, a flowering of fine Spanish names; the Casa de las Cabreras in the Plaza de las Nazarenas, now a convent school, recalls the family of that name whose coat-of-arms reveals in its quarterings that they were descended from the Dukes of Alba. Other noble families of Cuzco were the Castillas, Hereditary Admirals of the Ocean, who once lived in the Casa del Almirante, and who were so proud of their lineage that they became a byeword. After one of them, who had made himself unpopular by his murderous ways, had been found hanging from a gibbet in the courtyard of his own palace, the house changed hands and was owned by the Peralda de los Ríos, Counts of Laguna, or in full, Conde de la Laguna de Chancacaye, a title given by Carlos II, last of the Spanish Habsburgs, in 1687. What a vast distance we are here at Cuzco from the Escorial where the patent of nobility was probably sealed and signed! Other long sounding titles and names of Cuzqueñan families were Marqués de San Juan de Buenavista, of 1671; Marqués de Valle Umbroso for the family of Esquivel y Jarava; and the de la Cerda family who were Marqueses de Casa Jara; all of which names are associated with old houses in the

town that are still standing. It is for instance the house of the Marqueses
de Buenavista which is now the Bishop of Cuzco's palace, and is that
often photographed and sketched, most picturesque of old houses in
the city, on the lane which is bordered on both sides with megalithic
Inca walls. The interiors of the old houses in Cuzco would have been
considered splendid perhaps, but uncomfortable, even in the seventeenth century, by persons used to town houses in England or in
Holland. Those of them that survived to be inhabited by descendants
of their original owners in the middle of last century will have seemed
an anomaly indeed. Having once seen Cuzco one can never forget
this Spanish city with a *mestizo* population but, also, inhabited by many
families from Spain.

We were fortunate to be invited into one of the old houses of this
sort, and would not have been happy to leave Cuzco without the experience. It is entered by a huge old courtyard where in former times
the horses and mules were tethered. This court has wooden galleries
all round it and the stair is in one corner. At the top of that, what must
have been an open corridor is glassed in, and a room at the end of it
has heavy and ornate furniture of the mid-nineteenth century just as
in some old house in Italy or Spain. We were shown a long saloon
or drawing-room in the same style, and a dining-room where the
Prince of Wales and a large party had been entertained when he
came to Cuzco some thirty years ago. There were photographs of the
Prince with the Duke of Kent, and with two or three persons we knew
who were accompanying them, and a nostalgic feeling of how long
ago that was when everyone was young, and before the world had so
many troubles coming to it. A curious feature was that although this
old house had practically nothing older in it than what was equivalent
to mid-Victorian times, the effect was grand and noble. The gilt
mirrors and chairs and sofas, the enlarged photographs of bearded and
whiskered relatives, the far-fetched bronze statuary, also, were what
one would associate with Victor-Emanuel II in Italy, yet this was
undeniably an old patrician house in Cuzco, in Peru. How, or why
one did not know, though it could only be through some personal
projection of its large-hearted owner who, early as it was in the
morning, came with his two little fair-haired sons to see us off at
the station when we left for Puno.

In this Peruvian city of the ancient Incas what could be more typical

Church near Cuzco

Market place at Pisac

Above and below, Market place at Pisac

of Spain than the *dignidad* of the Cathedral who arrived, late it is true, but that also was in character, in order to show us the *tesoro*, jewelled monstrances and the like, just as in Palencia, or Plasencia, or Cuenca, or Calatayud, in any old cathedral town in Spain. The choir stalls of Cuzco Cathedral are very fine indeed, mid-seventeenth century in date, and not surpassed anywhere in Latin America. They would seem to be the work of Spanish, and not *mestizo* craftsmen. In Cuzco Cathedral it is difficult to believe one is not in Spain, a feeling which even detracts somewhat from a fair appreciation of its qualities for in Spain it would not be outstanding, whereas, here, eleven thousand feet in the air and in the middle of the Andes, it is something of a miracle that this could have been accomplished. As one walks in it there is the pure sensation of seventeenth-century Spain, and the only things missing are pictures by rather better painters and the tapestries that are nearly always to be found in Spanish cathedrals.

I cannot find it in myself genuinely to admire paintings of the Cuzqueñan school. They are too often copies of Italian or Flemish engravings, Rubens being a favourite model. The museums are crowded with such paintings which always induce in one a feeling of disappointment. But they improve the nearer they approach to folk art and the further they are removed from European models. The practice of covering large areas of the canvas with gold tooling does not compensate for inanimate subjects and bad drawing. It gives an icon-like or spangled Hoxton print effect, but one of insipidity. Nearly always, and in every case, the carved frame is better than the picture. On all accounts the most fascinating paintings on the South American continent are the life-size, winged Archangels dressed as musketeers, in plumed hats and embroidered coats with huge sleeves, loading or firing their guns, a local speciality of the Peruvian Altiplano only to be encountered near Lake Titicaca and over the border to La Paz.

The *prefetto*, a giant of a man dressed in black with a big man's genial humour, who, we were told, blows like a hurricane into the prisons to inspect their sanitary arrangements and general conditions, now sent us in his car to see the gigantic fortress of Sacsahuamán outside Cuzco, and on to Pisac. The road there climbs up above the town rather in the same direction as Machu Picchu, and then winds off on its own—and on your own you remain, it may be added, for the rest of the long morning. It has been said that 'certainly no other archaeological

H

structure in the two Americas gives the visitor the awesome impression
of stupendousness that Sacsahuamán does',[1] a statement which remains
true even after having seen Chichén-Itzá and Uxmal, the Mayan ruins
in Yucatán. Sacsahuamán is in the mountains only a little way north
of Cuzco and looking down over the city. The first impression is of
finding yourself being driven on a greensward past a fantastic kind of
card-house of huge stones stretching a long distance on your right-
hand side. The next sensation is to wonder what it can all be about.
The giant stones are as monolithic as the individual playing-cards of
which one builds a card-house, when a child, so that with no one
standing between us and the stones, and nothing to measure them by,
one does not grasp their titan size.[2] An angle of the fortress wall will
consist of no more than one gigantic stone. It is this that gives the
illusion of a card-house; and in fact there is nothing to do at Sacsahuamán but walk among the huge stones. It is as at Carnac, in Brit-
tany, or at Stonehenge, and it is no different in the cyclopaean ruins
in Malta. The same problems present themselves, that the nearest
quarries are, respectively, nine and twenty-one miles from Cuzco.
And Sacsahuamán is not on level ground, as Stonehenge is on Salisbury
Plain. It is in the mountains above Cuzco; the universal question with
cyclopaean ruins all over the world being how were the stones
brought here? But there is this difference between Sacsahuamán and the
cyclopaean temples. Those others were built at uncertain date by
unknown races. This was begun in 1440, no earlier than many of the
Oxford and Cambridge colleges. There are even huger monoliths at
Ba'albek, the work of later and decadent third century Emperors, while
Sacsahuamán was begun by the ninth Inca Pachacuti, and being only
five hundred years old is last in date of megalithic buildings all over
the world.

There are three tiers of walls one above another, and the fortress is
a third of a mile long and sixty feet high. The tradition that fifty
thousand workmen, or others say twenty thousand Indians changed
yearly for upwards of eighty years, laboured upon it—either, or both,
or neither of these stories must be true. It does not matter in the face
of those gigantic stones. But *was* it a fortress? Why all the fuss? Why

---

[1] J. Alden Mason, *op. cit.*, p. 159.
[2] One of the monoliths is 27 ft. high, 14 ft. broad, and 12 ft. thick, estimated weight 200 tons.
The Temple of Bacchus at Ba'albek, in Lebanon, on its enclosing wall has three blocks of stone
64, 63¾ and 63 ft. long, each of them 13 ft. high, and 10 ft. thick.

were they frightened of, and so anxious to defend themselves against? Surely not the savages from the Amazon forest. Even to my un-military eye it does not seem that Sacsahuamán, rightly speaking, is defending anything. There are so many other roads leading into Cuzco, and no such frantic effort made to protect them. It would seem easy for a hostile force to bye-pass Sacsahuamán. Or to shut the defenders up in it, if they insisted on being besieged there, and move on. Sacsahuamán in war might be more of a liability than an asset, and the stores and weapons be kept there and never used. It is not even the principal direction from which an enemy would approach Cuzco, but seems to be laboriously placed there at a hazard.

Other opinion would have it that Sacsahuamán is not a fortress at all but 'a place of refuge' for the inhabitants of Cuzco if there was an attack upon the city. But so far as I could see from a cursory look at it, there is no large open space within the walls and it is quite unsuited to this purpose. Certainly there is no room for houses or even tem-porary dwellings within the enclosure. Garcilaso saw Sacsahuamán in 1560, the year he left Peru, when the three great towers were standing. They seem to have been square towers, and there was a huge water cistern in the middle. The ground is honeycombed with underground passages and tunnels which were part of the defence walls, and it is impossible to think of thousands of old men and women and children cooped up there in addition to the garrison. So it was more probably a fortress, but one wonders if the choice of locality was superstitious and due to divination or the result of omens. It would be interesting to have the expert opinion of an engineer as to how much less trouble and labour would have been involved in building Sacsahuamán out of ordinary-sized stones. The inconceivable, inhuman task of dragging along the monoliths from their quarries would have been avoided, and the fortress although it gives such an impression of strength with its huge stones would be no less strong in an age when there was neither gunpowder nor battering-ram, and military weapons were the sling and bola for the distance and a club with a stone on the end of it for close combat. It is difficult to avoid the conclusion that the cyclopaean megalithic walls were built only to instil respect and terror. How much easier it would have been to build it of stones cut on the ordinary normal scale! It looks like a tradition thousands of years old which had become so fossilized with time that no one dared to contradict it, a part of the rulers' prerogative and a sort of equivalent of the Pharaoh's porphyry or the Caesar's purple. But it is fascinating to think that could the erection of Sacsahuamán have been witnessed in just the years when St George's Chapel, Windsor Castle, or King's College Chapel at Cambridge were building, we might know the secrets of the megalithic builders all over the world.

There is nothing more to see at Sacsahuamán and we went on to Pisac, passing on the way a stone water-trough which imagination has elevated in rank into an Inca bathing-place. But the road to Pisac is not so easy; it is mountainy and has many hairpin bends. There is no traffic along it except when motors bring people to Pisac to see the Sunday market, and in case of a breakdown one wonders if we might not be there till next week-end. It lends excitement and whets the appetite which, all being well, will soon be satisfied at Urubamba, 'ancient summer resort of the Incas', as the advertisement reads. We come down from the mountains into a green valley, which we follow for some miles with no sign of a town or village. It is this same Urubamba river that runs through the gorge below Machu Picchu, and that eventually joins the Amazon. But the contrast is extreme between this mild Pyrenean valley, now we have come down into it, and that astonishing landscape of the classical Chinese masters which to all appearances should be somewhere in the mountains of Sze-chuan. This mild and gentle valley should lead to mineral springs and a resort hotel where visitors come to drink the waters, and in fact there is a good hotel in the eponymous small town of Urubamba, which is much lower than Cuzco and the refuge of those who do not relish the eleven thousand foot elevation of the Inca capital. Lunching in the hotel the illusion was complete that this was some little place like Cambo in the French Pyrenees. The orchid-bearing trees in the gorge under Machu Picchu could have been a thousand miles away. But after Urubamba the road to Pisac is more precipitous than ever, and so full of hairbreadth turns and twistings that sooner than keep continually in a state of tension one tries to think of other things.

The three Inca fortresses of Sacsahuamán, Ollontay-Tambo, and Machu Picchu were all to guard this same river valley and now we were on our way to Pisac where was another fortress above the present market village. Peru, where the clash or discord of geographical contradictions and opposites is louder and more reverberant than in any

other land, has its own population mystery to keep one thinking.
Where did the labour force come from who, using only implements
of stone, shaped the huge stones and built the megalithic buildings?
For that matter, in our own time where do the Indians come from
who throng the Indian markets? The unnecessary labour of erecting
those huge fortresses is almost unimaginable in terms of the trouble
they involved. They are as battleships or aircraft-carriers deployed
against a fishing fleet. For surely the Indians of the Amazon jungle
cannot have been that dangerous. With their wonderful system of
roads, in which the Romans were their only rivals, the Incas had the
strategic advantage and could move their forces all things considered
at the pace of Caesar or Napoleon for, while it is true they had no
cavalry, neither had their foes. But the Romans had to protect their
frontiers against, not a large population but a veritable swarming of
barbarian or half-barbarian tribes, Celts, Vandals, Goths, and Huns,
while the Indians of the Amazon armed with blow-pipes and poison
darts can never have numbered more than a few hundred at a time.

The lateral nature of those stretches of the Pacific coast that are
suited to a large population—which on an atlas assume almost caricatural
proportions with the elongated shape of Chile—made it that Cuzco,
although longitudinally in the centre of the Inca Empire, was only four
days march from the nearest jungle tribes. Was the fear of arrows
tipped with *curare* the force that raised the Inca fortresses? The Incas
would have been as safe in forts built out of ordinary stones. It was
mere superfluity of energy to erect megalithic fortifications on the high
mountain ridges. In the meantime, for mile after mile we had met no
single human being. Not even a hut was to be seen, and yet this road
was one of the important channels of local communication. Where
do the Indians come from who go to Sunday market at Pisac? One
of their traits of native character is to sit for hours or days at the railway
stations; and another is to spend a night and day trotting to market
in order to sell a handful of vegetables, and the like time in getting
home again. It is a simple explanation of how a rural population can
collect, as though from nowhere, and be in two places at once.

Even on this road from Cuzco to Pisac we were not much more than
two hundred and fifty miles away from almost unexplored country.
That distance measured in a straight line would take one to the province

of Madre de Dios and the borders of Bolivia and Brazil. The unbroken
jungle lying to the east of the Andes, beyond the mountains into the
province of Loreto, and up to the frontiers of Colombia and Ecuador,
where is the Colombian province of Amazonas, is nearly unknown
territory. One of the most exciting adventure books of modern times
is *The Rivers ran East*[1] by the American *condottiere* Leonard Clark, who
had previously distinguished himself in Mongolia and Tibet. This
deals with precisely those regions that have just been mentioned. In
the appendices to this work, which are divided into seven sections,
he lists seventy-one Indian drug plants of which only twenty-one
have been identified so that fifty of them are new to science; gives
thirty-one 'useful flora' of which only eighteen have been scientifically
identified; enumerates fifty-eight valuable timber trees of which only
thirty-seven were previously known; gives details of forty edible fish
and six kinds of turtles where only ten of the fish and three of the
turtles were known before; and ends with the fourteen poisonous snakes
'most feared by natives of the western Amazon region' (out of thirty-
two varieties observed by himself), of which fourteen only five have
been positively identified. It is an astonishing list. The timber woods
alone are a fascination to read about with their different colours;
'rose-red'; 'red-veined with a golden yellow'; 'white with yellow
designs'; 'mottled with markings similar to those of snakes'; 'bright
red blood wood which takes varnish without losing its bright colour';
'yellow sepia veined and striped with marble black'; a wood 'of a
beautiful texture like elephant ivory'; or another 'of rich creamy
colour with a patina like velvet'. The Indian drug plants are no less
interesting with their possibility of cancer cures, mention of new
febrifuges and antiseptics, and other remedies. His list of poisonous
snakes is no less imposing; cascabel, 'thick-bodied rattler'; coralito
'with red coral rings around it'; fer-de-lance 'with cat-like eyes, and a
deep pit between organ and nostril which is thought to be the organ
of some unknown sense'; and viper bushmaster 'fatal to man in five
minutes'. Of all these snakes and fishes, drugs and trees, he gives,
throughout, the Indian names.

Now the great interest in all this is that the terrain of his discoveries
is in Peru. He does not go over the frontier into Brazil. It is all within

---

[1] Hutchinson & Co., London, 1954. Leonard Clark has also published a book dealing with
his adventures in China called *The Marching Wind*.

Peruvian territory. Moreover, the maps which form the end papers of his book, on two of the four of them have written large the Urubamba river; this same river flowing below Ollontay-Tambo and Machu Picchu, and now Pisac which we are nearing, but Pisac is on its higher reaches where it is called by another name, the Vilcanota. It is the Urubamba that flows to Atalaya where Leonard Clark started his adventures coming from La Merced, a place looming large on the map but where there were only some fifty inhabitants under the 'flowering, porcelain-blue jacaranda trees' to quote his phrase. As for Atalaya of the beautiful name, it consisted of a garrison of troops and a Franciscan mission.

But after Atalaya, which is a river junction, it is no longer the Uru-bamba but the Ucayali, in which guise it flows past Cumaria, not a town but a house, for 'every house in the western Amazon has a name which appears on the map as a town', as he says in a footnote. The 'house' of a family of Italian exiles, with rooms 'veneered with palo sangre of bright red colour and chairs of mashonaste, a rare wood with twisted grain of red and green, woods which put to shame rosewood, mahogany and other fine woods', a house where talk was of Leonardo and Chekhov, and Leonard Clark and his companion were entertained, given 'soup made from the choicest varieties of turtles found in the river, a pinkish rare roast of tapir, saddle of roast venison, partridge and turkey, and a dessert of sliced papayas, pineapples, sacha mangoes, grapes, zapotes, oranges, shimbillas, and salted Amazon cashews'. And so after many hundreds of miles, for it is more than four hundred miles in a straight line, to Iquitos, joining on the way the Tuaranón; to Iquitos, the Alice Springs, or Timbuktu of the Amazon. And all the way there through those hundreds of miles in Peru; with another three hundred miles still in Peru from Iquitos north to the Putamayo of sordid fame where it meets the frontiers of Colombia and Ecuador. Iquitos, in Peru and on the Amazon, 'the last port on the Amazon for ocean-going steamers', to which you can sail with one change of ship from Liverpool.

One can never be reconciled to the immensity of South America. And to the fact that despite that, a large part of it is one huge river basin. With Bolivia only a very little bit smaller than Peru, with an estimated area of five hundred thousand, against five hundred and six thousand square miles. But with Brazil with three and a quarter million

square miles, which is slightly larger than the whole of the United
States; and the whole of India together with Pakistan is no more than
half that size. Figures which are difficult to digest but they give the
scale. And in Peru which looks so large on the map but is only somewhere between a sixth and a seventh the area of Brazil, we are making
what seems an immense journey, but it takes up no space at all in the
atlas. There is hardly room for the names of Cuzco and Urubamba
and Machu Picchu, they are so near to each other on the map. It
could be said, in a phrase, that the two Americas have but four rivers;
the St Lawrence and Mississippi, and the Amazon and River Plate.
But the Amazon is incomparably the most impressive because so much
of it is still a mystery. How wonderful to have seen waters which
flow into it and join its lifestream! Where could there be a more
marvellous experience of this than in the gorge of Machu Picchu!
It makes the Urubamba into a name of poetry, and I was glad to have
seen it where it was no bigger than a Pyrenean stream of a size where
there would be trout upon the luncheon table. But within a few miles
it was in spate and hurling itself through that tremendous canyon,
above which it was almost too good to be true that Machu Picchu
should have lain hidden until 1911.

Time went quickly while thinking of such things, and here we were
at Pisac. It was a relief coming down to it at last from so many twists
and turns, and to have a little level ground before one at the bottom
of the valley. With a suspension bridge where there had been one of
the Inca rope-bridges till not long ago, a modern bridge that leads
determinedly straight into the town as though standing no nonsense,
though you can still see the stone foundations of the Inca bridge upon
the river bank. But in fact there is a lot of high flown, if frugal fantasy
at Pisac, but only on one day in the week, on Sundays when there is the
Sunday market. On other days Pisac is quite dead and empty. When
we went there it was mid-week and early in the afternoon. We got
as far as the market place without meeting one human being. Here,
more was going on because there was the police station, and Indians
were standing outside it in the Pisac dress which we knew already
from Cuzco. The women wear woollen skirts in bright colours and
flat mushroom hats, generally of green cloth or felt with a red edging,
like Quechuas of the time of Holbein. But there were only old women
about to-day, and the men wore their working clothes, not 'Sunday

best'. Their Sunday hats are mushroom shaped and bright red, the Holbein 'look' accentuated by their knee-breeches which are surely a mark of Spanish influence. The effect is certainly sixteenth century, and this is carried further in their *chullos* or stocking caps which are those of mountaineers the world over, not forgetting mountain valleys in Austria and Switzerland. What we missed seeing were the alcaldes (mayors) of the nearby villages marching to church, in knee-breeches, striped *ponchos* of alpaca wool, and enormous mitre-mushroom hats, with silver-bound staffs or maces of office in their hands. And the blowing of conch shells in church at the elevation of the Host, but all of this except that raucous sound is familiar from postcards which are on sale at newspaper stalls all over Peru.

The market place at Pisac is shaded by two enormous and magnificent trees, *ceibas*, perhaps they are, which must be at least two or three hundred years old, and look as though they have been here since Inca days. They have some of the beauty of gigantic ilexes. It must be emphasized that this is an Indian, a Quechua, and not a *mestizo* market. From Indian markets we saw at Puno, and also at villages in Guatemala, knowing the costume of Pisac already, it is not difficult to reconstruct the scene. Above the village the whole hillside is terraced with *anderes* where in Inca days maize and other crops were cultivated, and there is the ruined fortress of Pisac covering, it is said, an area larger than the whole of Cuzco with a stone-built gnomon, sun tower or observatory, still higher on the mountain. It is another of the *pucará* fortresses like Machu Picchu and Ollontay-Tambo in the chain that guards the Urubamba.

Another Indian market, better known because it is nearer Lima, is at Huancayo. It would have been interesting to see this because of the local differences in costume but it entails a railway journey of a few hours in a train which climbs to fifteen thousand feet. Oxygen is carried as in the aeroplane going to Cuzco, and a number of passengers always suffer from ear-ache and nose-bleeding, with the sure promise of a headache and sleeplessness when you have got there. As we were about to spend a fortnight on the Altiplano, going as far as Lake Titicaca and hoping to reach La Paz, all at great altitudes, we did not undertake this supernumerary journey to the Indian market of Huancayo. What is always remarked about it, is the perfect silence. But one has only to be a few hours in Cuzco to notice that; and one writer, an Irish woman, has stated her opinion that the legendary reserve of the Englishman is as a case of echslalia compared to the silence of any Indian. One may even be inclined to think their muteness must be psychosomatic and self-imposed since the Spanish conquest, whereas the truth is more likely to be that the Inca welfare state with its pigeon-holing of every activity and energy made them mute not of malice, but inertness. Their diet, and the constant chewing of coca leaf, has helped to make this worse. For by now we had come to regions where every male Indian has a quid of coca like a permanent swelling in his cheek. They are quite stupefied by it, and yet it is the only thing that makes their hard lives tolerable, apart from their regular bouts of *chicha*-drinking and non-stop dancing. We were told that the most rewarding sight in the Huancayo market would be the innumerable varieties of potatoes for sale. Many centuries ago the Indians of the Altiplano had evolved no fewer than two hundred and forty different kinds of potato, in all colours, pink, purple, black, and streaked or piebald, and many of these are for sale at Huancayo. Curiously, except later on at Puno, one is never given any but the more ordinary kinds, and it was with some difficulty and only through insisting upon it that we tasted one of the rarer kinds at the Country Club in Lima.

We were up in the hills again a few minutes after leaving Pisac, and in view of the *anderes* that terraced all the hillside. There may be a tendency to exaggerate the importance of these. They are remarkable as a proof of ant-like energies, and it is astonishing to see terraces carved almost out of the summit of the mountain at Machu Picchu at what must be thirteen thousand feet of altitude, there being incidentally, one variety of potato which will thrive even at fifteen thousand feet. But it is the altitude that is impressive more than the terracing, *per se*. No one has thought of imputing Incaic qualities to the peasants who banked up the lemon terraces in the peninsula of Sorrento. The most painstaking terracing and irrigating water-channels ever seen are on the island of Madeira but they pass almost unnoticed and are never brought forward in argument of a higher civilization. The *anderes* are works of the Indians and the real interest is their dizzying altitude. We were told the effects of this would wear off but they were no better. The slightest exertion, such as walking forward to look at something, or stooping to pick anything up, would bring on an attack of breath-lessness and a swimming of the eyes. Or it would come on suddenly for no reason, just apparently because it felt it was time to attack again. I was averaging an hour to an hour and a half's sleep a night. It induced weakness and a slightly, but not pleasantly delirious feeling. It was weakening, generally, and I hoped I would not have to make any important decision. A kind of breathless irresolution is not a pleasant sensation.

But at last we were back in Cuzco, entering the city by way of the Arco de Santa Clara, a satisfactory structure built obviously in the seventeenth century, and it is a surprise to find it dates from 1836-9. It was the late afternoon and growing chilly. Going out to buy *Time* at the street corner a small Indian boy with a fearful cold, or worse, looked up at me, wheezing and coughing, and drawing his pathetic *poncho* a little tighter round his chest. How long would he survive, and what treats had life in store for him? He cannot have been more than four feet six inches tall. But the little Indian woman by him with a baby slung on her back was no taller. She could be sixteen or seventeen years old, and as she had no other children with her had probably one or two dead babies. One estimate puts it that four-fifths of the Indian children fail to reach sexual maturity; or that seventy per cent of babies born alive die before they reach the age of two.[1] Which are the lucky ones, we may be inclined to wonder. The small boy would be twelve or thirteen years old, and if he lived, soon married. In two years' time he might be a father.

We sat round the fire again that night, and could not but wonder where he was huddled. One thing was certain; that he would be no better off in the Barrieras of Lima. The infant mortality is a dreadful problem, but the swarming of the population which is coming, and has nearly arrived, will be still more appalling. It is something that has never happened before, that there should be a huge Indian population. Their numbers have been kept down by natural selection. They have evolved their own forms of resistance to the high altitudes, and are, in fact, healthier in the Altiplano than on the coastal plain where they easily fall victims to tuberculosis. Later on during our journey we were to notice the difference between the Quechua and Aymara and the Guatemalan Indians who are predominantly gay and cheerful. Not that a silent passivity is universal among the Quechua, any more

---

[1] *Peruvian Adventure*, by Will Brown, Robert Hall Ltd., London, 1958, pp. 101, 135. The average height of the Quechua woman is four feet ten inches.

than that all of them are so poverty stricken. We were invited on one of our nights in Cuzco to a performance of ballet put on by Quechua students from the University. It was a most hopeful corrective to any gloomy forebodings. The theatre was a large upstairs room with a platform at one end. An old music master was violinist, and also there was a curious Indian instrument. The tunes were Indian, and had been collected by the violin-player in high villages in the Andes. A strong note of Quechuan pride in their old traditions was evident in the entire performance. The dances were those performed at harvest rituals, and the like, except for one or two of them that had been taken from Indian tribes in the Amazon jungle. It was a delight to watch these well-formed and lively dancers of the student class, the men being perhaps better dancers than the women, but above all they were students, a status to which one had not known the Indians could attain. There was nothing sullen or downtrodden about them, and it was good to behold their pride in being Quechuan.

Our stay in Cuzco was nearly over now and there were but one or two more churches for us to see. La Merced is the largest of them all after the Cathedral and La Compañía but there is something un-satisfactory about it. The pair of towers have their columns pitted with a fish-scale, and in their upper parts a species of worm-cast rustication which is unpleasing. It may have been the excruciating rendering of a Chopin Nocturne by a white-robed friar playing on an upright piano in what must once have been the refectory. This gave the illusion of a sobbing, drizzling rain and damped the sunlight. The ghosts of all who have ever hated piano practise were trying in vain to materialize as though the cloister was full of weeping children. I have never heard anything more depressing; and the friar exulting in his skill played on and on. But even without his music-making it would be difficult to agree that 'Hispanic colonial architecture knows nothing more beautiful than this cloister', or that the unknown architect 'showed genius . . . in constrasting the virile strength of the rusticated walls with the opulent decoration of the columns', rising to 'magnificent handling of open space, lightness and grace combined with sturdy virility of mass, the deep beauty of the colour, extraordinary richness and originality in treatment of textures, unerring taste in scale and propor-tion, all this and more make the Mercedarian cloister unique.'[1] This is

[1] Harold E. Wethey, *Op. cit.*, p. 53, 54.

high praise indeed; but it would be equally true to remark that the main cloister of La Merced is in an emasculated version of the Spanish *plateresco* which gives the appearance of having been built in about 1860, and to which it is hard to assign the correct date in one's mind. The double stair fails to impress and does not stand up to its own size, 'while the superb handling of rusticated stone' which is merely a division of the surface into stone bricks of equal size takes no account of what rustication is capable of at the hands of a real master. The interior of La Merced is another matter for it has fine choir stalls, many of them to celebrate the ascetic triumphs of obscure fathers of the Mercedarian Order, while in the upper choir there is a pretty chamber organ.

On our last evening we went to see the church of Belén which we liked as much as anything in Cuzco out of the Cathedral Square. This church, and that of San Pedro, have nearly identical façades to which the esoteric interest attaches that they are the work of an Indian architect who has been identified as Juan Tomás Tuyru Tupac, though as the announcer of this news has it, there is nothing specifically 'Indian' about them. They are just good architectural frontispieces of about 1690 in three storeys, with fewer or more pilasters as in the three or four voices of a fugue. The comparing of façades is a game one can play in Cuzco, if not to the extent this can be done in London with the steeples of the City churches in white Portland stone. But there is another almost identical façade to those of San Pedro and Belén in the case of San Sebastián, a village about three miles from Cuzco which is interesting in that it is said to be inhabited by the Ayllos, families of Inca descent, who were settled here after the Conquest. And curiously enough on one of the towers of San Sebastián are inscriptions of 1664 giving the names of bishops, priests, and noble Indians, and the name of the architect Manuel de Sahuarauza, who was an Indian. The mention of 'noble Indians' at this late date is interesting. All three churches, San Pedro, Belén, and San Sebastián, have pairs of towers, and are variants on the same theme which in turn is borrowed from the cathedral, but that of San Sebastián is the only one of them which in its flat ornament seemed to have anything distinctively 'Indian' about it. San Pedro is perhaps the most successful of the three for Belén is a little clumsy in the recovery of its second and third storeys after allowing for the large space taken up by the bas-relief over the door. What is extraordinary after all is that we should be discussing seventeenth-century façades by native Indian architects in Cuzco, which is how many thousands of miles away from the source of this architecture in Papal Rome!

In the yellowing light of that last evening it was a dusty drive to the church of Belén which stands in the low lying part of the town and can be seen from far away upon its terraced platform. An insane asylum, or we could not quite determine if it was that or a hospital for sick prisoners, now occupies the convent buildings, but the rather odd-looking female who is in charge of the church, and refused to accept a present, keeps it scrupulously clean. We were shown the sparkling silver altar and admired the gilding which was eloquent of the gold mines of Peru. Long after we left, the lay sister, if she was that, stood looking and waving to us from the door. We dined in a splendid new mansion with a swimming-pool, and met the *prefetto* again, and the Rector of the University, and a painter from far away Croatia who has achieved fame with his pictures of Inca themes painted, withal, in the heroic language of the Serbian ballads. He had interesting tales to tell of remote Andean villages, and the light fused and we were left in darkness and a fire of wooden logs was lit. When we came away it was bitterly cold and we felt the altitude. It was long after midnight and we were to leave early in the morning. I will never see Cuzco again, where I have wanted to go for as long as I can remember; a town of megalithic stonework, with tiled roofs, Baroque churches, a *mestizo* population, and now and again a herd of llamas in its streets, two miles high in air.

Chapter Seven

❖❖❖❖❖❖❖❖❖❖❖❖❖❖❖❖

PUNO AND THE ALTIPLANO

THE STATION FOR PUNO AND Lake Titicaca is down at the lower end of Cuzco, leaving the church of Belén to your right, and towards the village of San Sebastián. When we got there it was to find we were to travel not in a train but in a motor car. This is a novel experience but there is much to be said in favour of it. The car is fitted with special wheels, and once embarked you are your own master. On the previous evening we had met the official, our fellow countryman, who was to travel with us, and was in charge of a long section of the railway line. This ideal system of railway transport, combining the good points of motoring with the safer feeling at precipice edges thanks to the steel rails of the permanent way, was by courtesy of the Peruvian Corporation who built the railway, an exemplary display of British engineering skill, more than eighty years ago. The friend before mentioned, owner of the old house in Cuzco, had come with his two small sons to see us off, and the luggage once arranged so as to be comfortable for the long day's journey, the chauffeur-driver climbed in next to our compatriot, and we were off to Puno.

It is a curious sensation to be motoring out of a railway station past the sheds and the turntable along the railway line. We looked back, but nothing was to be seen of Cuzco. It had gone as completely as though it had never been there at all. The track was smooth and steady, laid on sleepers of eucalyptus wood till we reached regions where termites attacked the wood and the sleepers had to be of concrete. But that was far ahead. For some time we went along a fertile valley, not unlike the Pyrenean vale at Urubamba, passing after an hour or more the *estancia* belonging to the friend who said goodbye to us at the station. It looked charming enough out of the left-hand window in its grove of trees. But this idyllic valley was not to last much longer, and we were climbing gradually on to the high plain of the Altiplano in which this valley can have been no more than a slight trough or depression. Soon the familiar scenes began, known from the line to Machu Picchu, of crowds of Indians at the wayside stations, come out of nowhere, for often there was not another house in sight. We could move up close to photograph them, and go on. By now it was the hugest landscape ever seen, with but a line of mountains thirty, forty, fifty miles away, but not so strange for Spaniards as for other races because of the high plains of Castile and Aragon where a donkey, but here a solitary llama, is conspicuous as would be an elephant on a mown lawn in England. A succession of landscapes which are all the same landscape for hour after hour till one becomes almost mesmerized by the solitude and emptiness. Certain halts along the line stand out in memory. A long wait for a train to come by beside a river which could have been anywhere, for disappointingly, there were no flowers growing out of the rock. But, an hour or so later, magnificent flowering aloes ten or fifteen feet high, the most profuse of flower-spikes ever seen, where was a woman in a white hat and bright sapphire skirt.

We stopped for luncheon at Sicuani where the line from Arequipa joined us, if I am not mistaken, but at any rate it is a considerable railway junction. Our host was a railway official, English in origin but Argentine by nationality, with an Italian wife. They lived in a small but comfortable house within biscuit throw of the railway line. From the conversation it was apparent that from the point of view of the human resident we had already crossed the watershed, and that the longed-for centre of civilized life was no longer Lima, or even Arequipa, but B.A.—Buenos Aires. The loneliness, especially for the wives of such officials, must be quite appalling, and any compensating experiences few and far between. The only other white inhabitants of Sicuani are missionary doctors who certainly have large opportunities to practise. Impossible to stay in Sicuani even for an hour without an aching feeling of its loneliness.

We were now bound for the heights beyond any contradiction and began to climb in wide, sweeping curves upon an interminable grassland. An hour or two of this gradual climbing with no sensation of a precipice, and hardly realizing what was coming and that we were higher than we had ever been before. After a while there were herds

Above and below, Andean churches in Peru

Country church in Peru

Andean church in Peru

of alpacas grazing by the line. All four races of the llamoids, that is to say, llamas, guanacos, alpacas, and vicuñas, are related to camels, and after thousands of years of adaptation they look entirely natural against this marvellous, but empty landscape. The guanaco is, it seems, the ancestor or progenitor of the llamas, which are a hybrid, but from what mating?[1] And the alpaca is a hybrid of the llama and the vicuña. Personally, I could never distinguish between guanaco and alpaca, except that both are smaller than a llama. It is from the wool of the alpaca and guanaco that the fine rugs are made, and again I do not know the difference between them. But the vicuña has wool which is chinchilla-soft and unmistakable. So far we had not seen a live vicuña.

There were alpaca and guanaco farms beside the railway line, with lonely-looking farm buildings where the herds were fleeced. A white overseer might come up here for the fleecing but all the rest of the year the herds were with their Indian shepherds. This landscape of the alpaca and guanaco herds brought one nearer to pre-Columbian America than even the megalithic walls at Cuzco. To that age before the Spaniards came with their horses. It is probably from the eternity of this landscape that the Indians have no sense of time, a presence from which I, myself, would be suffering most acutely, even agonizingly, were I to live at Sicuani, or any other of the towns we were to see that day. But now the air was becoming so rarefied that one felt it even sitting there in the car, keeping, on advice, as still as possible, and not smoking all that morning or afternoon. Our companion, who had been a source of fascinating information all the way, made his chauffeur-driver produce a bottle of raw spirit and pour a little of it on our handkerchiefs. If one kept sniffing this it relieved the breathlessness.

In the clear air one could now see as through a pair of glasses where the whole beauty lay in there being nothing but grass and mountains. Alpacas—or were they guanacos?—with occasionally a wholly black one among them, and their lambs. And now a little more delicate animal to the right, in quantity, and only a few yards from the railway line, with *les fines attaches*, neater and smaller even than those of a gazelle, and this was a vicuña herd. What a spectacle when the Incas

[1] The llama has been domesticated for so many centuries that in the graves at Paracas, where were found the most splendid of pre-Columbian textiles, there are mummified llamas with five toes, instead of two. cf. van Hagen, *op. cit.*, p. 81. C. H. Prodgers mentions a district in Peru where the horses have not two, but four nostrils.

hunted as many as forty thousand head of guanacos and vicuñas in a
great circle of beaters! The vicuñas are a fawny-chestnut colour, and
their wool is more silky and fine than that of any other animal. Now
their skins cannot be bought in Peru; they are extremely scarce, and we
were lucky to have seen this herd. In winter this high plain must be
covered in snow, so we saw the vicuñas in their summer pasture.

Only a few miles beyond this we stopped at Crucero Alto, a station
just below the highest point on the railroad; and on the station wall
the height was given as 14,666 feet above sea-level, only a hundred feet
lower than the summit of the Matterhorn, with Mont Blanc at 15,781
feet only a little more than a thousand feet above us. We got out in
order to experience what it was like walking at this altitude, and
stumbled breathlessly a few yards to a little shed inside which a hot
spring was rising. We were told that the railway superintendent
from Sicuani had come here to take the waters and be cured of
rheumatism, and I remembered reading in C. H. Prodgers of the
marvellous cures effected by mineral springs in Peru. But the altitude
of the hot spring at Crucero Alto, and its degree of heat, made it seem
all the more remarkable. We were waiting for the express train to come
in with passengers from Bolivia and the Argentine, and here it came
puffing and blowing as though hardly able to reach the top of the pass.
Just such a train as you might see on the Simplon or St Gotthard with
the same passengers standing at the windows, all first or second class
passengers, with not an Indian on board, and a restaurant car. The
novelty lay in seeing Buenos Aires and La Paz and Arequipa painted
on the coaches. For some three or four hundred miles out of Buenos
Aires the train crosses the pampas; passes Córdoba with its Baroque
churches and Jesuit ruins; enters the province of Santiago del Estero,
a desert of huge cactuses; leaves the Argentine, enters Bolivia, and begins
to climb. A journey of four days and three nights by train; but scarcely
as many as four hours from Buenos Aires all the way to Santiago of
Chile, or to Lima, by aeroplane. The passengers, some few of whom
were probably suffering from the real mountain sickness or *soroche*,
or from nose-bleeding, and were being given oxygen, settled themselves in their seats, the young couple standing in the corridor pulled
up the window, and the train went on.

So did we, but in the opposite direction, and were soon passing by a
chain of little lakes with marvellous reflections of the clouds in them.

And on into another, and still vaster emptiness. But for some way one's thoughts were with that train descending, and I wished we had gone to Arequipa which we were prevented from doing by the earthquakes. We had been told so often that at 7,500 feet it had the pleasantest climate in Peru; a climate of perpetual spring with flowers blooming all the year round under the white cone of El Misti, which was described to us as more spectacular than, and twice the height of, Etna. But there are the earthquakes which, as I am writing, have been nearly continuous from Arequipa, down the coast of Chile from January to July (1960). Even more than at Lima, earthquake after earthquake since the beginning of the eighteenth century has spared little of Arequipa. I had hoped to see the Jesuit church of La Compañía, 'the only church which had survived intact from the repeated disasters' but it is to be feared this is no longer true, and the Casa del Moral, an old Colonial house of the eighteenth century with a stone overdoor carved with puma heads from which are issuing writhing serpents, 'while other native themes include Indian dancers in flounced skirts and the *ccantu*, the sacred lily of the Incas'.[1] For Arequipa was one of the centres, if it was not the fountain, of the *mestizo* style, the same author just quoted saying that 'if any art or race was ever crossbred, if ever there was a mixture of European and native Indian, the monuments of Arequipa and Puno are proof thereof'. But one can form some idea of the churches of Arequipa, and 'the lacelike reliefs against a background of stucco painted yellow', from the churches of Guatemala which are nearly identical in style and date, this remark applying more particularly to the façades of the village churches at Caima and at Yanahuara, a short distance from Arequipa, if they are still standing.

We are still high enough to keep thinking of altitude, and remember that the highest recorded habitation in the Andes is at 17,400 feet, a panting, breathtaking thought. But, also, it induced one in cold comfort to think of other and stranger isolations, not just a shepherd's hut even if that had stone walls, and was a permanent dwelling among the herds of guanacos and vicuñas. For in the Peruvian Andes there are Tibetan remotenesses and solitudes. We had been told of a town in Peru big enough to have its own newspaper which could still only be reached by three day's ride over the mountains. I had forgotten its name, but several persons made their suggestions as to which it could

Wethey, *op. cit.*, pp. 142, 151, 111.

be. That there may well be such places in the Andes is further supported
by mention in Mr Harold E. Wethey's book of churches 'in the remote
fastnesses of the mountains', two of them 'far in the mountains without
roads, and only to be reached by mule or on foot'. One of them is the
sanctuary of Nuestra Señora de Cocharcas, 'the most splendid of all
the remote Andean churches', and the other is the parish church of
Mamara, both places in the province of Andahuaylas,[1] and of the latter
Mr Wethey remarks that 'no historian either of architecture or of the
Church has ever braved the rigours of mountain passes by muleback
to visit it. Luckily it is known as the result of an expedition of a photo-
grapher of Lima'. Mamara looks interesting enough in the photograph,
with pillared façade of two storeys, twin towers, a porch with Solomonic pillars, and group of Indians in striped *ponchos*, the alcalde among
them, silver staff in hand, waiting by the wall.

What a huge country is Peru, and how hopeless to see it all in less
than a stay of many years! For that is only in one region of the Andes,
and there is Trujillo in the coastal desert three hundred miles north of
Lima, near to Chan-Chan, the ancient capital and necropolis of the
Chimú, covering with its ruins an area of eight square miles. But
Trujillo 'has suffered utter degradation, forgotten and forlorn in this
present world', and in spite of its churches and colonial houses 'has
less to offer' than Cajamarca, near-by in the mountains and at ten
thousand feet of altitude, the scene of Atahuallpa's arrest, ransom and
subsequent execution, and its three fine churches with *retablo* façades,
that is to say they are similar in style to the golden *retablos* of eighteenth-
century Peru. The three-winged, two-storied façade of the Cathedral
with an attic storey for its centre, and the whole of its front one mass
of fretted pilasters, does certainly resemble a *retablo*; still more so in a
detailed photograph which shows motifs of bunches of grapes, scrolled
leaves, and all the paraphernalia of wooden columns carved and
gilded and set up by an altar. San Antonio de Padua looks less interesting,
but is certainly *retablo*-like with its statues standing in niches, four of
them above one another to each side; while El Belén with unfinished
towers and the like number of statues of saints in rounded niches is
like the *retablo* of a high altar removed bodily and put up in the bright

[1] Not to be confused with Andahuayllas, a village thirty miles from Cuzco with a splendid
church. It has a frescoed interior, a *mudéjar* ceiling, a golden altar with mirrored canopy over
the Virgin, and an early organ which has painted shutters with angels playing musical instruments in the manner of a village El Greco. On a side altar 'seductive female caryatids with silver
bodies dressed in black netting hold out their arms'. cf. Kubler and Soria, *op. cit.*, p. 181.

sunlight outside. I could wish to have seen Cajamarca, Trujillo, and another town, Sana, on the coastal desert some way north again of Trujillo, a city destroyed after a flood in 1720, but with the remains of its ruined churches, in fact a dead city like Antigua in Guatemala and Old Panamá. But it was of no use regretting them; any more than Ayacucho with its twenty churches and golden altars, in particular that of the nunnery of Santa Clara with whirling shells and volutes and mirror-inlay, and its nun's choir at the other end with perforated wooden choir screen inlaid with mother-of-pearl and tortoiseshell to remind me of the marvellous golden *coro alto* of Santa Clara at Oporto and the no less imaginative golden lattices of Santa Chiara at Naples, now vanished for ever when it was destroyed in the last war. We could have gone to Ayacucho, but did not because it is ten thousand feet up and we wanted to reserve our strength and energies for the Altiplano. It was of no use to regret it, there was still so much to see.

The landscape in the meantime was something utterly wonderful and beyond precedent in one's experience, its scale such that one lost all measures of comparison. There were still the lakes with their cloud reflections, but it was not to be longer than an hour or more before our chauffeur-driver, looking over towards the left where were certain snowy shapes upon the horizon, would exclaim 'los montañeses de Bolivia', a phrase as haunting as any I have heard since we went on our way from Madrid with letters of introduction, bound for 'las fiestas de Sevilla'. The mountains of Bolivia they were indeed, but a very great distance away, mountains of eighteen and nineteen thousand feet, of which it is true we were two-thirds of the height ourselves, but in this clear air they had the full grandeur of their altitude and were of Himalayan stature.

It was somewhere over in those mountains that a mountain Indian came to C. H. Prodgers and told him there was a Condor Real which lived up in the mountains near his shepherd's hut. He said there were several common condors with the Condor Real, which was much bigger than any condor he had ever seen before. But Prodgers failed in his attempt to kill or capture it. However, he has a story to tell of a friend 'whose father heard from the mountain Indians that there was a big white bird far larger than any condor living in the mountains, at the back of Inquisivi near some old abandoned mines. There were several white-necked condors guarding the King of the Condors, and bringing him food. No house was near and nobody was working there. The father, who had a fine collection of birds in his house in Lima, knew at once that this bird was a specimen of the Condor Real. He got two of the men to accompany him and his mule men, and started off with provisions for a fortnight. They camped near some of the abandoned mines, killed two llamas they had brought for the purpose, and abandoned the carcasses about half a mile from their camp. The next day the white-necked condors began to fly down and circle round the dead llamas. . . . On the third day the big white bird was seen feasting on one of the dead llamas, with some of the other condors sitting at a distance, and others hovering overhead. He started very carefully to stalk the white bird, so as to get a sure shot . . . and was lucky enough to kill the bird stone dead. But as soon as the other birds saw what had happened to their King they began to circle round him, making angry noises and flapping their wings so fiercely that, though he saw the big white bird lying still, he was afraid to go nearer, and thought it prudent to return to the shelter of his camp in the mines. The condors came flying round his camp, flapping their wings angrily against the entrance of the mines. All that afternoon, and the whole of the next day, the condors kept flying about the mine close to the entrance, flapping their wings and shrieking. On the third day everything seemed quiet, and they ventured out again, only to find that all the white necked condors had gone, and the big white bird had disappeared too. He said there was no doubt that the condors had carried away their King.'[1]

This is what the great traveller and naturalist Baron von Humboldt has to say about the Condor Real. 'The condors of the Cordilleras are the biggest birds that fly. They are black with a white collar; the females are just as large, but are a coffee-colour brown and have no collar. They live at a height of fourteen to sixteen thousand feet and measure anything from tip to tip from seven feet to fourteen feet. The Condor Real or King of the Condor is a pure white bird and measures as much as twenty to twenty-five feet from tip to tip. In the whole range of the Andes, I do not think that twenty-five exist.' There are many tales of the huge white condor and whether it exists, or not, is a matter of speculation. But the ordinary condors with the

[1] *Adventures in Bolivia*, by C. H. Prodgers, John Lane, The Bodley Head, 1922, pp. 206, 207.

white collar are large enough and I have talked with persons who have
shot condors with a wing spread of eleven or twelve feet. Big enough
to cover the whole of the car in which we are travelling along the
railway line, and they could wheel and circle at twice our twenty-five
miles an hour. What winds and chasms they must experience in the
Andean wastes! And I remembered that my friend Tom Goff, the maker
of harpsichords and one of the foremost living craftsmen, uses condors'
quills in his instruments because of their lightness and resonance. How
apt that the biggest bird that flies should lend its pinions to the flights of
Johann Sebastian Bach and Domenico Scarlatti!

But now there was something else to think of because we were
nearing Pucará. A word which means a fortress in Quechua, but in
this instance it is the name of a town. At about six o'clock in the
evening, when the clouds were piling up, there was ominous darkness
and all the threatenings of a storm. The line lay straight for miles ahead
as in a prairie, and we were looking for Pucará and it seemed we
would never get there. Mile after mile, with still the pools by the rail-
side, but now with leaden or pewter shadows in them. And now, at
last, some buildings ahead must be the station, and we came into it
to find the spaces between the tracks—there were no platforms—
crowded with Indian women, and a multitude of pottery bulls put
down beside them. The bulls of Pucará, for this is where the pottery
bulls seen in most houses in Peru come from! They cannot have been
made before the Spaniards came because the Indians had no cattle. The
Spaniards brought their bulls with them, and the cult caught on in
this remote place on the Altiplano. We are to suppose the Indians
have made the Pucará bulls for two hundred years or more. They are
fond of bull-fights in this region, and no one could doubt it on seeing
the pottery figures with their Minoan associations and all the *mystique*
of the minotaur down to Goya and Picasso. In fact they much resemble
the bulls of Cuenca in Spain, yet not wholly, for there is the Peruvian
Indian about them. They are even characteristically Peruvian; pottery
subjects that, viewed depressingly, could come from moulds and be
made of gingerbread. But in another moment they are grand and
awe-inspiring with splendidly masculine curls on their foreheads
and dewlaps, their stance, heavy and earthshaking, and you can hear
their bellow.

The bulls are kilned in a variety of shapes and colours in the surrounding villages, and are brought in to market at Pucará where, as always in Peru, the railway station is the social centre. There are brown bulls and even green ones, and others of plain pottery with the curls and dewlaps painted on them, always with a lowering, threatening pair of horns, but perhaps the black bulls are the best of all, plain black, or with white lines incised on them. There were so many on the ground, and such a crowd of Quechua women, that we took refuge in the stationmaster's office where the most expensive of them, costing no more than a shilling or two, were on sale. Here, some were positively enormous, bigger than you could lift with one hand, and fierce in proportion. When we had made our selection and came out again, the train had run up behind us, a slow train with Indians pouring out of third class carriages and all chewing coca. There had been a feeling of hurry for we knew it was due in and close behind us. And so, clutching an armful of pottery bulls we were on board again and left Pucará in semi-darkness.

It had been a long day and we were not yet at Juliaca, an important railway junction, where our companion lived. But it was becoming too dark to see much, and we sat in silence waiting for the miles to go by. It must have been at least an hour, or an hour and a half, with curious flat areas of light low down in the clouds almost as though you were looking through a leaden pane. And then lights, a great number of lights, and the noise of trains shunting, and we were in Juliaca. The one-floored house in which our companion lived was just across the railway line, and we went there to be greeted by his young and charming German wife. Our journey was not over yet and we were quite exhausted, but stayed a little time to talk to her for, as at Sicuani, one felt the terrible loneliness of living in such a place. Juliaca is much the larger of the two, but this might make it even worse on the principle that one can be lonelier in a foreign town than in a village. Again as at Sicuani there was a medical mission, and our friend's wife who had already a small son was retiring for the baby she was expecting before long into the Seventh Day Adventists' hospital. Puno is their shopping town, and there can be no one to talk to in Juliaca except the missionaries and their wives. It would be expecting too much of an ordinary English middle class family to think that their years of work and exile in a town near the shores of Lake Titicaca would be lightened by studying the *mestizo* architecture of the

region. All their interests must lie within the four walls of their houses
and in news from home.

It must have been eight o'clock when we left Juliaca with another
hour, or an hour and a half, to Puno. The sky had become perfectly
dark and there was loud thunder and pouring rain. In this way we
missed seeing the beginnings of Lake Titicaca and could only know
that we were among shadowy, steep hills. It could have been midnight,
or two o'clock in the morning. There was not a light or a human
being to be seen. Our friend who must have longed for his home
had insisted on coming with us, which was lucky, for certainly we
would have been lost when we arrived. And at length there were
lights but no live beings for it was as though the pouring rain had
drowned them all. Our car had stopped as near as possible to where
we were going which was a little way outside the station, and there
was the choice of running with our luggage which would mean making
two or three journeys of it, or going back and trying to find someone
in the station. But somehow, and I do not remember by which alternative, we made the transit, running and splashing, carrying suitcases,
to find ourselves under the porch, and at the foot of the staircase, of a
comfortable hotel. No eighteenth-century traveller could have been
happier to arrive from the highwaymen's heath at the door of the
posthouse, or to struggle through a snowstorm and reach the Hospice of
St Bernard with, says the guide book, 'a Morgue, nearby, now walled
up, a receptacle for bodies found in the snow', and all of that, incidentally, at eight thousand one hundred feet altitude, which is only two-
thirds of our present height on Lake Titicaca of twelve thousand five
hundred and six feet above sea-level. We ate a late dinner and went
straight to bed.

But it was not so easy as that; I had to change my bedroom four times
during the night. The first change was because all the government-
run hotels in Peru have identical wooden bedsteads, which in the course
of years have developed musical properties and squeak loudly and
piercingly at every movement, and even at each breath. On Lake
Titicaca something of the extraordinary nature of the entire surroundings has affected them as when an ageing tenor—it happened
with Caruso—finds his voice changing into a baritone, or, at a particularly shrill complaining, it is just the ordinary bass voice breaking or
emerging from the treble. But, at any rate, I was over-tired and could

bear with it no longer, making my way along the passage to a room
beyond the staircase looking out onto the same side. Here the bat-
like squeakings were less obstreperous, but just the exertion of moving
room brought on a bad attack of breathlessness. I had to go back
along the passage for the cardamine, arousing on that double journey
the suspicions of the night porter, a full-blooded Indian engaged in
throwing pairs of boots down at the bedroom doors.

A little uneasy rest followed, and then after a few moments which
may have been an hour, at four o'clock in the morning the electric
pump began working with a noise like thunder, next door, it seemed
to my new room. This was not to be borne, and I stormed down the
staircase in my pyjamas to the night porter's desk. He was not there
and I stayed a while looking distractedly at the postcards of balsa
rafts in a frame over his desk. Presently I saw him watching me from
the end of the hall towards the engine-room, and after staring intently
wondering what I was going to do next, he came forward rattling his
keys and offering to sell me postcards. When I declined angrily he
followed me upstairs, barefoot as I, and escorted me to my (wrong)
door while murmuring 'veinte dos' the number of my (right) room.
I lay down again, but the engine was shaking the whole room, with the
maddening feeling that it must be taking one somewhere when the
truth was that I was to stay there listening to it until breakfast time.

Whereupon I made one more descent to the desk, determined to
change my room honestly and by orthodox method, but once more he
was not there, and after waiting like a wandering spirit for about a
quarter of an hour I chose the key of an empty room for myself, hoping
it was a lucky number, and went upstairs. It proved to be a large double
room with luggage and clothes lying about in it, but unoccupied. It
was daylight by now, bouts of breathlessness were continuous, and as
sleep was out of the question and this room was on the other side of
the passage, I pulled the curtains and sat looking at the view, where
the lake must be but all one could see of it was a corner of the harbour.
But the Indian brave had stalked me to my new apartment, and now
started to knock on my door, muttering the numbers of all three rooms
one after another, and would not stop. He would not pay heed to
'silencio', or anything said to him in English; and at length, frenzied
with tiredness and thinking the only sensible tactic was to break
the siege, I crept to the door, waited a moment, and then sprang out

nd darting across the passage bolted myself into what was happily an
mpty room. There, admitting to his defeat, he left me in peace. But
ow it was almost time for coffee after a sleepless night in Puno.

It was Sunday morning. From the windows of my different bed-
ooms even as early as five or six o'clock I had seen women in bright
oloured dresses all walking in the same direction, but had been too
ired to think where they were going. The market was just round the
orner from the hotel, and going to the chemist to buy more cardamine
ve were in the midst of it. We had grown as used to the drug, if it is
ne, as the Indians to their coca, without any evidence that it did one
ny good at all for we had to walk slowly along, pausing for breath
very few moments. The chemist's shop with Indian assistants behind
ne counter had as many cosmetics for sale as in any country town in
ngland, but there were no babies in perambulators at the door.
istead, there was a Gypsy-costermonger encampment of the Indians.
We were deep in it already, stepping over the Indian women
quatting on the doorstep of the chemist's shop, and quite submerged
a it when we came out again. But this was another race of Indians
om what we had seen before. Or, at least, their dress was different.
hey were probably Aymara, and not Quechua, for it is chiefly the
ymara who live round the shores of Titicaca and towards La Paz.
very woman in the market wore a brown bowler. This was what
aade them different. It is the mark of the Bolivian *chola* costume,
aat and the skirt or *pollera*, although we are not in Bolivia yet; Puno
in Peru. It is not exactly the costume of La Paz which is the metro-
olis of the *cholas*, but a Peruvian version of that, because the true
ola is a *mestiza* or half-caste and probably most of the women in the
uno market were pure Indian. It is the colours of the *polleras* which
e so startling. The skirts (*aksus*) of the Quechua women are straighter
id longer, as may be seen at Cuzco. But these are all bell-shaped and
ort, like a short, boneless crinoline, one pollera worn over another.
ve, six, seven, even ten of them, and all in different colours. This
ve of bright colours is apparently Aymara, and not Quechua.
owadays their skirts are aniline-dyed, and perhaps just for this once
en better in effect because of that. Certainly I have never seen any-
here such vibrant and stirring colour clashes, or such a colour passage
a skirt of some particular hue. The marvellous costumes of Guate-
ala, perhaps the most beautiful left in the world, are worked on

another system altogether, stitch by stitch. These are handloom costumes, *tachiste* affairs by the eye of genius—were there one among
them—compared to the microscopic inch by inch rendering of an
Antonello da Messina or a Van Eyck. At La Paz the results were to be
still more wonderful, but they were startling enough at Puno.

Appreciation suffers from there being no adjective by which to
describe the Indian markets. 'Indian' has a double meaning with all
its weight on Hindu India, so that 'Indian' applied to a Peruvian or
Bolivian market conveys almost nothing at all. South American, or
Central American where Guatemala is meant, means less still. It is as
if the Indians, again, for there is no other general term for them, have
been dormant all this time, or have been there and none have noticed
them. After only an hour in Cuzco or Puno or La Paz one is looking
for a word for them, and cannot find it. *Chola* would seem to be the
answer, but it is of doubtful application here in Puno, applies hardly at
all in Cuzco or La Paz, and is quite inapplicable in Guatemala where the
race is wholly native with no Spanish blood at all. One cannot say
'the Indian market' in the sense in which one can describe something
as Oriental, or just Moslem which has a wealth of meaning. These
are races which the outside world took no account of at all, and even
christened by a wrong name which was in use already. It is a deficiency
felt all over South and Central America, though it is finding its own
solution in Mexico.

Haggling and bargaining went on till evening. The same handful of
carrots or bunch of mushrooms was still lying on a cloth in front of the
same woman at four o'clock in the afternoon; by which time most
of the menfolk had drunk themselves half-silly. There was a good deal
of clumsy half-hearted dancing, and a wild-looking boy of about
fifteen ran past chasing somebody and brandishing an open knife.
But many *cholas* and *cholos* were already on the way home, and there
was the unpleasing sight of men relieving themselves drunkenly
against the wall of the hotel, and a *chola* with her babe on her back
squatting on the ground, defaecating. Their insanitary habits are conducted in public without shame. It was no surprise when we were
in La Paz to be told that diseases like infectious haepatitis were practically endemic in the city. The *chola* women never take off their clothes,
the most they will do is to wash their top skirt and put it on again
underneath the others. But they are 'hat-conscious' to inordinate

ngths; and there are time-honoured stories of Indian or *chola* women
who will undress for once in their lives to be examined by the doctor
ut refuse on any account to take off their hats.

For the next day or two we were to make excursions from Puno,
eing reduced by breathlessness to a state when we could do little more
han crawl round the market, stopping every moment or two and
oping not to drop anything and have to stoop to pick it up. I had by
ow exchanged my musical bedstead for another of less hoarse, fresher
imbre of voice and had a permanent apartment from which I went
no more a-roving by the light of the moon'. The manager of the
otel, a young Andalusian Spaniard lately come from Málaga, had
een sympathetic to my vagaries, and having himself just graduated
o the shores of Lake Titicaca from managing the hotel at Machu
Picchu we had more than one talk together, contrasting the amenities
f his beloved Málaga with Puno. He and his wife had gone off to Mass
hat morning with as much of solemnity as though he was attending
he Semana Santa of Seville, and on their return we arranged for a car
o take us round to see the sights.

There are some four towns or villages round the shores of the lake
vhere the curious *mestizo* architecture of the district can be seen. They
re Puno itself, Pomata, Juli, and Zepita, all of them on the Peruvian
hores of Titicaca. We made the mistake of going on foot to the
Cathedral in Puno, with the result that we were in a mood to minimize
ts beauties. Its façade is certainly curious because, begun early in the
ighteenth century like many of the most beautiful of Mexican churches,
o the charge of 'a rich miner', it looks as though it had been built in a
emote district of Northern Spain in about 1550. One of the side doors
vith odd-looking hooded entablature and a mass of intricate, flat
arving under it, has more character. Perhaps Puno was a half-hearted
ntroduction to the *mestizo* style, and except that it would have entailed
not getting to Puno till about five o'clock in the morning we were
beginning to regret that we had not insisted on stopping long enough
t Pucará of the pottery bulls to see the parish church of Santiago de
Pupuja. It would have been too dark, it is true, to distinguish the
detail of the high altar of 1760, wittily described as 'an amazing
spectacle in blue, white, red and gold, with brackets that look like
iger masks, conch shells like fans, and Ionic orders that have *estipites* of
shells with fluting', in fact the transformation or transcendentalization

of ordinary or standard motifs, while 'underneath the pulpit of red cedar, sprinkled with gilded edges like dew-drops, Atlantes in dress uniform serve as brackets'.[1]

Instead we started along the shores of the lake to Juli, a little town now much shrunken in population which had fourteen thousand 'converted' Indians living in it in 1579, and in consequence four churches. The church of San Pedro Martir is in the same square as the old Zavala mansion—it is certainly no palace—with its barbaric carved stone doorways; and San Pedro Martir is peculiar enough, but San Juan still more so with the most splendid imaginable carved and gilded picture frames upon it walls, and extraordinary round-headed arches in the baptistery that anywhere in Western Europe would be Romanesque and nearly a thousand years old. But the true flavour of Juli is in the ruined church of Santa Cruz, where the carved stone ornament enters into full *mestizo* repertory and on inner and outer portals there are monkeys holding papayas or biting into bunches of grapes, pomegranates split open with ripeness and showing a plentiful crop of seeds, and a riot of red-pepper pods and bananas.

The mystery is as to the origin of this exotic ornament. Some authorities would have it that the source of the *mestizo* style is Arequipa while, according to others, these tropical elements were brought to the Peruvian highlands by missionaries from Paraguay. Whereas the puma or native tiger and the *ccantu* (sacred lily)[2] are indigenous and of the country, the papayas and monkeys and bananas of which the *mestizo* sculptors made great play are only found at great distance from the Altiplano, the nearest locality being the *yungas* or tropical valleys of Bolivia, a long march from Titicaca at a llama's walking pace. But then, for that matter, neither do these exotic fruits and animals occur on the ruined churches of the Jesuit *misiones* in Paraguay, so that there is really somewhat of a mystery as to their source of origin. We are not to imagine that in the beginning of the eighteenth century there were monkeys and papayas for sale at market stalls in villages round the shores of Titicaca. There are not now, and there were not then; and yet the *mestizo* sculptors were perfectly familiar with these models.

It was almost with impaired faculties from fatigue and breathlessnes that we went on from Juli to Pomata. Here the church of Santiago

[1] Kubler and Soria, *op. cit.*, p. 181.
[2] The sacred lily of the Incas has a flower resembling a single fuchsia. It grows at Mach Picchu.

he masterpiece of the mestizo style', stands on a promontory above
'iticaca at thirteen thousand feet above sea level. It was built by the
)ominicans from a beautiful dark rose-coloured stone, and the unique
:ature of its interior is the flat sculpture between the ribs or spandrels
f the dome. They form a species of flat abstraction of stalks and
:aves with human heads where the heads should be, and these abstract
.gures are linked each to each by flower garlands, and have been
iterpreted as performing a native dance. Even if 'any suggestion of
ance rhythms was unpremeditated', that is their effect upon one, and
: is difficult to believe this idea was not present in the sculptor's mind.[1]
'he central boss in the middle of the dome looks like a cluster of
:ylized *ccantus* or sacred lilies. There are also sacristy doorways of the
ichest possible carving in this peculiar manner which now for a
1oment suggests a church interior in the Kremlin in 'old Russian'
:yle. But we now felt too exhausted to continue any further and so
1issed seeing the fourth of these churches at Zepita, regretting this
he less because it is only the outside of the church which is interesting
nd the interior is described as quite bare and empty. It is the side
loorway at Zepita that exhibits the rich ornament of the *mestizo*
:yle.

At Zepita we would have been within a mile or two of the Bolivian
•order, having, so to speak, bye-passed the promontory on which
tands the pilgrimage shrine of Copacabana. For some reason difficult
o fathom this place, which is famous all over Latin America, has a
limate of its own, and must seem to be in another world from the rest
•f Titicaca. It is in Bolivia and visited every year by thousands of
1dian pilgrims. Everyone who has been there agreed in telling us that
t Copacabana you cannot believe you are separated by only a few miles
rom Puno.

I think there can be few places in the world that give so remote a
eeling as these villages on the shores of Titicaca. But there are so
1any things that contribute to this impression. In spite of its having
•een their background for who knows how many centuries the Indians

[1] Mr Harold E. Wethey illustrates another and similar dome from the church of the Espíritu
.anto at Chihuata, 'a tiny and desolate pueblo' in the region of Arequipa. In this instance 'twelve
ngels in flounced feathered skirts stand with arms upraised, flanked by twelve strips of rectangular
lowers which rise from vases'. The stone at Chihuata is white, and the background of the dome
s painted blue, but he says that the carving is not as good as at Pomata, and that the design 'lacks
he almost terpsichorean rhythm of the more famous sanctuary on Lake Titicaca'. Wethey,
p. cit., p. 153 and plate 214.

with a plug of coca leaf in their cheeks cannot be described as normal
ized inhabitants of their Martian or multiplanetary landscape. I call i
that because even when you are in it the suggestion is of a landscap
viewed from an immense distance with the sort of distortion of M
Alamo, Jodrell Bank, or other giant telescopes. You may think Indian
only keep going at all because they are artificially sustained by thei
narcotic. You are feeling more than peculiar yourself, while knowing
that at this moment there are persons in bed in the hotel being give
oxygen by the doctor. This was the case while we were at Puno. I hav
purposely refrained up to this point from trying to write of the lak
itself so as to give full emphasis to the strange ornament of the *mestiz*
churches around its shores. The hallucinatory nature of that ornamen
with its exotic overtones from another and more tropical clime
whether from Pacific or Atlantic because it is on the watershed, stil
further accentuates the midday glare and distortion of this arid, and
at nights, this icy climate.

But there are more contradictions. For this feeling of utter an
entire distance and loneliness is to some little extent disproved so fa
as ourselves are concerned by the number of European travellers wh
have passed this way. During the centuries since the Conquest at leas
as many persons have come to Peru overland from the Atlantic coas
of South America by way of Titicaca as have made the long Atlanti
crossing to Panamá, crossed the Isthmus, and sailed down the coas
to Callao, the port of Lima. Such a remote town as Juli on Lake Titi
caca, where we have just been, in the seventeenth century 'was only
outranked in the number and splendour of its churches by Cuzco and
Lima,' while as early as 1612 the astonishing Jesuit missionaries pub
lished an Aymara dictionary at Juli. In fact it has been 'settled' fou
times longer than either Australia or New Zealand. So Lake Titicac
is not after all so remote, and on all counts it should not be so lonely
Yet it is both those things, and no amount of theoretical arguing o
marshalling of historical facts can dispel these feelings.

For a full flavour of which I will describe our excursion on an afternoon at Puno. It left an even sharper impression because the ide
of it had been to go nowhere in particular, but just to drive up int
the hills and look down on Titicaca. The way led up a steep street on the
outskirts of the town where the characters standing in doorways gave
us to infer it was the 'red light' district. Our driver, and the companior

Asillo church, Peru

Andean village scene

Peruvian village at harvest
time

Above left, Making a balsa raft at Lake Titicaca; *above right*, Lake Titicaca;
below left, Chola women at Puno, Peru; *below right*, Tiahuanaco (Bolivia)

he insisted on bringing with him, began to talk from this moment on mutual recognition of acquaintances, and never ceased to keep their chatter through all the hazards of the afternoon. If the lake lies at twelve and a half thousand feet, the road with its many curves must have climbed another thousand and a half until we were at fourteen thousand, a height conducive to hysterically sluggish, or indeed anything else but clear, thinking. The lake waters below were pale blue like the cup of a blue poppy, and that the blue poppy is Tibetan seemed only right and sensible. Where else could it come from, with lamaseries upon its shores confusing the two countries in our minds? Never before has one seen waters of such a colour. Yet even at this height, which is higher than any but the highest of the Alps, across the lake there are the snowy mountains of the Cordillera Real, the *montañés de Bolivia* of the romantic phrase. They looked to be gigantic and could be a thousand miles away.

We were now on a sort of moorland where we continued for some time, then coming down onto a straighter-than-Roman road across the plain. An illusory village lay far away in the distance, and at a certain point we made an abrupt left turn off the road and then went for some miles along a causeway beside a river. As we passed, some curious little rodents scuffled into their burrows in the reeds beside the river. They were as numerous as rabbits used to be on summer roads in England. Then we came, under a hill, to a large hacienda, and as we reached it the American who owned it came out in his motor. This was a last outpost, and after that we were in the wilderness, first appreciating our situation only when we were some eight or ten miles beyond it and perhaps three hours walk away. A church tower on a hill very far in front seemed to indicate a village, but at this point the driver and his friend, neither of whom spoke more than a word or two of Spanish, interrupted their duologue to tell us they were taking us to see an Inca ruin. The tower in front, although we were approaching it, kept on getting further and further away, and to every enquiry both of them turned round and with sweeping gestures of their arms seemed to imply that we could make a round of it and come back along a better road. We were by now too far to turn back and might as well go on. But the river landscape had changed to endless marshland, the road was one string of puddles and the car wheels were beginning to get caught in the mud.

K

The crisis came quickly, and there we were with the wheels churning vainly, as incapable of going forward as any bluebottle buzzing on its back with legs in the air. We had all to get out, dig the wheels free and put stones beneath them. After some half-hour we got started again, and the driver then went off the road and made us walk behind him. In a few minutes we were a quarter of a mile off the road and he was steering from one bit of hard ground to another and trying to rush the distances between them. Inevitably, he came to a halt again, and now it was beginning to be serious. The hacienda we had passed was further back than we could go on foot before it was quite dark, and we had gone by only to see the owner leaving in a car heaped high with luggage. I did not relish a night out in the marshes of Lake Titicaca. Not a house or a hut was in sight, and the hallucinatory tower on a hill had long vanished. We were in danger, too, of losing the road altogether, and in spite of the early hour the mosquitos were gathering. I will never know how or why we moved on again, and with many halts and much pushing and heaving got on to harder ground. We had the return journey to look forward to, and yet with wills weakened, I suppose, by days of breathlessness we allowed ourselves to be led on.

We now began climbing the stony bed of a road which more nearly resembled a mountain torrent, but in the dry season without the water and only the stones. Soon there were stone walls to both sides as on roads in Ireland, but they were old walls. And not only walls but the ruins of stone houses, too. We were in the ruins of an Inca, or more probably pre-Inca, town or large village. It continued for half a mile at least, and even when we had climbed above it at breakneck speed on the stony track with blue flowers like harebells growing out of the banks, and great clumps of a lovely saxifrage out in the stony fields, there were more ruins. We were by now entirely tranced, unable to make up our minds one way or the other and at the mercy of our driver who kept on pointing in front and saying the only two words we could understand which were 'Inca cemetery'. A mountain lake of marvellous colour now appeared, with wild duck upon it, and skirting its left bank in such a remoteness and solitude as were nearly unimaginable, we came round its shores under or on the side of a hill, but of such shape that it made only a shadow against the light of evening. Never in all my life have I seen anything so far away or lonely, and in a dread of the late hour and of never getting home again we drove into what seemed to be the courtyard of a farm-house under the tower in a sudden radiance of the evening while two Indians, first human beings we had seen for hours, came out of the building. We did not dare to stop for more than a moment but turned the car and drove away.

The dark tower must have been connected in some way with the Inca cemetery. If, indeed, it was a cemetery at all, but I preferred never to make enquiry or find out where we had been. Any more than I attempt to describe the return journey which went as though by enchantment, without untoward incident, and as if we were being forwarded back safely from an adventure into another sphere. We got back late, it is true, but how late can one be in returning from the lost world! No doubt there are other and strange experiences to be enjoyed round Titicaca. Had there been time, I would have liked to continue back along the shores, away from Bolivia, through Juliaca again and back to Lampa. For here, and at Ayaviri, a near-by village, are domed churches of a surprising size until we are told that the present inhabitants number only a fifth of the original population. But the interest is in the façades of the two churches, in the Cuz-queñan, not the *mestizo* style, yet by architects of pure Indian blood, strange exercises in the discipline of the classical orders to find hundreds of miles from anywhere on the Altiplano of Peru. Built of the red stone of the region during the two decades immediately before 1700, they argue a degree of Indian talent which the Indians have been slow to display in the two and a half centuries since that time. Both façades are stone frontispieces in three storeys, that at Lampa composed of single columns in pairs, while at Ayaviri it is a fugal upsurge of two lots of triple columns, but without real fluency or distinction, enuncia-ting, so to speak, the Latin syllables but with strong Indian accent, though astonishing enough so far from Papal Rome. A more Indian affair still must be the red stone village church at Asillo, a remote village under the snow mountains, once thatched, now roofed with corrugated tin; three storeys again of triple columns but with rings like cigar-bands or paper crowns around them, and the hand of the Indian sculptor has been unable to resist giving some of the angels feathered head-dresses.

On the last afternoon at Puno we drove round the lake towards the floating islands. Large crowds were gathered at the cemetery, buying and carrying in flowers as we passed by, coming at last to the lake's edge, and going past large rocks by the roadside all along the shore. But the water with the snow mountains of Bolivia far away over it was at some distance out, and there were large beds of reeds, none other than the famous *totora* reed of which the *balsa* rafts are made. At one point there was a track or footpath through the reeds to where an Indian was making a *balsa* boat, and we went down to watch him. No process could be simpler; and without the skill to make or do anything with my own hands, here, at last, in a long and full life was something I could have done myself. It consisted in cutting and tying together four bundles of reeds to make the hull of the boat, and it looked as if one could make a *balsa* boat in a morning. The sail is only a reed curtain. But the Indian at work with his small son beside him was not so pleased, and resented our interference. He looked angrily at us; and like a child about to launch his paper boat on a pond dragged his *balsa* raft away, and stood with back turned putting the finishing touches to it. There was nothing else we could do but turn round and walk away.

About half a mile out in the lake were some of the floating islands, and we could distinctly see men and women walking about on them, and their conical huts made, also, presumably, of *totora* reeds. But 'floating islands' carry a suggestion of lotus-eating and listlessness, if not of lilies and languor, whereas the water-Indians, as we could see even from this distance, were busily employed mending their fishing nets, as we imagined, or just, mariner-like, pacing the reedy decks. Children, also, were clearly visible, and one thing was obvious that for better or worse they never went to school. We could see human figures but not the clothes they wore. A traveller well describes the scene: 'The tips of the white cordillera are reflected in the blue surface, and the conical-shaped houses of the Indians give a character to the scene not found elsewhere in Peru. There are areas of yellow water-weed from which numerous scarlet feathered herons arise as the traveller passes.'[1] The scarlet feathered herons we did not see—or could they be flamingos, or, more likely still, the scarlet ibis?—but our hope was that the water-Indians on their floating isles were dressed in feathers.

What could it be like to live upon those islands? They are formed of reeds and water-weeds with enough soil upon them to grow a few

[1] C. Reginald Enock, *loc. cit.* p. 124.

vegetables. How hideously the Indians must suffer from mosquitos! But, at least, in the cold nights of Titicaca they could sit in the smoke of their fires, and then wrap themselves from head to foot and even cover their faces with their ponchos. The floating islands are, it seems, more common on this western side of the lake, and down particularly in this corner, though the best place to see them is some two hours away. Their inhabitants are a very primitive sort of Indian at little higher level of intelligence than Indians of the Amazon forests. Certainly it would be an experience to spend a night on one of the floating islands.

But we are back in the hotel, being told by the manager from Andalusia that we were heroes to have come to Puno, and half-agreeing with him, and being joined by the English railway manager and his wife from Juliaca who have come to see us off. We drive down to the quay with our luggage, and go on board a large steamer which was surely once a paddle-boat. It had been carried up piece by piece from the coast and assembled here, forty or fifty years ago; and in its way I have not been so much surprised by anything since we went in 1932 on a Sudan Nile Steamer, three hundred miles south from Khartoum to Er Renk on the White Nile, where the giant Dinka stand stork-like on one leg upon the river bank leaning on their spears, and when I asked how old was the steamer in its coat of new white paint I was told it had belonged to General Gordon. We dined with our friends on board in Puno harbour, and then it was time for them to leave us in the pouring rain. With the cranking sound of raising anchor on all the seas of the world we were crossing Titicaca, and would be in Bolivian waters by tomorrow morning.

Chapter Eight

✦◆✦◆✦◆✦◆✦◆✦◆✦◆✦◆✦◆✦◆✦◆✦

TIAHUANACO AND LA PAZ

BUT NOT SO FAST. IT was one of the most unpleasant nights I have ever spent in my life. There are persons who have felt seasick on Lake Titicaca, but I am not of their company. It was the cold and breathlessness that made me ill. We had been given the best cabin on the ship, with one of the ship's officers next door, away from all the other passengers. It had two bunks, of which I occupied the lower, which may have added to the shut in, claustrophobic feeling. On the top deck with a heavy curtain over the door one could have left the door open if one felt breathless, anywhere else except on Titicaca, for usually it is heat that goes with breathlessness. But here one was faint from cold. It was cold that made one feel sick and break out in a sweat. My teeth were chattering, and I felt ice cold on my wrists and temples. I could not lie still, and it began to distort my senses. For some ten days I had not slept more than an hour or two a night, and it was beginning to tell upon me. If this was to go on much longer I was afraid of injuring my heart. Because of the incessant fidgeting and turning over and over in my bunk it was impossible to dwell on anything pleasant in one's mind, which kept on jumping from subject to subject and dragging one breathlessly along with it. At about three or four o'clock I began to wonder seriously what I would feel like in the morning. We had a long and exhausting day ahead of us in the ruins of Tiahuanaco, and I was not sure I could stand it. But worst of all was just before dawn when I became really afraid of getting up or moving. The attacks of breathlessness every few moments were exactly like the sudden sensation of being winded, and then one turned over again only to have the same feeling a moment later.

The only sensible course was to get dressed and go out on deck, which I did by fits and jumps, with a fearful effort like performing the two halves of an exercise in pulling on my trousers; then, in my overcoat, emerging from that Bastille-cabin, and sitting on one of the benches on deck only a few feet from the cabin door. It was six o'clock in the morning. The awful night was over and done with, and although still icily cold the huge snow mountains across the lake were so stupendous that they lifted the heart and put new life into one. Mountains of the Cordillera Real thirty or forty miles away in Bolivia, and after all this night of crossing Lake Titicaca we have not really crossed it at all, but come from about half-way down its length to the far end of it, making a wide sweep on the way in order to come round the peninsula where Copacabana lies on its isolated corner of Bolivian territory. But although it cannot be very far away there is no sign of it when we sail into Guaqui, the Bolivian port whence runs the railway to La Paz. Copacabana must be somewhere over there to the right along the near shore, with its pilgrimage church where formerly had been a pagan temple of the sun-cult, appropriate enough to the Gulf Stream clime of this one locality along the bleak lake shore. Great fairs were held here in the plaza in part of the church which must have been a wonderful spectacle with the Indian and *cholo* costumes; while à propos of local colour, it is interesting to be told that a side altar in the church has polychrome work by a seventeenth-century sculptor of Indian royal blood, Don Sebastian Acopa (tupac) Ynga, 'charming predella reliefs' of sacred subjects with 'views of Lake Titicaca and the snowy mountains'.[1]

Nearer still to where we are looking out over the rail of the ship must be the village of Desaguardero, on the border between Peru and Bolivia. Here, a river flowing out of the lake had a pontoon bridge of *balsa* boats with a floor of grass laid over it, constructed by Inca Capac Yupanqui in 1160. The *balsa* floats were renewed every two years, and this bridge, which aroused the interest of the first Spaniards as much as did the famous bridge across the Apurimac (the 'Bridge of San Luis Rey'), remained in use until 1875. It was sad to be leaving Peru, and our thoughts went back inevitably to the Alcalde Don Hector García Ribeyro from whom we had received so much help and kindness, and to other friends in Lima whom it is likely we may never see again.

[1] Kubler and Soria, *op. cit.*, p. 179. The balsa bridge mentioned in the next paragraph is illustrated in E. G. Squier, *Peru*, 1877, who saw it still in use.

As the ship berthed at Guaqui we could see two persons scanning the
deck, and obviously looking for us. They proved to be another English
railway manager from the Peruvian Corporation, and a delightful
and interesting Señor Montes attached to the British Embassy in La Paz.
In a few minutes we were on board the train; not a motor car on rails
this time but a vintage observation car with kitchen attached. Our
new Bolivian friend had travelled up in this train from La Paz the
night before, and slept in one of the armchairs. Our coach was joined
to the mail train, and we were to go with it as far as Tiahuanaco which
is only some ten or twelve miles away.

Tiahuanaco is the archaeological centre of South America, and one of
the interesting and extraordinary places of the world, even if there
is not as much to see as at Stonehenge, Carnac, Avebury or the stone
circles and underground hypogeum of Malta. How could it be otherwise when it has inspired the wild and romantic theories of Arturo
Posnansky; and even the staider Harold Osborne in his volume on
Indians of the Andes in the International Library of Sociology and
Social Reconstruction[1] calls one of his chapters *The Megalithic Empire
of the Piruas*, and believes the very name Tiahuanaco of mysterious
origin to be a word from the 'esoteric, secret language spoken by the
Inca royal family, according to Garcilaso Inca de la Vega', and argues
that the use of this name is accounted for by the 'special religious
sanctity of the place!'

We arrive at the railway station of the sacred name with the hermetically sealed museum in an odd style of architecture to the right of
the line, and disembark for a walk to the ruins across the scorching
plain which gives an immediate impression that it is seared by both
ice and fire. To the left is the *pueblo* of adobe houses with a church
which, although it is half a mile away, we can see in the clear air has a
pair of pagan statues standing at the door. All round are mounds and
terraces and trenches, and soon we are in the middle of the excavations.
We are thirteen thousand feet up, do not let us forget, with few Alpine
peaks higher than where we are walking, hatless, in the direct rays of
the sun. And here, in front of us, is the Puerta del Sol—shade of the
Madrileños!—the Gateway of the Sun, a megalithic portal, ten feet
high, carved from a single block of stone, but, truth to tell, paltry and
disappointing in that gigantic landscape. The doorway has been hewn

[1] Routledge & Kegan Paul Ltd., London, 1952, pp. 56, 57.

out of the middle of it, and over that is a frieze carved with the figure of a god, 'probably the sun-god Viracocha', 'flanked by forty-eight small rectangular figures running towards him,'[1] but they looked to me more like conventionalized domestic fowl. Further on there is a monolithic human figure with an iron railing round it, but this, too, is disappointing in scale and suggests a race of human beings of diminutive stature trying their hand at something giant and big. It is nowhere so impressive as that unique megalithic statue in Malta, the Colossa or stone Venus of Tarxien.

None the less this figure is typical Tiahuanacan in style with its box-like head, flat face, and no room for the shoulders. For, although there is so little left above ground, and few if any textiles are found here, in the pottery and textiles belonging to the same culture but discovered elsewhere, are all the ingredients of a distinctive style. It is indeed the most easily recognisable of the Indian cultures of South America for which reason the modern textiles and goldsmiths' work sold at Lima and La Paz are so often copied from weaves or patterns in Tiahuanacan style. The craftsmen would in fact be hard put to it if they relied only upon Inca designs, for the Inca was the least ornamental of all Indian cultures. But neither in all this is it necessary to distinguish between the five periods of Tiahuanco that Posnansky professed to find. Nor, alas! need Posnansky be believed when he ascribes ten or twelve thousand years of antiquity to Tiahuanaco, and indeed calls the ruins antediluvian and dates them from before the Flood, in which case with certain living specimens of the fossil trees they would be survivors from before the Ice Age.

The theory of Posnansky and the wilder elements of it which have encouraged other writers on the same path of improbability is that not only the whole Altiplano but even Lake Titicaca as well were much lower in altitude and have been lifted up bodily by some convulsion of nature which yet, miraculously, has not much disturbed the ruins. The landscape setting of Tiahuanaco is so extraordinary that after an hour or two among the mounds and Megalithic remains one might be inclined to believe almost anything, but this is too tall a story. The truth would seem to be that they are about ten or twelve centuries old, and no older. By now we are at the back of a mound up which there is a broad flight of stone steps, and trenches have been dug all

[1] J. Alden Mason, *Op. cit.*, p. 90.

round it by the archaeologists. But even if it is not antediluvian
Tiahuanaco was certainly the centre of a Megalithic Empire, and we
may picture it to ourselves peopled by personages wearing feather head-
dresses and the wonderful textiles of Paracas. The same air blows over
it as over the downland circles of Avebury and Stonehenge. Megalithic
races all over the world loved the open spaces. At this extreme altitude
it is not easy to keep the normal level of one's senses. Any work of
human hands must look small against that giant background of the
mountains and the plain. Stone portal and Megalithic figure, now we
have time to think of them, and to know that stones weighing a hundred
tons were dragged here without the use of wheels and shaped without
iron tools, begin to lose their comparative smallness and to loom
in size. A few more hours at Tiahuanaco and one might credit any tale
one was told.

When we had walked back to the train our attention was temporarily
distracted by a marathon dance just beginning in a yard next to the
station. Indians at differing stages of intoxication were reeling in and
out of the door and we went over to watch them. A cracked kind of
violin supplied the music, and the same tune like a disjointed mazurka
was reiterated over and over and over again. It was likely to continue,
we were assured, for twenty-four hours on end. Some couples of the
Kermesse were lying on the ground asleep or in a stupor, and others
were shuffling round with their eyes shut. But, also, there were angry
and almost murderous glances from the few Indians who were awake.
It seemed a curious celebration of a saint's day. So far we had only
looked in at the door, but when one of us went back to fetch a camera
and we wanted to walk into the yard again, they had locked the
door. Half an hour later when we left Tiahuanaco for ever the same
tune was playing. But in the meantime we were changing trains.
Our luggage was being carried from the observation car into another
smaller coach. An altogether unnecessary number of Indian porters
sprung from nowhere in this wayside station transferred each piece of
luggage separately as though to draw attention to each individual
object, carrying each one past us and trying to catch our eyes. It was
by this technique that my umbrella was not so much stolen as with-
drawn from me and, I suspect, hidden somewhere in the undercarriage
of the observation car. So neat was the manner of its removal that I
could only feel I had left a new Briggs umbrella behind on purpose in

he ruins of Tiahuanaco. And as I write this a whole Indian family may be sheltering under it on a rainy day.

Our new railway coach was motor-driven and like that in which we had made the journey from Cuzco to Machu Picchu. And leaving Tiahuanaco we were soon lost in that illimitable plain. The very straightness of the track in front of one giving the effect of hauling us in on an enormous windlass, probably a result of fatigue and the high altitude. It was a marvellous storm scene on an unprecedented scale with great storms of rain pouring down in a dozen places at once, and so many waves and breakers of cloud above us that it was like a reversed world with an ocean over our heads, and a railway line in the sky crossing the endless empyrean in front and behind, below our feet. We passed one small town with not a soul abroad in it, awash and deserted in the rain. Far off *pueblos*, made of grey mud, were islands where no ship called, lost and sinking. Yet this long day's journey, for so it seemed, upon a map of South America is not the length of a small fingernail. It is no longer than the space taken up in spelling the five letters of La Paz.

Now the awe-inspiring, huge snow mountain of Illimani moves into sight, whiter and taller than the other mountains. One of the giants of the Andes, more than twenty-one thousand feet high. As huge as any mountain in the Himalayas. It has four peaks or pinnacles of virgin rock. No mountaineer, I believe, has yet subdued them. And just as the landscape is emptier and more storm-tossed than ever an aeroplane comes down out of the grey clouds, losing height, and we are told that it is landing at La Paz airport. That is over to the left, and soon we see the aeroplane safely landed, but still moving at high speed behind some sheds and one-floored houses. Not so many years ago in our own lifetime, one would have looked out of the train window and wondered in horror and astonishment what it could be, this long thin white object with fixed wings come down out of the lead-grey sky! We were kept waiting for some time on a railway siding, then moved through the station of El Alto and began the extraordinary descent. We had been told of this, but it must be one of the spectacular experiences of South American travel, and may be no less of an astonishment in its different way than the arrival by sea in Rio de Janeiro.

It takes half or three-quarters of an hour to come down into La Paz.

But in a few moments the town is seen filling the whole cup, or, rather
the trumpet or cornucopia-shaped valley below. The first sensation i
one of bewilderment at so large a city miles away from anywhere, and
with no apparent reason to be there at all. As we grind down neare
into it at slow tram-train speed, even in the backyards of the suburb
we can see the *chola* women wearing more brightly coloured dresse
than ever before. Down and down we go, gradient after gradient, a
little more than walking pace with the railway station only a little way
across a valley but only reached by a long and sweeping, slowly descending curve, and are at last on La Paz Station platform being greetec
by our host Sir James Henderson, with whom we are to stay. W
get into his car, and are driven through the town, going lower anc
lower down the valley to the residential section of it where is the
British Embassy.

Here there is something of an optical illusion for we could be in a
comfortable country house in England, or more accurately in the
Lowlands, in Berwickshire or Mid or East Lothian, somewhere not
far from Edinburgh and, astonishingly, there are even scones for tea
How this can have been achieved in a kitchen staffed by Aymara
Indians is hard to understand but it must be from the mingling in the
ambassadorial couple of the North Briton and the Dane. Still more
difficult is it to credit that only a few months before our visit the
Embassy Residence was slowly sliding down the hill. The descent wa
somehow arrested and the building is now at anchor in a lovely flowe
garden. English seed packets have had their share in this on the flowering
terraces at the back of the house but, also, there are semi-tropica
flowers that do not grow in our gardens and great coloured anc
tethered clouds of bougainvillaea against the walls. Humming bird
are darting about, but not, alas! while we were there, and at times the
lawns are invaded by flocks of small green parrots. One afternoor
at the end of a luncheon party at which we were present the guest
all went out into the garden and looked up into the sky. This wa
in order to see the planet Venus which at that great altitude is sometimes visible in daytime, but there was too much cloud that day.

The learned voice of authority intones that, 'physiologically, La Paz
at a height of more than twelve thousand feet is equivalent to a heigh
of about five thousand five hundred feet in the Alps'. I wished I coulc
agree with this. He continues: 'The slight physiological discomfort

often experienced by travellers . . . are mainly due to a combination of suggestibility and a too rapid change from the atmospheric conditions of the Pacific coast . . . to conditions analogous to those which cause little discomfort to holidaymakers who visit Switzerland for winter sports.'[1] But the first night at La Paz, as at Cuzco, I had no sleep at all; and thereafter slept fitfully for an hour or two hours, panting much, and turning restlessly from side to side. Whenever I think of it I still hear the kind voice of Lady Henderson saying: 'Now remember! Only one step at a time,' as we pulled ourselves by the banisters upstairs to bed. Speaking for myself, I do not believe I could ever get used to these altitudes, and after four weeks on the Altiplano I felt hardly, if at all, better at the eight thousand five hundred feet of Bogotá. That it is a personal question I am ready to agree, and that some may stand it better than others. Equally, there are persons who take naturally to life on board a submarine. I did not feel well at La Paz, but this did not prevent my enjoyment of it. Rather it added a slight, hysterical edge to all we did and said.

It is a town of great fascination in unobvious ways. In the first place there is the mystery of its being there with its three-quarters of a million inhabitants at all. Then we met many writers and poets, and La Paz has decidedly learned and intellectual life in it. The sculptress Marina Nuñez del Prado may be among the foremost artists of the day, if uncompromisingly abstract-international in outlook, and of that school which could be in Paris, London, Warsaw, La Paz, or, in fact, anywhere or everywhere without accent of race or tongue. There seemed to be inordinate numbers of Bolivian writers, or was it only that Sir James and Lady Henderson collected them? Through the haze of three languages, Spanish, French and English, all spoken at once, they seemed intelligent and charming.

The old part of the town is some hundreds of feet higher up the valley, and according to information much has been pulled down and destroyed. But there are odd things to see, such as a large wooden double doorway carved with figures of a man and woman in bowler-hat and bustle of the 1880's which could have been carried out after a drawing by Seurat. There should be paintings in the same style, and contemporary 'Douanier' Rousseaus. A rather sad museum has portraits of the 'proto-martyrs' of the Revolution—whatever this

[1]Osborne, *Op. cit.*, pp. 205, 206.

obvious superlative brand of martyr may be!—paintings of 1820 t
1840 which exceed in their natural primitiveness anything of thei
kind that I have ever seen. They are rather creepily distasteful, thoug
interesting. This is painting at a further remove from the studios o
Paris or of Italy than oil pictures anywhere else in the world. Portrait
of Persian or Indian potentates by native painters have this at any rate
that their subjects have the trappings of Orientals. They have curve
scimitars, jewelled turbans, fan-shaped whiskers, whereas the general
and 'proto-martyrs' (for they seem to have combined both professions
wear Napoleonic uniforms and cocked hats and have only, it may be
an excessive amount of Bolivian gold in their epaulettes. In othe
words they are like everyone else, that is to say, the portraits one ma
have seen in Lisbon or Naples, or any other town in Southern Europe
only more so, with just that added, or rather subtracted touch o
Indian blood in some few of them to make them different.

Another, and private museum belonging to an old gentlema
resembled a native Indian *multum in parvo* or compendium for it ha
every conceivable object salvaged from tombs neatly arranged accord
ing to subject, and displayed in one room by a system which woul
have delighted the orderly if dusty mind of Sir John Soane. Suc
expanding or contracting show space is worthy of the Soane Museun
in Lincoln's Inn Fields. But the interest is archaeological more tha
aesthetic, and probably the medical section is the most complete o
all. There are artificially deformed skulls, trepanned skulls, and, o
course, a few of the shrunken heads from the Amazon forests, if nothing
quite as sensational as the whole body reduced to eighteen inches o
two feet long seen by Leonard Clark and mentioned in his book o
travels.[1] There is still a belief, which he refers to, that these are th
mummified bodies of a race of tiny men, a tale for gullible swallowing
with the eyes shut, while it is certain that most of the shrunken head
offered for sale in Peru or Bolivia are those of monkeys.

Deeply interested, but with a shudder or two and a longing for fresh
air, we emerged and made for the church of San Francisco which is th
finest in the town. Here a problem of another and unexpected sor
was pending. Outside the church, and always it seemed to the left o
the main door, was sitting a line of women beggars. But I am maligning

---

[1] With regard to the shrunken bodies, a former traveller has this to say: 'There is a tribe nea
Cusicuari, on the river Orinoco, which reduced entire human bodies in this way.' cf. C. Reginal
Enock, loc. cit., p. 281.

hem. For they were not beggars at all. They were selling church candles. Prosperous, well-dressed *chola* women of generous proportion, like London flower girls of long ago at the foot of the statue of Eros in Piccadilly Circus, one and all of them wearing brown or grey bowlers. And the lady at the end of the line nearest to the church door, 'her choice', in the words of the fashion writer, a smart grey 'derby', had grey hair and wore steel-rimmed spectacles. She had blue eyes and a pale white skin. Her nose was pointed, and she was taller and thinner than the other candle-vendors. She seemed to us the perfect picture of an English spinster, and we began to form our own ideas of what she was doing here, and how she got here. Perhaps she had made a hobby of folk-dancing, or collected folk-tales, or took down Indian tunes, or was noting knitting patterns. But none of these theories could explain how or why she was sitting here at the end of the line of women in front of the church of San Francisco at La Paz.

The interior detail is very definitely of Indian or *cholo* workmanship. It was curious to see the *chola* women in shawls and 'derby' hats, but barefooted, and most of them with a baby on their backs, in ecstatic prayer in front of some saint's statue, much of the sculpture being most creepily, even horribly, realistic. Long raven wigs, bleeding wounds, emaciation, and agonized facial expression, in contrast to simpering innocence, and a purposeful and loathsome goodness, with the evil one portrayed as a creature with horns and a forked tail whom you might meet casually at the street corner, or find like a bird or a bat got into your bedroom, were the spirit of these carvings, all of them with an urban not a rustic significance as befitting a large town. But this I think to be the curious essence of La Paz, that it is a huge town in this cup or valley in the high plain, near Titicaca, under snow mountains such as the giant Illimani, with a large *cholo* or *mestizo* population of costermonger, flower-girl, fishwife, street-vendor connotation, with learned persons, writers and literati, and where there should be Latin *boulevardiers* and *flâneurs*. When I came out of the church of San Francisco and looked again at the English spinster, her eyes met mine and I saw that she was no Englishwoman at all but only the ghost or suggestion of one where her ghost or *doppelgänger* could easily have been.

Perhaps I was so interested by Bolivia because we had not intended to go there, and only decided on it at the last moment when it emerged

that La Paz was so short a way beyond Tiahuanaco. I had though
before this that it was a question of spending two nights on Titicac;
and making a day's excursion to the ruins. In the event we avoidec
that second night on board ship for which I was grateful, and hac
some little experience, however superficial and tenuous, of a new
country. Its character is perhaps well expressed in saying that 'there
is probably no other country in the world which has so high ;
proportion of non-white population so essentially integrated in it
productive life as Bolivia'.[1] It is calculated that eighty-two per cent o
the inhabitants are Indians and *cholos*, and fifteen per cent are white
or near whites. But the degree of mestization now becomes toc
complicated to follow, and the term *cholo* must be taken to includ
town-bred Indians as well as those with some slight dilution of Indiar
blood in them. So, if Cuzco is a *mestiza* city, La Paz is *cholo*, by and large
This it is that gives peculiar character to La Paz and makes its street
gay and cheerful with bright colour. Something here adds itself to the
repertory of town types, such as the *lazzaroni* of Naples, the *varina*
(fishwives) of Lisbon, or the Cockney flower girls and pearly coster-
mongers of Lambeth. I will do my best to describe the street scenes o
La Paz when the time comes, but in the meanwhile there is the res
of Bolivia to consider, which can be achieved only at second hand fo
I did not go there.

Bolivia is only very slightly smaller in area than Peru, that is to say
each of them is ten times the size of England. One's imaginatio
sets forth instantly for those distant provinces bordering on Brazil anc
Paraguay. But, in fact, there are more interesting places nearer at hanc
though in all conscience far enough away. For instance we enquirec
about the possibilities of going to Potosí, and were told it would take
two days and nights by train, with perhaps the chance of being giver
special facilities in the form of a private coach as had been done fo
us from Cuzco to Machu Picchu and back, and all the way from
Cuzco to La Paz. Three days, at least, one must spend in Potosí to se
it properly, where incidentally the hotels are so poor that one mus
stay either in a private house or in the train, and then two days anc
nights back, making a whole week in all. Potosí, moreover, stands a
more than thirteen thousand six hundred feet of altitude, and we di
not feel we could endure the height and cold. There are no crop;

[1] Osborne, *op. cit.*, pp. 203, 204.

Above left and above right, Tiahuanaco, Bolivia; *below left*, Interior of the church of San Ignacio, Quito; *below right*, Cloister and church of San Lorenzo, Quito

Negro footman embracing his mistress's bust, by Landaluze, National Museum, Havana

University of San Carlos, Antigua, Guatemala

growing within twenty-five miles of the city, and an Irish writer says bluntly that 'the region is fit only for condors and llamas'. She must be quite certainly correct in this.

Yet what an extraordinary place it must be! With thirty churches, monasteries, and nunneries, and the famous Mint or Casa de Moneda. San Lorenzo is the most elaborately ornate of the churches, and is seen by some authorities as the culmination of all Hispano-American art and the masterpiece of the Andean-*mestizo* style. Its main doorway has twisted columns on either side, convoluting themselves until they turn to caryatids 'with arms akimbo' and wearing flounced skirts in two tiers that form the capitals. A side altar is 'all in white and red with gilt edges and touches of greyish blue. The columns have a lozenge pattern, and in the side flaps gorgeously plumed giant birds or webbed volutes are bitten by white profile heads looking rather like Japanese Nō masks'.[1] It must be worth seeing.

One or two of the churches, La Compañía of the Jesuits and the nunnery of Santa Teresa, show a most curious architectural feature for which there is a special expressive term in Spanish that could be applied to Baroque buildings in many other parts of the world. *Espesaña* denotes a bell-wall or flying façade, rising above and often doubling or even trebling the height of the building, and is derived from the verb espesañar, 'to spread the tail-feathers' which most exactly describes the feature in question. At Santa Teresa the espesaña rears up in two storeys of twisted columns; while at La Compañía a composition like a frontispiece of Solomonic pillars with a broken pediment over them is only the start of a flying screen of twisting pillars, and there are Solomonic columns carved in order to be seen in profile in the main opening of the bell-tower, all, apparently, from the hand of an Indian carver, Sebastián de la Cruz.

The secret of this strange city lying, relatively, some fifteen hundred feet below the summit of Mont Blanc was the silver mined from the mountain of the Cerro Rico just above the town. It was the richest silver mine in the world, and the present parlous state of the Bolivian economy could be blamed on the Spaniards who for three centuries took all the silver out of the country. Early in the seventeenth century Potosí had the astonishing number of one hundred and sixty thousand inhabitants, a bigger population, so it is said, than either London or

[1] Kubler and Soria, *op. cit.*, p. 181, and Kelemen, *op. cit.*, pp. 44, 190, 191.

Paris. But human suffering was in proportion, though no more than that endured by the women and children who laboured in English coal mines till early in the nineteenth century. The Viceroy Don Francisco de Toledo assigned ninety-five thousand Indians to work in the silver mines of Potosí, and their quota was a year's work in every seven. 'In the rich entrails of this admirable mountain', says a Spanish chronicler, 'resound the blows of the picks, the voices and groans of the workers, the shouts of the overseers. . . . Some perish in the ground itself, because they do not know the openings underfoot, and falling into wells and lagoons of great depths, are drowned, while others are buried under falling rocks. You will see them, laden with metal climb up ropes and descend great depths by thin sticks, and through missing their footholds fall to their death. You will see them crawling on all fours like beasts with a load on their backs, or dragging themselves along on their stomachs like worms.' It all sounds very reminiscent of the *Report on the English Working Classes* by Marx and Engels. Another seventeenth-century chronicler tells of 'winds of bitter coldness, which they could never stand were it not for the coca, which renders them insensible.'

The silver, once mined, was stored in the Escorial-like Casa de Moneda, with elaborate accounts of it preserved in duplicate there, and in the Archivo de Indias at Seville that forms one side of the Court of Orange Trees (Patio de los Naranjos) of the Cathedral. Thence it was removed by llama-train to Lima on the Pacific coast some twelve hundred miles away. Then it was loaded onto the galleons, and carried to Panamá with a screen of small boats eight leagues ahead of the treasure fleet to give warning of danger from pirates or English ships. 'This part of the journey, though it could be made in fifteen days, invariably took a month, the delay suiting the commanders of the galleons, for they could make considerable profits selling playing-cards to the passengers. They received for each pack ten patacones (patacoons)— and the quantity sold was prodigious, for play went on continually and it rarely happened that there were any on board who were not interested in gambling.'[1] The next stage was by mule-back over the Isthmus to Portobello, on the Atlantic Ocean, where a fair was held for fifteen days on end, at the end of which another fleet of Spanish

[1] *Relation des Voyages du Sr . . . (Acarette) dans la Rivière de la Plata et de la par terre au Perou* Paris, 1672. English translation published 'at the Dolphin over against St Dunstan's Church in Fleet Street,' 1698.

galleons embarked for Havana and thence to Cadiz. And so it continued for centuries the sailing of the last of the Spanish treasure fleets being in 1796.

What a pity it is that no wandering draughtsman of the calibre of Jacques Callot, or indeed, a painter of any kind at all, was on board the Spanish treasure fleet to draw the dons and hidalgos at their games of cards, gambling for patacoons! The Feria of Panama would have made a more inspiring subject for Callot than his Fair at Impruneta. And the silver-rush in Potosí must have been a spectacle fantastic to behold. 'The people here live on another level from the rest of the world, and the getting and spending of money is a fever that burns and possesses the whole population.... Everybody, whether they are señores, caballeros, Crown officials, or whosoever they may be, are engaged in commerce from which they draw such gain that there are some who have made, two, three or four million crowns. They always go very fine, either in cloth of gold and silver, or in scarlet, or silk trimmed with a great deal of gold and silver lace, and the utensils of their houses are very handsome, because in general they eat and cook off silver plate.... But the wives of gentlemen, as well as of the common people, are kept very close, to a degree beyond what they are in Spain. They never leave their houses except to go to church, or on rare occasions to attend a *fiesta*.' He continues: 'The women here are generally addicted to taking Coca ... they are so heated, and sometimes absolutely fuddled by it, that they have no command of themselves at all, 'tis likewise often us'd by the men, and has the same effect upon them.' (Acarette). When this Frenchman, passing himself off as a Spaniard, reached Potosí he was able to bring the news of the birth of a Spanish Infante, one of the sons of Philip IV, and immediately a fiesta was held lasting for a fortnight 'during which time all work stopped in the city. There were processions, masquerades, games of bulls, comedies and dances, all with the greatest magnificence and costing prodigious sums of money. First there appeared a ship tow'd along by savages, of the bulk and burden of a 100 tuns ... her anchors, ropes, and sails swelling with the wind which very luckily blew along the street through which they drew her to the great publick place, where as soon as she arriv'd, she saluted the company through the discharge of all her cannon.' Floats were pulled through the streets, and a sham castle was attacked in which Oliver Cromwell, then at war with Spain, was imprisoned. The *fiesta* ended with a religious procession from the Cathedral to another church along a road paved with bars of silver. Life in Potosí seems to have been as strange a mixture of riches and squalor with as much of squabbling and braggadocio as in that other European and half-caste settlement with a very different climate, Goa in the Portuguese Indies.

While in La Paz we also heard much of Sucre, the old capital. It was not indolence that prevented us from going there, but having still so many aeroplane flights ahead we were nervous of the local air lines. And that this was not unreasonable was given demonstrable proof, as we shall see, on the day we left La Paz. Sucre lies much lower though not quite in the tropical valleys of the Yungas. The churches are whitewashed with white towers, and the perpetual mention of orange blossom speaks of another climate from the breathless rigours of Potosí and the chill airs from La Paz. But Sucre is a place for the archivist more than the art lover, for here are preserved the documents and correspondence between the Spanish Crown and the Royal Audience of Charcas. This was a high court of justice with jurisdiction over all the Viceroyalty of Peru, i.e. all Spanish South America, independent even of the Council of the Indies, and with five judges called *oidores* who were personages of vast importance. They wore long robes called 'togas', like those of the priests, and had the exclusive right to ride the famous Salta mules, animals brought up especially from Salta in the Argentine, and caparisoned in splendidly sombre, black trappings. The *oidores* must, also, have been somewhat of a personal nuisance for we are told that on meeting one of them in the street any person on horseback was expected to dismount, and 'all who met him were under obligation to escort him at a respectful distance to wherever he happened to be going, and there they were dismissed with a slight movement of the head, having lost their time and perhaps their business'.[1]

Bolivians will always draw a distinction in conversation between their countrymen from the Altiplano and those coming from the lower and tropical regions of the Yungas, whom they look upon almost as another race. The alteration in climate should certainly produce a change in human temperament. I liked to think that just the beginnings of the Yungas showed in the semi-tropical flowers of

The Road to Cuzco, by Ena Dargan, Andrew Melrose Ltd., London, 1950, pp. 113, 114.

the garden our windows looked out onto, and that this was where the humming-birds and the green parrots came from. There, too, coca has been grown since Inca times. The nearest of the Yungas are no more than five hours by motor from La Paz, and we would have gone to them but for the fact that owing to the extraordinary spring of 1960 with its history of earthquakes and landslides the roads had broken down completely and it was impossible to get there. Beyond them again are those unknown, almost unexplored jungle and swamp provinces of El Beni and Santa Cruz that stretch for hundreds of miles on the map to the borders of Brazil. On a National Geographic map of only a few years ago there is but one road leading for five hundred miles through the province of Santa Cruz to the Brazilian frontier, and no road marked at all in El Beni; while the two provinces from end to end, north to south, can be little short of a thousand miles. They must be among the emptiest spaces left anywhere in the world today.

Further south still we would come to the Chaco Boreal of Paraguay, a swamp four hundred miles one way, by three hundred the other, with nothing marked in it for a hundred miles at a time except the names of a few forts,[1] and with the salt marshes of the Salinas de Guaramocas taking more space in the mere printing than a whole English county. Here Quechuas and Aymaras are left far behind; Paraguay is bilingual and the Indian language is Guarani. Here the Jesuits established the Misiones which were virtually an independent republic of their own. They had landed on the Atlantic coast of South America towards the end of the sixteenth century, and travelled far inland on their missionary enterprise till they came to the huge pampas plains of the interior, rolling plains with blue or red hills far away, perhaps one hundred or one hundred and fifty miles into the clear distance. The scene of their labours was of extreme beauty, hundreds of miles removed from snow mountains or volcanoes; and apparently so far from human interference that war or pestilence need not enter into their calculations. These regions were inhabited by the Guarani Indians, a race of savages whose conversion they at once set about, and within twenty-five years of their first arrival in the country the Guarani had altered their mode of life, and were living in the Misiones,

[1] Upon a National Geographic map of October, 1950, twenty-four forts or *fortins* and, enigmatically, settlements marked Kilometres 76, 75, and 160, reminiscent of the lonely Bidon 5 in the middle of the Sahara.

or settlements designed for them by the Jesuits. These villages were uniformly alike in arrangement; the church with its monastery was in the plaza, and the long tenement houses of the natives lay along the roads radiating from this centre. The houses were built on a fixed plan, and the Indians even wore a costume which the Jesuits had designed for them. There were in all thirty of these settlements, eight of them being in the present Paraguay and the rest in Brazil and the Argentine, with eventually twenty-five more in the Chaco and Beni rain-forests of Eastern Bolivia.

This territory which was ruled like a republic by the Jesuits lay far concealed, some one thousand or fifteen hundred miles inland from the Gulf of La Plata. The Guarani language was studied and written down, with results which have made it now to all practical purposes the spoken tongue of Paraguay, and the Indians themselves were taught to print books, or, where this was impossible, to copy with a pen the printed letters of a book in so close a fashion that the copy could not be told from the original. These books which are among the most valuable of bibliographical rarities were printed and finished entirely by the Indian workmen, and they bear the imprint of the various settlements, principally that of the Misione de San Loreto.

The Indians were taught also every art connected with the science of building; they carved the statues and painted the altar-pictures. A few of their churches had as many as five aisles, for the Jesuits were rich from their cattle-ranches and from the various objects which they exported on a fleet of their own making down the La Plata river to the harbours at its mouth. Maté, the South American tea, coffee, and sugar were part of the sources of their wealth; while some of their medicines, as for example quinine, were of such value that the Jesuits were directed to send every year a quantity of their balsam of the Misiones for the use of the pharmacy in the Royal Palace at Madrid. They had an army of Indian troops, and on more than one occasion drove back bands of marauders or mamelukes, as they were called, who had come eight hundred miles through the wilderness to attack them from the river state of São Paolo de Piritinanga, the so-called Paulist Republic, a colony of all the desperadoes who could get there from every country. It was their wealth and military strength which brought about the downfall and expulsion of the Jesuits, against whom charges of cruelty and extortion of the Indians were raised by their jealous neighbours. It is well established that those charges were un-justified; but in 1767 they were expelled, and as soon as they were removed—there being apparently only some four hundred of them among a population of as many hundred thousand Indians—the whole region fell back again into barbarism.[1]

Like all Indians, the Guarani had a highly developed cult for flowers, in connection with which they believed in many pagan traditions as to the origin or the different uses of each blossom. On particular feast days they would decorate the whole interior of the church with flowers, and would build up triumphal arches of flowers along the roads leading to the church door, while even the trees by the roadside would be hung with flowers in such profusion that the branches, says one writer, would be festooned with different coloured snows. The uniforms worn by the Indian notabilities on such occasions as this were of a gorgeousness in keeping with the colours of nature. 'All the militia of the town were in attendance mounted on their best horses and armed with lances, bolas, lazos, and a few with guns. The officers of the Indians rode at their head dressed out in gorgeous clothes and troops of Indians at stated intervals performed a sort of pyrrhic dance between the squadrons of cavalry. In front of all, on a white horse, rode the Alférez Real dressed in a doublet of blue velvet richly laced with gold, a waistcoat of brocade, and with short velvet breeches gartered with silver lace; upon his feet, shoes decked with silver buckles, and the whole scheme completed by a gold-laced cocked-hat. In his right hand he held the Royal Standard, fastened to a long cane which ended in a silver knob. Behind him came the Corregidor, arrayed in yellow satin, with a silk waistcoat and gold buttons, breeches of yellow velvet, and a magnificent hat. Other officials—the Comisario, the Maestro de Campo, and the Sergente Mayor—were in scarlet cloaks, with crimson damask waistcoats trimmed with silver lace, red breeches, and black hats adorned with heavy lace.'[2]

[1] At their expulsion in 1767, the Jesuits owned: cattle, 719,761; horses 27,204; sheep 138,827; and oxen, 44,183.

[2] *A vanished Arcadia*, by R. B. Cunninghame Graham; and *In Jesuit Land*, by W. H. Koebel, with an introduction by R. B. Cunninghame Graham, London, 1912. I have adapted some sentences from my *Southern Baroque Art*, 1924, pp. 257, 261. For a contemporary description, with maps of this region, see *La descripción geográfica del Gran Chaco*, by Padre Pedro Lozano, Córdoba de Argentina, 1733. A great bibliographical rarity must be: *Histoire de Nicolás Neenguirui* (Nicholas I), *Roy de Paraguai et Empereur des Mamelucs*, São Paolo de Piritinanga, 1756, which according to Cunninghame Graham, if really printed in Piritinanga, is the only specimen known from any printing press in that region. For recent accounts of the Jesuit Misiones see *La arquitectura de las Misiones de Moxos y Chuquitos*, by M. Buschiazzo, 1952; and *La arquitectura en el Paraguay*, by J. Giuria, Buenos Aires, 1950. cf. also Kubler and Soria, *op. cit.*, pp. 100 and 362.

In fact the Guarani were taught everything, and have forgotten it again. How better to end this description of a vanished Arcadia than by remarking that one of the plain Jesuit chapels of the Misiones with wooden pillars and adobe walls, at Yaguarón, near Asunción in Paraguay, has been copied in the new church at Assy in Haute-Savoie, 'even to the colouring of the outer walls', and has thus become the model for one of the most unconventional of modern buildings! Or, in thinking of all the things the Guarani Indians were taught to make and do, to end by recalling the bagpipe bands of regiments in our Indian Army, and at La Paz, the British Ambassadress's scones for tea!

By now, needless to say, we had found our way to the shops in the Bolivian capital. It is remarkable in the South American towns how refugees from Central Europe own the shops that sell gold or silver objects copied from Inca and Tiahuanaco designs, and native textiles. La Paz is no exception to this rule. The little, flexible golden fish, of Bolivian gold of a high carat, copied from Inca patterns, and intended for brooches, can be bought here cheaper than at Lima; and so can alpaca and vicuña rugs. But, also, there are unfamiliar objects not hitherto met with, carved and painted masks that one would take at the first glance to be Southern Indian or Cingalese. If shown a mask of the sort anywhere but in Bolivia one would guess that it had to do with Kathakali dancers. The principal type is a devil-mask with tusks and a blue face, perhaps, and they have fanciful and elaborate crowns. Others have antlers or bull's horns; and there are whitened masks with pink cheeks and oval faces, portraying Spaniards. They are carnival masks coming chiefly from Oruro, a town about half-way between Potosí and La Paz, where they are worn in pantomimes and folk plays. They are something entirely typical of Bolivia, where the carving and painting of them is a hereditary profession.

Upon countless coloured postcards the carnival maskers are to be seen, and often a *chola* woman spectator is in the background in her shawl and short petticoats and white felt hat. Not at all the same shaped hat as that worn here at La Paz, though it may have been so at one time for the Frenchman Alcides D'Orbigny, writing of La Paz in 1830, remarks that the *cholas* wore 'a man's hat, usually of white felt.' This must have been before bowlers became the fashion. Harold Osborne states that the bowler 'which is now universal and one of the most distinctive adjuncts of the *chola* costume, was introduced about 1925'. One has got used to the bowlers which are worn coquettishly on one side, and are always a little too small for the head, and although the rest of the *chola* costume is basically the same another shape of hat gives quite a different air to it. To say that 'south of La Paz the pointed witch's hat is the rule' is not quite true for the hats worn at Oruro are not witch's hats at all. They more resemble the Córdoban hats worn by male spectators at bullfights in Spain, except that the Oruro hats have a softer brim, a much lighter crown and a ribbon trained into a long v-shaped metal clamp upon the left-hand side. A market with a large number of *chola* women in their white hats must be an odd sight indeed. The Welsh women of a hundred years ago wore witch's hats that had come down in fashion from the tall hats worn by men and women alike, in James I and Charles I's reign; but those were black hats, these are white, of, as it were, another order of witch's coven.

We drove every day we were in La Paz to one or other Indian market in the high part of the town. There are whole streets where one sees nothing but the *chola* women in their bowler hats and bright dresses. The economic situation of Bolivia may be bad, and unless oil is struck its future uncertain, but even with thirty-three thousand *bolivianos* to the pound sterling the impression is of a thriving Indian population. The inconvenience is in carrying so much paper money. After a visit to the bank in order to change money you need a taxi to take away ten pound's worth of *bolivianos* with you, and the bank-notes are quite incredibly dirty. So also are the Indians passing in the street, but one has never seen anything to surpass the flaring colours of their dresses.

Light chocolate brown is the favourite hue of bowler, with a gold band round the crown, and always or nearly always a babe slung upon their backs. We would wander round, watching out for the occasional white hat of a *chola* from Oruro. But there was something even rarer, which we saw but twice during our time at La Paz. This was the real, pointed white witch's hat from Cochabamba. A special and affectionate *mystique* attaches to the *cholas* from this town who are known as 'Cochabambinas'. Pottery figures of them in their bell-shaped skirts and top-hats are for sale, usually for some reason in green pottery. One of the literati of La Paz even gave me a learned article in a magazine

about their hats,[1] from which it appears that they are made chiefly
in the Indian village of Vicurena. The writer visited one of the makers,
spending there *una mañana de generosa hospitalidad*, in a phrase that
hardly needs translating, and being shown all the processes of manu-
facture. The maker and his family, he writes, were *muy comunicativo*
and he sat down to a meal with them of maize and artichoke hearts
and fried eggs. Thereafter, he went round the factory of which he
gives plans and drawings. But now it seems there is a distinction between
El Sombrero Ovejar and *El Sombrero Blanco o 'Tarro'*, but this means
no more than the difference between a round hat and one shaped like
a cylinder, or, in other words, the type of hat worn at Oruro and that
which is the real witch's hat of Cochabamba.

Once again, in thinking of the Indian scene in Cuzco, in Puno, in La
Paz, and obviously in Cochabamba, there is a missing adjective, or
one not yet invented. It is not Oriental, nor African, and neither
mestiza, nor *chola* quite describe it. The flowergirl, costermonger,
fishwife (but without fish for sale), *chola* population is the secret of it,
and their hats the clue to that. To recapitulate; in Oruro and Potosí,
the hat is 'of hard straw, enamelled white with a high crown like a
Welsh milkmaid's hat' and the black ribbon round it varies from
village to village; in Potosí it is black or dark green felt; in Sucre they
wear no hat at all; in La Paz and Puno the headgear is a brown or grey
bowler with a gold band, in Cuzco hard felt hats, and mushroom
hats in Pisac. In conclusion, white witch's hats for Cochabamba, and
the traditional black witch's hat for Potosí. How much I would have
liked to go to Cochabamba, of lower altitude and a lovely climate,
from all accounts the most pleasant town of Bolivia, if only to see its
Indian market!

In La Paz you can stand in the doorway of a shop, and every *chola*
passing by is as rare a sight as the flamingo Gypsies and, more un-
expectedly, a tribute to the violence of aniline dyes. Under the arch
leading into a kind of Indian *fondouk* or native inn a beldame in a black
pointed hat is cooking unthinkable concoctions stained with pimiento,
or it could as well be cochineal; and there are tumblers of a light
pink drink for sale, the secret of which we did not discover, but it
could be *chicha* topped up with aniline; 'with fermentation produced

---

[1] *Folklore en el Valle de Cochabamba: El Sombrero*, in *Khana, Revista Municipal de Arte y Las
Lettras*, for October, 1956, by Antonio Paredes Candía.

A market woman in La Paz

by means of *mucko*, balls of maize flour which have been held in the mouth and after prolonged insalivation dried in the sun, then boiled slowly with chunks of meat, herbs, and portions of stale *chicha*, and finally fermented in clay vessels' (*Indians of the Andes*).

On our last evening in La Paz we went to a high quarter of the town where we had never been before, with an open market like an encampment on a sloping hillside. But for their copper skins, one expected the stall-women to be talking rhyming slang so alike are they in physique to the vendors of whelks and jellied eels. The older and more prosperous of them wore shawls made of brown vicuña wool, which is as valuable as many sorts of fur. And it was here on our last visit to the markets that we saw first one, and then another of the 'Cochabambinas', in her high crowned, white witch's hat. Both of them were sitting on the ground among the crowd of other *chola* women in their flaring skirts, and brown bowlers worn rakishly with a gold ribbon. Their pointed white hats made a mystery of the 'Cochabambinas' as though they came from a land, probably of conical houses and unknown fruits and flowers.

The day of our departure from La Paz was no holiday. There was, first, the long and serpentine ascent to the airport at El Alto, with lingering views of the town a long way below. The sky was stormy, and leaden with scurrying clouds. And it began to pour with rain. Then, the car-engine began to fail and we wondered if we would ever get up the hill. All this accompanied by a strong smell of burning, and when we reached the airport some fuse or loose end of wire in the boot had scorched our luggage. The airport building was crowded out with waiting friends and relatives for there were too many of them to be all travellers. That same afternoon there was a fearful accident with an aeroplane coming, I am afraid from Cochabamba, with fifty persons killed. Luckily, for ourselves, the news was not yet known, and we were spared harrowing scenes. Even so, our aeroplane coming from Buenos Aires was delayed some two hours by the storms, and when it landed could not take off again because of the wet runway.

I have never felt the altitude so much as in the airport at La Paz. It is many hundreds of feet above the city, after a climb which takes a good three-quarters of an hour by car, and must lie at nearly fourteen thousand feet. It is the highest commercial airport in the world. There was no room to sit down in the airport building, and we had to stand with our luggage heaped almost on top of us, holding on to a pillar sometimes with both hands. Cardamine was no longer of any use, and had become no more helpful than crunching a lump of sugar. We could not make the effort of talking, dreaded to pick anything up, were entirely breathless, and yet could not keep still. When at last we boarded the aeroplane the air-conditioning gave some relief, but at once, on leaving the ground we were in the middle of a great storm. Lightning played in every direction and long chains of hail struck and rattled on the portholes. The only solace was in looking out over the blue distances of Lake Titicaca, and over it to the far off snows. They must be the bluest and most open landscapes in the world. But they were soon past for ever, and we were among the dark and stormy mountains, much too near them for comfort, and not caring to look out at them, and at the lightning. The pilot must have flown perhaps two hundred miles off course in order to avoid the worst of this storm in the Andes.

We arrived late in the evening, but immediately the aeroplane door opened could breathe again. After the austerities of the Altiplano we were back among the airs and flowers of Lima.

Chapter Nine

✦✦✦✦✦✦✦✦✦✦✦✦✦✦✦✦✦✦✦✦

QUITO

IT HAD SEEMED ENTIRELY NECESSARY to go to Quito after seeing Cuzco. But this extension of plan involved endless visits to the office of the airline in Lima because our flight did not stop at Quito, but went straight on to Panamá. The whole return journey had to be re-routed in order to get us to Jamaica through Quito and Bogotá. But it would have been a pity to miss Quito, one of the singularities of South American travel being the impossibility in any one country of finding out anything much about the country that lies next door; in Peru no knowing about Ecuador, and in the latter country blank ignorance about Colombia, and so forth, even as to names of hotels, let alone anything one wanted to see. This is perhaps only natural, because if you are going away at all it is likely you are bound for Europe or for New York. But indeed the various republics are surprisingly different from each other. Chile, where we did not go, must be entirely unlike Peru, while Peru is certainly very different from Ecuador. Our reason for going to Ecuador was, of course, in order to see its churches which even in photographs could never be mistaken for those in Cuzco. Also, though little impressed by Colonial painting, Quito had a school of painters and sculptors of its own. But the real interest lay in visiting a country one had never seen before.

The Avianca air hostesses wore red cloaks and a kind of tricorne hat, but they used their cloaks only in transit to and fro across the tarmac and had discarded them long before we were flying up the coast. It must be some eight hundred miles from Lima to Guayaquil and for nearly all that way it is along the coastal desert. We flew almost straight along and above the shore with an occasional river running down through green banks on each side of it into the Pacific Ocean. They were like oases in the stony grey waste below. We passed above

a town which must be Trujillo with its churches; and perhaps an hou
later were over Talara, near which, off Cabo Blanco, there is big-gam
fishing for tarpon, a sport more strenuous than any form of shooting
for neither tiger nor elephant pull you along behind them on a heavin
sea. Soon after this we must have entered Ecuadorian airs and water
and were flying up the river estuary to Guayaquil.

Hyacinths, one reads, float on that river and the climate is tropica
but we saw and experienced none of these things. The airport is o
what appears to be a mud flat some way from the city, and all w
knew of Guayaquil was from reading advertisements of the Nev
Humboldt International Hotel upon the waterfront with 'a beautift
swimming pool' at back of it. More interesting were the Jipijapa an
Montecristi hats which were very expensive, and the Otavalo Indian
selling their woven textiles at the airport. Soon we were off again i
company with several white-clad nuns and a demonstrative honey
moon couple who were determined not to let anyone forget the
were newly married. The bride affected terror during the short fligh
to Quito and lay with her head on her husband's lap while he revive
her with his embraces.

All too soon it was over and we had arrived in Quito, a capital i
which the one-way traffic is arranged on the principle of a stage arm
so that, whether you approve or not, you are driven past the chie
buildings. The hotel is in the very centre of this concentric system
and on the wrong side of the road. Whatever happens, and whereve
you are going, you may only stop for a moment, luggage has to b
hurled out of or into the taxi, and if not done in time the driver has t
come round the block again. This is a major distraction whether a
arrival or departure. It sets one's pulse going at fear of losing most c
the luggage, and here again 'greenhorns' might find the altitud
trying. Quito lies at nine thousand four hundred and twenty-eigh
feet, with presumably a foot or two to add to that according to whethe
one is on the top floor, or even off the floor and climbing into bec
But we were old hands by now, and looked on nine thousand fee
with a few hundreds more or less on top of it, as a near normal altitud
after La Paz and Puno.

The hotel, we were told, had started life as a department store, an
there is something a little odd about the approach to it down a lon,
slanting passage, past the side windows of shops, and by a booksta.

run by the only Pickwickian character we encountered in South
America who greeted our passing by with obsequious bows. During
the time of our stay this passage was further enlivened by bullfight
posters announcing the coming of Ordóñez and Dominguín, brothers-
in-law who were then on tourney fighting *mano a mano* through
Venezuela, Colombia, Ecuador and Peru. The sloping passage leads
to the back of the hotel, once obviously a yard behind the department store, whence you go up by lift to the bedrooms and top floor
restaurant. Meals were monotonous and malpeptic (if there be such a
word) until the day when we were allowed *locro*, and other Ecuadorian
dishes with avocado, when the food became very good indeed. The
bedrooms, too, were a little peculiar, perhaps haunted by order
telephone and office desk, but they were comfortable and one became
attached to them every time one remembered with a little shock that
this was Quito.

Never in any town can there have been such noisy church bells. Not
even in Cuzco. They began at five in the morning with the noisy
clattering of some great ecclesiastical centre which, indeed, Quito
proves to be. But morning brought disillusionment of a minor sort
when I asked for *naranjillas*, a special kind of orange which only grows
in Ecuador, and the waiter produced a sticky green substance of
marmalade consistency which one mixed with water. It was not the
season for fresh *naranjillas*, and we missed one of the tropical fruits
we had most looked forward to.

But the bells stopped their clatter for a few moments and the view
from the window was superb. We were lucky to have bedrooms
looking out onto the main squares of both Cuzco and Quito. In Cuzco
we had the Cathedral with the churches flanking it in front of us, and
the Jesuit Compañía to the right-hand side. In Quito the plaza is less
important in point of buildings, but more pleasing and much more
picturesque. You see the side of the Cathedral with its arcades, but
not its façade, the square laid out with flower beds and clipped trees,
and many tiled domes and campaniles rich in promise of the golden
interiors for which the town is famous. There would seem at a glance
to be as many churches as there are in Salzburg; and this at nearly
ten thousand feet of altitude and only a dozen or fifteen miles south
of the Equator. I had already, in fact, been out for a walk yesterday
evening before dark, and had looked into the Cathedral, or, rather, the

Sagrario next door, and been confronted just inside it with the *mampara*
This is a carved and gilded entrance screen of a sort peculiar to thi
part of Latin America, and to be seen as nowhere else at Quito. The
mampara is always under the choir loft and just inside the door; and the
golden *mamparas* remain one of the memories of Quito, for each one
of them has become the excuse and been made the vehicle for a tour-
de-force of carving. Making a mental note that this first of the *mamparas* was in red and gold, a colour scheme much favoured in Quito
to the degree that one or two of its church interiors are almos
lacquered red and gold, I went along the street for a first glance at the
façade of La Compañía, and then came home.

But there was time to spare in Quito and it was not necessary to rush
out and see the churches this first morning. Instead, the British Ambassador kindly called for us and we were taken for a drive down
through the streets of shops and to an outlying part of the town where
a new American Hilton-style hotel is building, a project looked forward to by the foreign colony for Quito is sadly short of restaurants
We were taken to the studio of a Dutch painter who teaches textile
design of abstract import to the Indian students, met his English wife
and saw a lovely green humming-bird that, or one should write 'who,
in admiration of its beauty, flits about his garden. In the afternoon
and yet further down in this quarter of the city, we visited the shop
of an expatriate from Hungary, who, as noted with other refugee
from Central Europe, runs a business in which clever use is made of
native materials for women's dresses. That evening we dined with
the Ambassador and his French wife in a German-run hotel at the
other end of the town, where is the best food in Quito. We had, in
fact, first reserved rooms there ourselves, but had left because we
had no bathroom, and it was pleasant to be welcomed back there by
the management with no sign of rancour.

It is to be noted that Quito, although a capital, is in many way
like a country town. The *mestizo* element which plays so large a par
in Cuzco is missing in Quito. The inhabitants are either Indian or
Spaniard, and little in between. Yet it is not so Spanish as Cuzco
which speaks in unmistakable accents of Castile. That is because of it
Spanish austerity of manner. There are many towns in Spain on the
high tableland of Castile and Aragon that are reminiscent of Cuzco
until you see the *mestizas* and the llamas. It is a continual surprise to be

told that Quito has half a million inhabitants for it seems to be the size of a town like Salzburg or St Gallen. Those are the two cities that occur to mind because they, too, give the impression of towers and domes and seem to cover the same area. Also, like Quito, they are in a green countryside. From our window the green hills showed just behind the domes and towers as though you could be among them in five minutes' walking. It is in respect of this that Quito could never be mistaken for anywhere in Spain excepting perhaps in Galicia, the Basque provinces, or Asturias, somewhere along the Atlantic seaboard. The remarkable greenness of the surrounding country may be because it rains almost every day for about an hour.

The apparent prosperity of the Quiteñans which is visible in their clothes and general demeanour is in contrast to Bolivia. So, also, is the exchange rate which stands at dollar parity, and a sensible government must surely be reflected in the small number of *sucres*, twenty instead of thirty-three thousand to the pound. There are not the consumptive children coughing at the street corners, pulling their *ponchos* around their shoulders in the cold wind, and putting out a hand to beg. We saw no mean suburbs outside Quito, though we were told that this was deceptive and there was great poverty up in the hills. On a country drive a man came to the side of the road and asked our companions if they could take his small daughter of twelve years old into their house. It was as though to all intents and purposes this small farmer was selling her, for they had not enough food for her at home.

Outside the hotel every day there were eight or nine Otavalo Indians with scarves and lengths of material for sale, and we were long enough in Quito to become known to them. They seemed to be quite different in character to other Indians we had seen. Not silent to the point of dumbness; nor chewing coca and half-doped with that. But alert, if not talkative, and with a sense of humour. One feature with them was that they were alike as brothers; and another, that they did not resent to the slightest degree our examining the goods of one of them, and then buying from another. So good tempered were they over this that we wondered if they belonged to a co-operative and shared all profits.

All were dressed alike, as well as resembling each other. They wore white hats—the Indians are every bit as 'hat conscious' in Ecuador as they are in Bolivia and Peru—Panamá hats, in fact, but not the

M

expensive kind which has to be pleated under water with the docilit
which only Indians can command, and cost as much as fifteen or twent
pounds; striped *ponchos*, of course; and white pantaloons with an apro
worn over them so that from a distance you would think they wei
wearing skirts. The effect of it is rather like the hunting-aprons wor
by King Alfonso and Spanish sportsmen, except that those are (
leather and these are cotton. Their slightly heterosexual air, Panam
hats and all, is accentuated by their having like other Indians n
moustache or beard, and by their wearing their hair in pigtails, in
pair of pigtails if I remember aright. It gives them, too, somewhat (
an eighteenth-century air, but as though they were servants of som
grand person—Lord Mayor, *cacique*, or *alcalde*, for they are ver
cleanly dressed.

They would gather round us whenever we came out, or returned t
the hotel. I admired their woven stuffs, some of them with square
lines like tartans, and delicate scarves with gold or silver thread in then
though these did not meet with the approval of our new friend th
Dutch painter, who had graduated to Paul Klee and wanted to promu
gate new ideas among his Point Four pupils. Another feature of th
Otavalos is how much they resemble Red Indians. Their coppe
skins are of that hue, and most of them are aquiline. Their village is th
other side of the Equator meaning, here and now, some sixty mil
from Quito; and it was only a pity we could not visit Otavalo for tl
Saturday morning fair, where they can be seen at their looms and th
weaving is encouraged by Point Four.

But the time has come to go round the churches. We walk throug
the plaza, up to the high end of that, and turn left in order to loo
in again at the Sagrario. The *mampara* is the attraction, and a gloriou
golden screen it proves to be with the touches of red in it giving a
effect almost of lacquer. Its carved columns are those of the riche
imaginable golden altar candelabra, but to this something more h.
been added in the form of another, but this time pierced or open wor
pilaster to each side, carved so as to be seen in profile, the scrolle
foliage and the volutes of these pilasters having cupids hiding amon
their leaves. This whole conception of an openwork column to k
seen in profile with the light coming through it, a scheme which
also carried out in some of the chapel altars of Quito, is a featur
peculiar in my own experience to the churches of Ecuador, or, at an

rate, put into practise here as nowhere else, even if, as one authority
would have it, the volutes seen in profile are derived at second hand
from designs by the Dutch mannerist Vredeman de Vries.[1] This is as
much as to say that some learned priest in Quito must have been in
possession of de Vries' book and taught an Indian craftsman to adapt
designs from it.

But there is only the *mampara* of interest in the Sagrario, and we
go on to the Jesuit church of La Compañía which is further along the
same street. Here is the finest classical façade in all Latin America
although it is in full-blown Baroque, and we wonder for a moment
if we are not in Rome. It was, in fact, begun by a German Jesuit,
Leonhardt Deubler, in 1722, and finished after an earthquake by an
Italian from Mantua, while one writer sees Apulian Baroque motifs
in it which means the Baroque of Lecce in the heel of Italy. It is a two-
storey composition with banded and twisted Solomonic columns,
in threes, on the lower storey to each side of the main door, and flat
ornamented pilasters above, under a broken cornice and framing
the big window over the door. The running frieze over the triple
columns seems specially designed to throw shadow, and looking at
this façade from the side, it does certainly recall Santa Croce at Lecce,
but more from the richness of it and the colour of the stone than from
any close resemblance when we come down to detail. The Apulian
motifs, if such they be, appear in the carved overdoors above the side
entrances; and now we examine them more closely in the ornaments
on the flat pilasters of the second storey which resemble details on the
façade of the Prefettura, formerly the monastery of the Celestines, at
Lecce.

The point it is necessary to make is that this façade of La Compañía
at Quito is a wholly Italian work though, no doubt, carried out by
Indian masons. One criticism of it could be that it is a little old fashioned
for its date. If in Italy it would be eighty to a hundred years earlier.
But we are not in Italy; we are in Ecuador. And the snuff-taking
monsignore hobbling past could fancy himself back in Rome; and if he
had not been to Papal Rome, this was his nearest to it. The illusion
is Italian, how many miles from Italy! Its origin is from a time when
façade-designing was a hobby of the *cognoscenti*; and in any anthology

[1] Vredeman de Vries, Dutch architect and draughtsman, b. Leeuwarden, worked in Holland
and Germany (1528-1607).

of façades—and none has yet been published!—La Compañía could take its place. That it is the work of Indian craftsmen, and carved in a harder stone than that which permits the exuberance of Southern Italy is a point hardly occurring in the argument so orthodox is the Italian treatment.

But when we walk inside the sensation is of another kind altogether. From admiring a façade which is as Italian in its very different medium as are the arias of *Il Barbiere*, or the terraces of Isola Bella on Lake Maggiore, we find ourselves in a Jesuit interior where the purpose of the learned fathers has been to attract the Indian audience and keep its attention. To which end they must not let go of it for a moment or it will be lost to them, so that they have to keep moving or doing something interesting, as with a conjurer performing to an audience of young children, any or every means being legitimate to this end. Thus, before there is time to look at anything else, the screen or *mampara* immediately within the main door gives the sensation that you have been allowed in behind the drop scene and invited onto the stage. But you are at the same time on the boards and in the audience; or, in other words, the *mampara* or curtain has been contrived inside out; it is the wrong way round and facing you. Its columns are festooned with bunches of grapes, and the scheme is carried out in gold on a white lacquered ground.

The next sensation is of walls and ceiling in red lacquer, but before there is a moment to look at this, attention is drawn by a pair of paintings on each side of the main door. They are huge canvases in the lurid accents of Baron Wiertz, and would take a high place indeed in any world collection of 'horror-comics'. Their subjects are heaven and hell and, as always, the latter prospect is more interesting. Painted in about 1840 they must be among the very last works of their kind. They do indeed strain credulity to breaking point, yet are never without a few Indians kneeling before them. The countenances of the damned, both Indian and pale face, are rendered with so much more enthusiasm than in the case of the blessed across the aisle, and one wonders how many of his friends and fellow citizens the painter put among them. All the same, in spite of its comical attributes, which are many, I would have these paintings destroyed. One has only to see the Indians praying in front of them to know they have done more harm than good. Some shades of both Thomas and Oliver Cromwell cannot but enter the souls of most Anglo-Saxons in front of paintings such as these.

It would not be true to say that the interior of La Compañía at Quito has an interior in scarlet lacquer, although this is what one has been told of it, and this is the effect it gives. But, rather, it is as though stencilled with an all-over design; or stamped or incised with the raised portions of the pattern—or is it the sunken parts of them? —painted and varnished red. It is not a lacquer technique, strictly speaking, which comes as a little of a disappointment if one has heard that Quito has scarlet-lacquered churches, leading one to expect interiors carried out in red *vernis Martin*. As far as one can make out, the same pattern is cut into the stone of the piers, and then cut or incised into the stucco of the walls and ceiling, in gold on a red background. The church of the Jesuiti in Venice, out on the Fondamenta Nuova near the Madonna dell'Orto, has its interior lined with white marble inlaid with a repeating brocade pattern in *verde antico*; while another instance of the kind is in the Co-Cathedral of St John's at Valletta (Malta), where the arches and columns of the nave are carved with Maltese crosses and other motifs, as if stamped or impressed into the soft stone with monotonous result. One might assume that the architect responsible for the scheme of decoration at La Compañía at Quito had at least heard of, if he had not actually seen with his own eyes, the interior of the Jesuiti at Venice. One of the altars at La Compañía is fairly closely copied from altars at the Jesuit church of Sant' Ignazio in Rome. We are to think that the Jesuits from their headquarters were in constant communication with their daughter houses in Latin America and that they were in full knowledge of what was being built in their name in Quito. The note struck at La Compañía, no doubt with their approval, is of a façade in civilized Latin fashion with an interior of lively character designed to attract an Indian audience and hold them fast.

Quito has a more ecclesiastical character than Cuzco. It has little or nothing either of the Incas or the *Conquistadores*, although it was the other Inca capital, but much of the Jesuits, the Franciscans, and the Dominicans. For proof of which it is only necessary to proceed a little further along the same direction to the church and monastery of San Francisco. This is raised on a terrace with an imposing stairway topped with obelisks to lead to it, both stairway and façade having a

sixteenth-century Italianate air. The interior of San Francisco i
magnificently golden with a wooden ceiling which is, in part, pure
mudéjar with its inlaid geometric lines and gilded fir-cones. There
must have been Moorish blood among the craftsmen. If, already in
1581 this church had a richly carved cedar ceiling covered with gold
(Kelemen p. 158) of which this is a surviving portion, then it dates
from before the final expulsion of the Moriscos from Spain and the
Spanish Dominions, which did not take effect till 1609. The finest
of the altars is that in the left-hand chapel where more of the pierced
openwork woodcarving intended to be seen in profile, as in the
mampara of the Sagrario, gives a golden effect of astonishing depth
and intricacy.

After some parleying, we were conducted round the monastery by a
charming and intelligent Spanish friar who came from Burgos. He
showed us the four cloisters and innumerable chapels, taking a sensible
view of the more extreme and sanguinary paintings of martyrdoms,
and it was good to hear that he taught in the schools. There are many
sculptures of the Quito school in this monastery, including a few by the
Indian Manuel Chil or Chili, known as Caspicara ('Rough Face',
from his being marked by small-pox), the pride of the Quiteñan
school, but I found it difficult to enthuse about him, and admired
the *encarnación* enamelling of the faces in his sculptures and the *estofado*
colouring of their garments more than the actual carving. Paintings
of the local school seemed almost negligible to me.

Where the Indian craftsmen excelled was in purely ornamental
carving as, for instance, in the *mamparas*. And on a subsequent visit
to San Francisco we were able to see the little Cantuña chapel, entered
by a door further along in the same wall as the main church, and
called after a rich Indian who paid for it, and was buried there in
1699. This has a very richly carved gold altar, with corkscrew or barley-
sugar columns in pairs that twist in opposite directions, and is well
worth seeing. Another, and even more dramatic golden tour-de-force
is in the chapel of the Rosario in the church of Santo Domingo. This
has a special little *cachet* of its own from being built out on an archway or bridge across the street. But it is in fact a *camarín* where the
clothes and jewels of the Virgen del Rosario are kept, and the peculiarly
Spanish invention of a *camarín* has always called for special care and
attention on the part of architects and craftsmen. There are many

instances in Spain and Mexico. A flight of steps leads up into this chapel of the Rosario that entirely coruscates with gold in the only phrase to describe it, which is *rutilante de dorures*, only here the gold has scarlet or carmine added to it.

This is again the legend of the scarlet lacquered interiors of Quito, with here a little and definite step towards those. But in this chapel of the Rosario it is no more than an alternation or variation on the gilding, and not carried to the same lengths as in Mexico. There, for instance, the *camarín* in the church of Tepozotlán has three golden altars or *retablos* rising to the ceiling, their gold touched with scarlet, blue, light and dark green, and silver; and similar effects are to be seen in two nunnery churches at Querétaro where the gilding is heightened with touches of metallic lustre, giving ruby and emerald-green effects of lacquer varnish. What is certain is that this chapel of the Rosario at Quito is theatrically inspired, what with the staircase leading up to it, and the first *coup d' oeil* through the proscenium arch. The altar and the side-wing door in the altar itself are part of a built scene, and every possible adjunct is made use of, including panes of mirror, in order to secure the utmost brilliancy. This is only a small chapel at Quito; and not knowing how the rules of *clausura* apply in this country, one wonders what may still be hidden in the convents.

This is, therefore, the moment to speculate on what else there may be in Ecuador. More than one person has told me that climate and living conditions were so perfect he would like to live either on the Pacific slopes of Colombia, or in Ecuador. In the former country I have heard Popayán mentioned more than once as a beautiful and untouched Colonial city, to be referred to again when we pass over or near it in the aeroplane. Ecuador, where the climate is categorized as an eternal spring did not suffer in the recent epidemic of earthquakes, but it has certainly an unusually high number of volcanoes within its borders. It has also its share, if a small one, of the Amazon forests and jungles, but the prevailing impression during at least the season when we saw it was its greenness. This was the more remarkable perhaps coming from the Altiplano and the stony deserts of Peru, though there again there was the sensation of green mountain summits on the flight to Cuzco. But Ecuador seems more pastoral, more suited to sheep and cows, and less fit for llamas and alpacas.

After Quito, the Colonial town of Ecuador is Cuenca, about two hundred miles south of the capital on the way to Guayaquil. All accounts agree about its setting on a flowering plain. During the seventeenth century it had large churches and five monasteries and nunneries. There were gold and silver mines near-by, quicksilver was found, and there were marble quarries and fields of sugar-cane. Other local industries were weaving, the extraction of quinine from cinchona bark, and the making of straw hats, the famous Jipijapas or Monte-cristi woven in superfluity of Indian passivity or patience, as said before, with the hands of the craftsman under water during a part of the preparatory process for weeks at a time.[1] A town of waters anyway, for there is a river from the mountains running through it; and that it had reached a degree of civilized amenity probably exceeding that of its namesake Cuenca, in Spain, is evident when we are told that in Colonial times 'the nuns instructed their young pupils in the making of artificial flowers, delicate lace and embroidery, delicious confection-ery, and dried fruit'. This, in Cuenca of Ecuador, and how much more must it have been so in Quito, the capital! Some of the old houses in Cuenca have frescoed patio walls, and the church of El Carmen has a portal with pairs of columns like bars of barley-sugar twisting in opposite directions that a commentator remarks were the hallmark of a particular architect in Valencia in 1680, and they certainly look reminiscent of the smaller churches there and in Palma de Mallorca.[2] In fact, as we have noted in Quito, there is very little that is specifically Indian as compared with what is to be seen on the Altiplano of Peru, and although much of the work was undoubtedly carried out by Indian craftsmen there is nothing in Ecuador approximating to the *mestizo* style.

Half-way between Cuenca and Quito is the town of Riobamba which is famous for its Indian market of a more voluble and lively character than the silent marts of Pisac and Huancayo in Peru. It could be partly the lesser altitude, and in part that the Indians have not the coca habit and are not affected by it on top of their native silence, these being in any case another Indian race. Another Indian market is at Saquisili, in sight of Cotopaxi; and yet another at Ambato, on Mondays, between Cotopaxi and Chimborazo, where as many as twenty thousand Indians foregather on Market Days. Once again,

---

[1] Jipijapa and Montecristi are two towns, close together, north of Guayaquil, and near the coast of Ecuador.
[2] Kubler and Soria, *op. cit.*, p. 88.

how little is implied in the word 'Indian'! 'Red Indian' does at least
convey something, although its full import is lost since Catlin drew
them early in the last century. But 'Indian', by itself, there being a
whole sub-continent of real Indians, has little or no meaning. There
should be some other name by which to call them. The Indian markets
all over Spanish America; in Mexico; at Puno and Pisac and Huancayo
in Peru; at La Paz and, surely, at Cochabamba in Bolivia; at these
places in Ecuador; at Panchimalco in El Salvador; and at innumerable
villages in Guatemala, but chiefly at Chichecastenanga; all these surely
deserve some collective noun for they are among the most picturesque
scenes left in the world today. Speaking for myself I can say that I
had no conception of their interest till I saw the Indian markets at
Puno and La Paz, and later on in Guatemala. At the Ecuadorian
markets textiles are the chief artifacts, notably those woven by the
Otavalo Indians. The native dances are the *Pasillo, San Juanito, Albazo*,
and *Yaraví*, and one is curious to hear the music.

Such of course, are the civilized Indians, not much changed perhaps
since they formed part of the Inca Empire, but there are tribes of
jungle Indians as well, together with human curiosities like the Colorados, a tribe living in the village of Santo Domingo de los Colorados,
surprisingly, not down towards the Amazon jungle but between Quito
and the Pacific coast, a tribe numbering only two hundred in all,
though this is more than the total of some of the Amazon tribes with
languages of their own who are fast dying out in the forests of Peru
and Brazil. The peculiarity with the Colorados is their painting their
bodies a brilliant red with a paste made from the achiote bean, and
combing their hair into a sort of tight-fitting bowler or helmet which,
also, they dye red. Towards there we would be entering the region of
tree-ferns and Blue Morpho butterflies, particularly *Morpho Helena*,
one of the most beautiful butterflies in the world, if not quite the
paragon that is *Morpho Cypris*, where the marvellous blue colouring
'is produced by the scattering of the light by air-spaces in the wing
scales, which are yellowish-brown, the female having no air-spaces
and her wings therefore not being blue', this blue vision that sails
around the tree-tops while the females 'sit in the undergrowth waiting
for them[1] being found by a sympathetic magic on the part of nature,
in Colombia near the famous emerald mines.

[1] *Butterflies and Moths*, by Alfred Werner, André Deutsch, London, 1956, pp. 73, 149.

We had been unfortunate during our journey in Peru in seeing no interesting butterflies, and not many birds. In Ecuador alone we were told there were no fewer than two hundred different kinds of humming-birds, an estimate which is borne out more or less, if not *in toto*, on looking through Gould's *Trochilidae*. But there is one particular race of humming-bird, the Chimborazian Hill Star, which is found only in the crater of snow-capped Chimborazo, where it feeds on fuchsias and chuquiragas, a sort of shrub; a bird, for I have been looking again through Gould to find it, with a white breast or shirt front, a blue head with a green metallic patch, like the lustred altars of Tepozotlán one could say, and green and white tail feathers, a humming-bird divinely inspired out of a swift or swallow. In form and colour like swallows or swifts dipped in fire, but diminutive in size, their blue-green wings curved like a swallow's wing and their snow white breasts in emblem of the perpetual snows and of their prison from which they never issue forth, compound of fire and ice; much resembling another humming-bird, the Pichinchian Hill Star living only in the craters of Pichincha and Cotopaxi. It is nearly too good to be true that there should be races of humming-birds only found in the craters of Chimborazo and Cotopaxi, and nowhere else in the world. Of the other races, for it is at least good to hear their names; Sword Bills, Star Frontlets, Sun Angels, Incas, Star Throats, Puff Legs, Emeralds, Tooth Bills, Helmet Crests, Coquettes, Racket Tails, Thorn Tails, Jacobins, Sickle Bills, Swallow Tails, Topazes, Saw Bills, Green Hermits, Mangos, Caribs, Visor Bearers, Violet Ears, Sylphs, Shear Tails, Sappho Comets, Plover Crests, Sun Gems, Flame Throwers, and Train Bearers, there need be no end, and many of them are Ecuadorian. Though, as I say, we saw but one humming-bird in Quito.

And going to the garden where this humming-bird lived, and had built his nest in a wooden box near the front door, in the hope of seeing him again, we were taken by the Dutch painter and his wife for a drive into the hills. It was only a short distance, not more than four or five miles, if as much as that, but we were promised a marvellous view. It was a steep road which soon became a stony lane, and then stopped altogether and we drove on the green turf higher and higher till we could climb no further. It was the green top of the hill and we got out and walked, and came to the edge of it where it dropped sheer down. Certainly it was a breathtaking view, and the most striking thing about it was its greenness. It was as green as that view coming from Lismore over the Knockmealdown mountains down into the Golden Vale of Tipperary. And there were moments when it seemed to be upon the same scale. Down in the valley below were the ruins of an ancient Inca settlement that by no grand transference of the archaeological imagination could be early Irish, and it would come as no surprise to see a Round Tower down there. Or one of those small oratories in ruins, of awkward construction because the early Irish like the Incas had not discovered some of the basic principles of architecture.

But then the giant scale showed through the greenness. Suddenly one remembered that we had come here in order to see volcanoes. On a clear day eight or nine of them were visible from this hilltop where we were standing. They were Cotopaxi, a little to the south, and towering more than nineteen thousand feet into the air; Antisana of nearly the same altitude; and Pichincha with the same race of humming-birds as at Cotopaxi living in its crater. And what other volcanoes, extinct, dormant, or still active? Cayamba could be one of them, of nineteen thousand feet; or Cotocachi; or Sumaco, which is still fiery; but Chimborazo, I take it, was too far away, and never in view. That is but six names of volcanoes, and there were others. This was not all. Our friends had often come up here at dawn to see the sunrise which in Ecuador is at about six o'clock in the morning all the year round. Perhaps with luck the whole lot of volcanoes could be seen at sunrise. And at least a few of them later in the day. I could not but think of our younger son at the moment. He is working at Kericho, in Kenya, near Lake Victoria. For Kericho is nearly exactly the same distance that we were at this moment, namely only about a dozen miles, south of the Equator. It is the same green country there, at nearly the same altitude, in the midst of tea-plantations, and I wondered not having its geography in my mind, if he could see Kilimanjaro or Ruwenzori. But I have to tell the truth which is that not one volcano was visible to us. They were all hidden. One and all they were obscured from sight. And it may be stretching the facts beyond improbability to say the view was as wonderful without them. Nevertheless, they were there as surely as the stars are in the sky. It was only that we could not see them.

That afternoon we went to visit the churches again for that w
after all our reason for coming to Quito. We looked in once mo
at La Compañía and San Francisco; admiring the façade of the forme
the gilded dropscene of its *mampara*, and red and gold walls an
ceiling; and losing ourselves in the golden rain-forests of San Francisc
for that is nearly the effect of its golden vegetation and this was sure
its intention. And we went for the first time to a church we had bee
keeping till last, La Merced, with its fine cloister. But the super
object in La Merced is the organ, more still the organ-loft. High u
among its pipes are cupids, trumpet to mouth, blowing a fanfar
Three of them to each side of the organ, they look like the litt
automata of a puppet-show, and you expect them to put down th
trumpets and lift them to their mouths again.[1] But the gilded balcon
of the organ-loft is the wonder of La Merced, as closely entwine
and entangled as a golden thicket. It is a golden casket with the under
neath of it worked even more richly than the sides, and the gold
on a dark red ground recalling, thereby, the stories one had bee
told of scarlet lacquer interiors at Quito. How curious to think th
must be by the hand of an Indian craftsman! For all objects in Europea
lacquer seem undecided where their own *chinoiserie* came from. Th
provenance is uncertain and somewhere between China and Sian
or, in fact, East Indian; and, at that, as 'Indian' as this red-gold balcon
in the La Merced at Quito, in Ecuador. Coming away with the organ
loft still in mind, some part of that legend of red lacquer had com
true.

The journey was now achieved and over which I had been plannin
and hoping for since 1947, and had first set my mind on accomplishin
as long ago as 1922. Such is the span of time an ambition may requir
in order to fulfil itself. It had hovered, and come nearer, and ther
gone back again. But at last it advanced resolutely and our plans wer
laid. Two countries I had always wanted to write about since I too
up the pen were Mexico and Peru. When young and lacking th
means to get to Mexico, I had written of it without going there
in my first prose book that was published in 1924. In that, youthfu
imagination had to stand in and take the place of fact. But, ever
now, I am inclined to think no harm was done. The wonders o

[1] Kelemen, *op. cit.*, p. 231 and pl. 155, describes the organ at Cuenca which has 'ten paire
little figures, girl and boy, blowing *chamade* pipes, and at the top two reclining mermaids back
to back, holding bunches of pale blue grapes'.

ature and of architecture are not seen only with the eyes. Also,
was writing before and after a serious illness, and because of that was
n a curious and traumatic state which, if anything, helped the writing.
ndeed, it is the only time in my life when I have experienced the con-
lition that could be called inspiration. At all other times it has eluded
ne, and the little accomplished has been due only to constant practice
nd hard work. Perhaps because of those unwonted months of fluency
nd ease in writing when I was twenty-two years old I have always
lad a particular desire to see Mexico and, that achieved, her sister
country, which is Peru. Mexico I went to during the winter of 1952
rom the United States; and now in 1960 the second part of my
mbition had come true.

Both Mexico and Peru have a history more improbable than any
work of fiction. This, in respect of their conquest by the Spaniards.
But while the Aztec and Inca empires perished in a matter of months
nd the violent extinction of their civilizations is among the tragedies
of history, it is permissible to doubt if other colonizing races, the
English, or Dutch, or Portuguese, would have dealt more gently
vith them. Nor, if the tables were turned would they have spared
he Europeans; or in the case of the Aztecs not have held great sacrifices
of the Whites. The same cruelty and cult of death were not present in
he Incas. The first sight of ancient remains in Peru does not bring
with it the dread sensations that are inseparable from Mexico, in saying
which we have the Aztecs in mind and not the Mayans in Yucatán
nd Guatemala who are, all things considered, the most interesting
because the greatest builders and sculptors of pre-Colombian America.

It was our good fortune after seeing Peru to be able to continue
our journey into just exactly those two countries, Guatemala and
Yucatán. They form the subject of the shorter and concluding portion
of this book. Before embarking upon which there is this opportunity
to summarize what has already been experienced and seen. Any
feeling of wonder at viewing the huge scale of Inca remains must be
tempered by two considerations; that the Incas were themselves only
he latest and by no means the most interesting of Andean civilizations,
nd that the Spaniards had a more far-reaching influence than any of
the Latin races since the ancient Romans. The Italians were greater
n the arts, until in the reign of Louis XIV the French began an as-
cendancy that has continued into our own times. But the Italians lacked

all political cohesion, and only had one power among them which wa the Venetian Republic. The Spaniards were, and remained, a singl nation. Like the Romans, the Spaniards were builders and soldier Cortés had with him four hundred foot and fifteen horse, with seve pieces of artillery, when he landed in Mexico; Pizarro had but hundred and eighty men in his expedition when he set foot in Peru But even these small numbers are less remarkable than what th Spaniards accomplished afterwards, some reflection from which hope has penetrated to these pages.

With regard to 'Indian' Peru, and again one must regret there no more descriptive adjective, certain things that may not have bee anticipated remain in one's mind. First of all there is the entire absenc of ornament in Inca buildings. There is not a carved stone left i Cuzco or Machu Picchu, and this is in strong contradistinction t the Aztec and the Mayan remains. What are gone from Cuzco are th lifesize figures of llamas and shepherds with their slings and crook all in gold, the golden straws among the grass thatch of the templ roofs, and gold-plated walls; the legendary kingdom of gold which th Spaniards reached and pillaged. That is all gone, and the bare stone are left.

Secondly, the rigours of altitude along the Altiplano are littl mentioned, and the more unexpected because of that. It is, one con cludes, a Tibetan landscape of Tibetan heights and emptinesses. Bu the experience, though a little painful, is unforgettable. I found mysel wishing that Turner for once in his life had not gone to Venice or th Alps and come instead to Lake Titicaca. For only a painter, and not writer could do it justice. And another thing; were I asked would sooner see Cuzco with its gold spangled walls in all its glory, o Tiahuanaco, I would choose the latter in this most wonderful of al landscapes of the megaliths. What is Salisbury Plain compared to tha Andean setting! The textiles of Paracas are enough to give a pictur of the Stone Age people. For it was in their textiles that the unknown even unnamed Indian cultures were pre-eminent, and in their golde ornaments. But I am no admirer of Peruvian pottery. Despite it anecdotal or factual interest, the aesthetic level is that of Toby Jug o strip cartoon.

Something else one is unprepared for is the *mestizo* or *cholo* pop ulation. They form the townspeople of Cuzco, Puno, and La Paz

One is not told that Cuzco is a Quechua-speaking city. But the costume of the *chola* women is the living part of Cuzco. One will never forget the groups of women in their white hats sitting on the ground. And near them, Indians from villages like Pisac in flat, mushroom or saucer hats. In Bolivia where the Aymara outnumber, or, at least, outshine the Quechua, they give life to the street scenes of La Paz. I have tried to set on paper the brilliance of their dresses, and the colour of a large city that over much of its area has the exciting air of a Gypsy encampment.

Cuzco, fascinating as is its history as an Inca city, must ever remain an impressive monument to Spain of the sixteenth and seventeenth centuries. Not so much in respect of anything exceptional or extra-ordinary in its architecture as in astonishment that it should be there at all in those altogether exceptional surroundings. For with the omission of the Inca walls it could be any one of a dozen towns in Spain. But it is as though one arrived at Lhasa in Tibet and found that was a town of Spanish churches. However, even this is less interesting than the hybrid of Christian and Indian along the Alti-plano and round the shores of Titicaca, though it falls short of the fire and brilliance of Mexico. Nothing in the *mestizo* style of the Andes compares to the best in Mexico. Quito, high up as it may be, is softer and more amenable than Cuzco. And in La Compañía and San Francisco it has churches, Italian of form if Indian in workman-ship, that are more immediately attractive than the Cathedral and La Compañía in Cuzco. Quito is more ordinary as a town and does not leave that indelible mark upon the memory. In two chapters I have tried to leave a picture of Lima where I was treated with so much hospitality and kindness. It is a beautiful city and, like Seville its Spanish sister, seems ideal for an opera setting. No less than that, and a companion work to *Don Giovanni*, and *Figaro*, and *Carmen*, is due to this flowering city of the Spanish Viceroys, of *La Pérricholi* and the *tapadas*.

BOOK TWO

Chapter Ten

✦✦✦✦✦✦✦✦✦✦✦✦✦✦✦✦✦✦✦✦✦✦

BOGOTÁ AND HAVANA

OUR JOURNEY TO PERU NOW accomplished, we are on our way to Havana
and Central America, by way of Bogotá. But there is an inevitable
monotony in the mere announcement of departures and arrivals at
airports. This is one of the banes of twentieth-century travel, even if
its hazards remove us from the railway age and in some ways bring us
nearer to the more distant past. On that stormy flight over the Andes
from La Paz to Lima, with hail beating on the portholes and thunder
booming loud even above the roar of the engine, did I not remember
with envy that sentence in the old Spanish-English phrase book
'Postmaster, our postilion has been struck by lightning'? For, at least
they were on land, but we were miles up in the clouds. There had
been, and this was horrible, an accident only a few days before and a
well-known matador, who was on board the aeroplane, had been
killed. This was at the next place we were bound for after leaving
Bogotá. Also, it was at just the season when certain odd-minded
individuals had put a friend on board an aeroplane with a bomb in
his suitcase, or even blown up themselves and everyone else on board,
all for the sake of the insurance money. The Miami newspapers,
the only ones on board, were full of it.

It was better to look out of the porthole even if there was nothing
there to see. Only, now and then a green mountain top, and I began
searching on the map for Tunja but could not find it. Tunja is in the
department of Boyaca, and now I see that it is beyond Bogotá where
we are going. But the interest is that it is one of the oldest Spanish
cities in the New World, and has some fine old buildings; 'city of
palaces and convents, the Nuremburg of New Granada' it is christened
in the recent Penguin book, and another writer bears this out with
mention of its 'Colonial houses . . . their balconies, colonnaded patios

Indian headman at Chichicastenango

Headman of Indian *Cofradía* in
Guatemala

Women's *Cofradía* in Guatemala

and proud coats-of-arms, which retain to-day the atmosphere of the sixteenth and seventeenth centuries' (Kelemen). It has five churches in a 'frozen Renaissance manner', probably conditioned by its 'bleak mountainous landscape swept the year round by cold harsh winds', and an old frescoed house which is unique in Latin America but might not be so interesting anywhere else.

It seemed probable that we were passing almost directly over Popayán which I have long heard of as one of the most delightful of Colonial towns, and unlike Tunja, in a good climate. I had enquired in Quito about the possibility of getting there, and it would have entailed endless journeying backwards and forwards, for it was necessary to come down at Cali. Not that this would have been any hardship in itself for Cali is, from all accounts, one of the most charming of towns, at an altitude of only three thousand feet with a river running through it and in the midst of sugar plantations, but it was a question of expense and time. So we missed both Cali and Popayán, but we were on our way out of South America and must not linger behind, more particularly if, as we hoped, we were to end our journey in Guatemala and Yucatán. And again, here and now, as always in Latin America, we were about to land in a country entirely different from that we had just come from. Colombia has hardly any Indian population at all. We are leaving the Indians behind, bound for the West Indies and what are, basically, black men's lands.

And now we see below us a positively gigantic airport and have arrived at Bogotá. It is by far more magnificent than London Airport, and nearly brand new. The aeroplanes taxi right up almost touching its huge terrace so that it is like coming into harbour and tying up at a mole or pier. We are handed a packet of Colombian coffee, 'the best in the world', and after an impressive delay among carpets and armchairs drive off over what looks like an empty prairie into the town. It could be the United States or Canada, still more so when we begin to pass the new factories. But, already, we see from afar a huge flat section of a building in UNO headquarters manner, and guess it to be the new American-style Tequendama Hotel, although we are at once driven away from it in the opposite direction, but this is only because the street is taken up, and at last we are brought back to its door. Here one of our bags is bumped on the ground with consequent breaking of a bottle of whisky inside it, and in the confusion

N

the taxi-driver goes off with another of our bags still in the boot of
the car. When this is discovered everyone is most helpful, and it is
arranged for the loss to be announced on the loudspeaker to the cars
waiting outside the airport, but the head porter can only remember
the nickname of the taxi-driver and there does not seem to be much
hope of our recovering the lost piece of luggage. Meanwhile we are
taken upstairs in the lift to a comfortable room with built-in cupboards
and beds and armchairs designed as in a ship's cabin.

Superficially it is as though we are no longer in South America,
or, at least, no longer in the part of South America we are used to.
Coming downstairs again after looking out of a back window while
waiting for the lift, and seeing a round red O of a building which is
palpably the bull-ring, there are elegantly dressed young women
flitting about the long ground floor of the hotel or meeting their
friends, and this is like nothing we have seen for many a week in
Cuzco or La Paz or Quito. We are back somewhere in the latitude
of Buenos Aires or of Madrid, for they are most definitely Spanish,
if with a smart veneer of the U.S.A. We look into the dining-room
though it is far too early for dinner, and find it to be one of those
dark dungeon-like restaurants with no windows and an imitation
of being candle-lit that have spread from New York into every
American-style hotel all over the world. This is too expensive for us,
and we walk across the campus in front of our hotel which has been
completely bull-dozed and thrown upside down with huge pits and
excavations in it for drainage and foundations for new buildings and
electric mains. We cross this by a kind of footbridge with hooded
cranes and cement-mixers all around us, tarpaulins thrown over them as
though to induce them to stop grinding and shovelling and go to
sleep. Bogotá is in a fever of rebuilding. A cold wind is blowing and
rattling the lanterns hanging on the rails for even here we are eight
thousand six hundred feet up in the air, and we dine at a Soho-like,
Italian restaurant, having learned by now to order only one portion
of each course for the two of us to eat, where the cheapest bottle of
French white wine costs the equivalent of six pounds and we drink
beer instead.

Walking back again in and out among those craters and looking
up at our flat-iron of a hotel in the new mid-twentieth-century style,
we enquire at the desk where there is no further news of our lost piece

of luggage, and go up in the lift. An hour later just at midnight while I
am reading quietly in bed there is a knock at the door and a page-boy
comes in with the taxi-driver and the missing suitcase. He is in an
emotional state having evidently begun celebrating already on the
way here, and we have a tearful reunion, on his part at least, while
he will not go away and we make the tactical mistake of ordering
him a drink in order to get rid of him. But he has become sentimentally
attached to us both and cannot face separation from us, or so we
understand for his Spanish is not much better than ours, and he is
probably Italian. We will have to make use of some ruse in order to
be rid of him, for he had already been rewarded for bringing back the
suitcase, and far from showing any sign of impending departure
seems intent on staying. So I give him my pair of shoes to admire,
saying they come from London, and while he lifts them under the
light to look at them make a sign to him to put them down outside
the door. Which he does for me, and then firmly half-shutting it in
his face and giving him his chauffeur's cap through it, I then shut
and bolt the door. We are rid of him, and can relax once more. We
may be in a mid-twentieth-century Spanish-speaking but American
town; but there are at least one, if not two, if not three persons, two
men and one woman, from earlier, more gullible times. This was a
scene which should have taken place in some mountain village, and not
in Bogotá which has more than a million people in it.

The Tequendama Hotel is seventeen storeys high, 'completely
modern and equipped with custom furnishings designed to IHC
specifications'—whatever those may be—'and many other outstanding
features,' I am quoting from the hotel brochure. Such American-
style hotels are something new in the world. The first of them I came
across four years ago was the Hilton Hotel in Istanbul, which is outstanding as a modern building, not least because it stands in that
city of Turkish mosques and Greek churches on the Bosphorus. Here
in Bogotá we are on the edge of that part of the world where the new
hotels are swarming; in the West Indies, in Havana especially, just
beginning to do so in Jamaica, and in Venezuela where they are,
comparatively, most numerous and long established. They are so
marked a feature of the new era that it is not possible to ignore them.
But it would be wise to consider just where we are in Bogotá.

First of all, it is with somewhat of a surprise that we read of Colombia having fourteen million inhabitants which is about as many as in the whole of Canada. I found, and still find that, unexpected. As to area, it is only slightly smaller than Peru or Bolivia, much of its space being taken up by the three huge provinces, one of them the Amazonas, bordering on Brazil and Venezuela. From extreme north to south they measure not less than eight hundred miles, and there is a remarkable paucity of names of towns in them. As for that, how many in England or the U.S.A. have heard of Bucaramanga? Medellín is a name familiar perhaps to most of us because it has a climate of perpetual spring and is famous for its orchids; but Bucaramanga? It is in the mountains near the Venezuelan border, in another province, and the leaflet by my bedside tells of 'tropical restaurants where you'll enjoy barbecued goat, fried yuca, and famous Culonas ants,' with further mention of unfamilar fruits, *guayabas* and *curubas*; while *cumbias* and *marecumbés*, it seems, are native dances. Colombia is not the best known of South American republics, and there is much here that may be new and strange though in another world altogether from Peru.

By way of Colombian antiquities there are the golden ornaments of the Quimbaya Indians, highly formalized figures of men and birds transformed into abstractions but always with that curious, unmistakable signature of the Amerindian upon them. At their best they are as beautiful as anything produced in pre-Columbian America, and belonging obviously to the same continent as the totem poles of British Columbia. However, the Quimbaya Indians worked only in gold with any distinction. They were gold-workers, but not interesting in other ways.

We have now at last discovered that Tequendama is the name of a waterfall not far from Bogotá, which sets our minds at rest. It had been puzzling not to have heard the name before. And now we began to look about in Bogotá. It has one long street of shops, and is growing at prairie speed with the result that very few, if any, old houses are left. But it is an old town and there must be old convents. When Victor Perowne, a friend of mine at Eton, took up his post as head of the South American department at the Foreign Office, he went for a tour of Latin America just after the Second World War ended, and I remembered two anecdotes he told me about Bogotá. First, he was taken to the salon of the literary lady, now dead, and I am afraid I have forgotten her name, who had known Wilde and Verlaine, and other writers and painters of the end of the last century. The other story he told me was of his being given *marrons glacés* of huge size, bigger than any chestnuts he had ever seen, made from a tree that grew in a convent garden in Bogotá. They had been famous for generations, and it made me think of the sweets, rather of the same sort, wrapped in gold paper, that we had in Lima. I would have enquired about these had I known anybody in Bogotá. But in fact we knew no one, and so had to seek out our information at first hand.

What is left in Bogotá are some churches with fine wooden ceilings. One of them is among the craters just in front of the hotel, by now filled in, no doubt, and with skyscrapers rising from them. It is a pretty double-aisled church which in some indefinable way stands as though it should be looking out on the Caribbean. The other churches are downtown among the traffic. We entered two of them, and both had very pretty wooden ceilings, one of them on a light blue ground. The effect is charming, but they are in a provincial country style, although from 1717 Bogotá was made capital of the Viceroyalty of New Granada. But, as against this, of all the Spanish capital cities of Latin America, it was the most difficult of access, and this continued until the aeroplane age for even now, I believe I am right in saying, it is a journey of some forty-eight hours by train from Bogotá down to the coast of Cartagena. These facts of geography would account for a certain provincialism in the old capital of Colombia, though the more profligate of the Viceroys may have brought it liveliness. If Lima had the Viceroy Amat and *La Pérricholi*, Bogotá had its Viceroy Marqués de Solís y Folch de Cardona and his Creole mistress María Lutgarda de Espina, known as *La Marichuela*. The Viceroy de Solís made extravagant gifts and built a Rococo *camarín* for the miracle-working statue of the Virgin, in the church of San Diego outside the town, following his propitiatory offerings by becoming a monk in imitation of *La Marichuela* who had led the way into retirement as a holy nun.

There were to be no more churches where we were going, till we came to Guatemala, and in their absence I found my imagination playing with a new phenomenon, the huge hotels. That, and the bull-fight posters announcing Ordóñez and Dominguín who were to appear tomorrow, Sunday. Prices of tickets were soaring and had reached about double their face value by the middle of the previous afternoon. We thought of putting off our departure till Monday morning, and even looked out of the back window by the lift to see if that would not serve as a balcony seat, for nothing. But it was no use although the bull-ring was only some two hundred yards away. Also, the flights to Jamaica were but three times a week, and we could not arrive there on the wrong day. So we had to miss the bull-fight and the spectacle of the Spanish matadors marching into the ring.

And disconsolately on that last night in South America, and having no books or newspapers, I began reading a brochure on hotels in Venezuela. There is the Hotel Tamanaco in the capital, Caracas, a winged white structure rising above a ramp and looking like some kind of aircraft-carrier. It belongs to the same group as the Tequendama, but these others that follow are hotels of the Venezuelan National corporation or Conahotu. The Humboldt, on a green mountain top four thousand feet above the city, is one of the round gasometer-observatory-type buildings, fourteen storeys high, of the kind feebly imitated in London at the corner of Lowndes Square. There is the Maracay in a town some seventy miles away, like a double section, intending that it must have apartments back and front, two deep, indeed a double flat-iron, and it has a swimming pool and a theatre, looking like a nest of boxes from the air. The El Tama, in San Cristóbal, down inland in the south-western corner of Venezuela, near the coffee plantations, is a grid-iron building with eight ramps of cement balconies and a swimming pool of maniacal proportion. The Trujillo, in the town of that name, near vast pineapple plantations, whence 'excursions can be made to Boconó, a town justly famous for the beauty of its women' . . . the Hotel del Lago (of another company) in a grove of cocoa-nut palms on Lake Maracaibo, near the oil wells . . . and another hotel of mammoth size on Margarita Island of the pearl fisheries. . . . Venezuela which is a thousand miles from east to west. . . . Caracas with hotels at millionaire prices, but beggars sleeping under the arches of its bridges. . . . Caracas with the new motor-road up from the airport and the harbour, where taxicabs go at a hundred miles an hour along the ten miles round the curves and in and out the tunnels. . . . Venezuela which too, has its empty, probably unexplored province of Amazonas! And I could read no more and let fall the pamphlet.

In the morning after driving through the Sunday'd town to its

gigantic airport, and regretting once more not to have seen the Spanish
matadors, we were in two or three hours at Barranquilla which is on
the Caribbean. We disembarked and walked to the air-building, and
were in another world altogether which is still Colombia, but the
kingdom of Jim Crow. The population was negro, in other words,
and there were young negresses with supple figures in pink dresses
and smart hats. Their chattering high voices were of a different pitch
from the Indian market voices of Cuzco and La Paz. We were at sea-
level for the first time for many weeks and it was tropically hot. A few
minutes later we were over Barranquilla with its straight streets and
rows of shacks, and heading out into the blue Caribbean, leaving
South America behind us. It was a flight of some nine hundred miles
across the water which in fact was invisible most of the time. And
in two hours or so we came down at Kingston with intent to go on
in the aeroplane to Montego Bay, where we waited in the airport,
drinking a planter's punch, and watching a negro wedding party. We
were to stay with a Spanish friend in Havana for a few days before
going on to Guatemala, but the aeroplane developed engine trouble.
Instead of arriving in Havana, which is only two hours' flight away,
in time for dinner it was after four o'clock in the morning before we
took off and we got to Havana long after five. Our friend who had
waited long hours for us had gone off, and we drove through the
empty streets in dawn light to the hotel.

Havana, like fifty or a hundred other towns in the modern world,
has a million people living in it. By going there I had achieved an
early ambition which was to see Mexico City, Lima, and Havana, all
three of them Spanish Colonial cities, and now only the fourth has
eluded me which is Manila. Havana is less interesting by far than either
Lima or Mexico City, but its claims are as great in quite other directions.
Its nightmare hotels are incomparable in size and ugliness, and its
claim to be 'the Paris of the western hemisphere' is to some extent
borne out in its lay-out and disposition. Rather, one should say, to
have been the Paris. A Paris, all the same, without Frenchmen in it,
and presenting a strange spectacle at the time we went there. The
followers of Fidel Castro with unshaven beards and hair down to
their shoulders were in every bar and restaurant, heavily armed, too,
with revolvers in their holsters. Most of them in their late twenties;
and we were told that a meeting of the Cabinet with hardly a minister

in it more than thirty years old, and all bearded, must resemble a fore-gathering of the bearded Twelve Apostles in the Passion Play at Oberammergau. All, too, in the flesh, or on photographs, are cigar smokers. Fidel Castro during our stay talked one night on the radio for seven and a half hours, and he seems to have adapted the technique invented by d'Annunzio, while he was dictator of Fiume, of demanding from his audience what it wanted, a voice would answer him, and in this manner a direct intercourse would be established between the public and the orator.

Rule by rhetoric, put into action by means of 'intervention', has no appeal for Anglo-Saxons, even if the original motives may have some degree of justification behind them. And that the previous rule of Batista may have been corrupt and cruel goes no way towards proving that two wrongs, on on top of the other, add up into a right. If the Americans complain about the second regime they are to blame for allowing and encouraging the first. The riches and poverty, the tawdry splendours and miseries of Havana, are only too apparent. Not that the former are all gimcrack for, in fact, the long drive along the water front called the Malecón would be sensational in any city. The ocean, of course, is half of it but not every city would have the sense to make this use of it, and it confers a dignity upon buildings that do not really deserve that commendation. It has dual purpose, too, for it looks equally well by night and day. But considering that Havana is one of the oldest and most important Spanish cities in Latin America there is not much to show for it. The Cathedral has a lime-stone front, while the interior is so little interesting that it is by no wrench of the will that one is lured away from it to an old house at the far end of the square. Here, on an upper floor, and in premises resembling those of a London club transferred to the tropics, every kind of Cuban rum can be tasted *gratis*. This is in the old part of Havana nearest to Morro Castle, facing which our Spanish friend showed us the house built by his ancestors a century and a half ago, now become a tenement, but still possessing its grand staircase and wooden galleries lined with pots of geraniums.

One of the squares has fine governmental buildings of the late eighteenth century which, were they in Spain, would be associated with the architect Ventura Rodríguez (1717-1785), 'coldest of the Vitruvians', and a positively enormous private palace, now become offices, one of those houses on so huge a scale that it is impossible to conceive of living in them till one remembers curtains, gold mirrors, and oil paintings upon the same scale, and knows that such a mansion was no more or less than a private town hall. This palace is fine and imposing, and noble in its Spanish manner, but the heart quails at thought of its huge and uncomfortable bedrooms. None the less, one would wish to have seen it eighty or a hundred years ago on the night of some grand entertainment, seen the crinolin'd ladies with camellias in their hair, and overheard talk, in high Castilian, of Madrid society and of the far away Court of a Spanish Empress in the Tuileries. Under the arcades is a flower market, but it is of artificial flowers. They may be better perhaps in Havana than anywhere else in the world, and as though inspired by the real flowers that grow in such profusion. Their direct flower copies or imitations are pluperfect; flower improvements as, for instance, blue roses, or green lilies are less imaginative; but the flower inventions are remarkable and, I would guess, the poetic fantasies of *mulâtresse* or hybrid feelings and imaginations. They are imaginary flowers; and it would be interesting to have the Latin description of them from a professional botanist, as in a botanical magazine, and his views as to their inherent possibility, or otherwise.

The twenty million dollar Capitol is so portentous that we kept as far away from it as possible, content in the knowledge that it has the third highest dome in the world, and that 'a 24-carat diamond set in the centre of the rotunda marks the zero kilometer from which all distances on the Central Highway are measured'. It was a more heartening experience to be taken to the bar where daiquiris were invented, and shown the corner where Ernest Hemingway sits below a bust of himself, but that evening the niche was empty. It is perhaps this mention of a bust and its original sitting so near to it, as though to invite comparison, that recalls to me the paintings in the National Museum at Havana where, incidentally, hangs what must be the masterpiece of Goya's pupil or imitator, Eugenio Lucas, a painting of *majos* and *majas* with all the excitement of the popular music of Spain and passages of painting worthy of Manet in it, a wonderful and exciting picture by any standard. But the immediate train of thought leads to a little painting by a Spaniard from Málaga, Victor Patricio Landaluze, who arrived in Havana in 1863, and died there in 1889.

He had been noted in his land of origin as draughtsman and caricaturist but took to painting in oils when he reached Havana. The little painting reproduced here, one of a pair, is difficult to put a date to at the first glance for it could be by some French petit-maître of the end of the eighteenth·century, like Boilly *fils*. But its date is really about 1870. The furniture and pictures on the walls suggest that it may have been an actual interior that Landaluze was painting, which would account for the French chairs. It may even have been an amusing incident that actually happened in one of the old houses in Havana. A negro servant with a feather brush is embracing the marble bust of a lady with droll effect. The very Spanish sense of humour of the painter shows the risks to which portrait busts are exposed and we realize that the veteran sportsman and novelist's bust in the café is at the mercy of every flâneur and passer-by. Another painting by Landaluze in a private collection in Havana shows the artist in a more brutal humour. Its subject is a wild chase after an escaped negro slave.[1] The wretched black man, who had a record of criminal violence, is being chased by dogs, and the picture is unpleasant enough to have raised protests when it was exhibited not long ago. But the *Negro kissing a marble bust* is another matter and reveals a minor and forgotten painter.

Two topics in Havana are really interesting, the music and the hotels. At the time of our visit the latter were an astonishing spectacle for they were entirely empty. Since then, most of them have been taken over by the government. When we saw them they were running at a total loss. There are four or five of these huge hotels, each with several restaurants, and all with casinos or gambling rooms attached. Waiters and croupiers were standing about listless and yawning for, however empty, they must keep open during the appointed hours. Only on a Saturday night was one of the hotels crowded when a cruise came in, and then most of the gamblers were our fellow countrymen. For the hotels and all this paraphernalia were intended for Americans. Posters and placards everywhere advertised Havana as only an hour from Miami, but not an American tourist was to be seen. At the very time the Cuban government was still spending tens of thousands of dollars in trying to attract American tourists, every public utterance of the ministers was calculated to frighten them away.

It was an extraordinary and revealing sight to visit the empty

[1] Slavery was abolished in Cuba in 1886.

caravanserais in the absence of their occupants, and an insight into the
mentality of mid-twentieth-century holidays. The first of them we
entered had enormous gambling premises, all figuratively, if not
literally, upholstered in dark crimson plush. Empty drawing-rooms or
lounges, whatever one likes to call them, stretched out endlessly
without a living soul in them. This particular hotel did have some
persons gambling, of vulpine or reptilian feature, even a little dangerous
of expression, self-exiled, we were told, from Las Vegas and not
improbably of Mafia association. It was the most congenial of the
night haunts. Another hotel of positively staggering size, towering
like a skyscraper, and all lit up at night with its lift shaft showing like
the green spine or backbone of its opaque body, had a ground floor
restaurant in Polynesian style advertising Cantonese food, 'fish from
the rivers, lakes and seas', a choice of fifty-four different rum drinks
all numbered on the menu, or *puai* drinks of the ancient Hawaiians.
Upstairs were streets of shops at virtuoso prices, and the hall rising to
several storeys was made to simulate a tropical forest with a stairway
rising in arbitrary fashion and changing direction for no reason so
that you could feel you were climbing in a cocoa-nut grove. Or so I
surmised. On the first floor, once you reached it, were gambling rooms
with frescoes and mosaics by *avant-garde* painters who certainly could
not complain of not being given their opportunity for they had been
allowed their heads completely, and a 'help yourself' restaurant, if
that is the right term for it, looking out over the enormous first floor
swimming pool. But we ate instead in a secluded grill-room; and
remembered to go up on a subsequent evening to another bar and
restaurant on the top floor whence you look down on the lit streets
of Havana.

Lower down in the town, near the sea, is yet another of the hotels
with the stamp of respectability upon it because it is the oldest of them.
It has a double row of shops, the cigar-counter, alone, being a major
attraction for anyone who appreciates the pleasing incongruities and
absurdities of cigar-labels. One can only hope the Cuban revolution
will not throw the designers out of work. In this hotel the restaurants
and gambling rooms have pullulated and there seems no end to them.
This was the hotel that was so crowded that night with passengers
from off a cruise. And the fourth of them that we entered, again in
the spirit of going to see Pompeii or Herculaneum, was not the least

fantastic of them all. Since then it has been taken over as a home for illegitimate children. It had the most bizarre and extreme of decorative schemes in mosaic, and the artists who surely had never had such an opportunity before in their lives were set to work on the scale of the grandest of Roman *thermae*. If only they had been better painters! But it is as though the hotel companies had jumped all their fences in one, and come straight from 'quatorze the fifteenth' Ritz style to action painting, except that this is now several moves behind. And landing plum in the middle of an international movement where there are no clues by which to know whether the artist is Brazilian, or Japanese, or a Greenlander, had commissioned the first painters who came to hand, while insisting that the note should be sub-tropical. These remarks are in no sense meant to be derogatory to the artists concerned whom in any event it was wise policy to engage, but their energies could have been better employed and co-ordinated.

The country clubs of Havana are upon the same lavish scale as the hotels, and I think, at the time of writing, that all of them have been confiscated by the government. It was no pleasant sensation, too, to talk with persons who had had their fortunes 'frozen'. Havana, like Lima, has its flowering suburbs where, as I have said, we saw for the first time a flamboyant coming into blossom. It is past these large houses in their gardens that the Country Club lies in a kind of oasis of green lawns and palm trees. There are, as well, at least two yacht clubs on the same huge scale with the amenities of a luxury liner. And the Tropicana night club! This would require a special pen functioning over the centuries, and laid up for hundreds of years at a time, but kept alive on ice or in the frigidaire. Trained at Baiae where the baths and villas of the Romans had their foundations laid far out in the waters of the Siren bay; in fact, aqua-architecture as that can be studied in paintings from Roman villas in the museum of Naples, where the frescoes of architectural oddities and extravagances are on a par with the mammoth-nightmare hotels; sent to sleep and woken to rub its eyes and open them in the Tropicana night club in Havana. There are two stages; one of them in the fresh air in a kind of aisled cathedral of palm trees but so illuminated, and with so many reflections thrown by mirrors, that it is impossible to determine its real proportions. This stage was lit up, but not in use. The other is an indoor stage, air-conditioned, of course, with positively Roman draughts and dinner tables laid down a sloping floor towards the proscenium. The cabaret outnumbered the diners in the proportion, I would say, of four to one; and it was to be noticed that the waiters with nothing much else to do were the only persons really interested in the cabaret. So might one become, oneself, if a programme seller or theatre fireman, someone forced by his or her profession to watch every performance. And, also, as well, there was the lubricious interest of the mulatto or half-caste at seeing so many nearly naked bodies spinning and gyrating in the dance. There was a special and desperate hopelessness in the performers as though this was 'last house' before the Fall of Rome, and indeed long since the Tropicana must have been taken over, though it is difficult to imagine what it could be converted into. Back in the hotel in the early hours of the morning, and still haunted by the Tropicana, I sent myself to sleep in thinking of Caligula and his bridge or pier, 'upwards of three miles long', built out into the Bay of Naples. It was rumoured that something of the same sort, no doubt an air-conditioned casino and night club, on an artificial island in the sea, had been planned in the last years of the Batista regime.

The nightmare luxury hotel under American tourist stimulus is already so marked a feature everywhere that it can be built on a semi-tropical island between the Pacific and the Caribbean that it is worth considering what has been achieved here in the West Indies for, given peaceful conditions, it will be carried still further in the future. At St Anne's Bay and Ocho Ríos in Jamaica the process is already under way. The island of Puerto Rico comes, of course, high upon the list with 'the fabulous' Caribe Hilton of three hundred air-conditioned rooms, each with private balcony. The nearby Virgin Islands are in full throes of 'development'; St Thomas, St John, and St Croix, bought by the U.S.A. from Denmark in 1917, St Croix having belonged at one time to the Knights of Malta. It must be curious in these little specks of islands to find old Danish houses and Lutheran churches in the two capitals, Charlotte Amalie and Frederiksted, side by side with luxury hotels. The Dominican Republic has also been developed by its dictator-'benefactor' Colonel Trujillo in no uncertain way where huge hotels are concerned, salt-water swimming-pools, air-conditioning, 'the cold of the rich' as Jean Paul Sartre has called it, and so forth, and must be in decided contrast to the other half of the island of Hispaniola, which is the negro republic of Haiti. But

these huge hotels which in the right hands would offer great opportunities to modern architects, and are too often a sad and ugly failure
would seem to be redeemed by the newly opened hotel on the Dutch
island of Curaçao. This is built right on the ramparts of the old town
and consists of two great red-roofed wings like two arms of a pentagon
with the ramparts forming the three other sides. There is a terrace
along the ramparts, a garden and swimming pool in the middle, and
on the lower floor is the casino. This has a passage with portholes in
it through which the swimmers, not all, we dare hope, aged sixty
years and upwards, can be seen. The hotel at Curaçao, not on this
score alone, would seem to be more imaginatively conceived than
the others.

For contrast to luxury thinking in hotels we could not afford we
attended a cockfight in Havana. Having been an amateur of fighting
cocks, myself, but never fought them, I found it interesting but
repellent. Having owned ginger-breasted reds, spangles, Cornish
hennies, blue Furnaces, silver duckwings, and smock-breasted blood-
wing pyles, no less, these latter in direct descent from the fighting
cocks of King Charles II, I wanted to see the plumage in the cockpit
at Havana, for it was because of their gay colours that I collected them.
The cockpit was an old one dating perhaps from a hundred years ago,
and among the crowded public my wife was the only woman. Several
of Fidel's apostles were present, profusely bearded in spite of the
hot weather, and with revolvers at their hips. The mains were monotonous and ugly to watch, with one cock chasing the other all round the
ring, pecking at it, while the plucking of the cock's thighs and rump
so that they are like bald patches, makes it an unattractive spectacle.
Shouting and uproar were continuous as bets were laid. Luckily
fights were not to the death, but the birds were taken out when things
had gone more than far enough already. We left after two bouts of
pecking and chasing, and were more interested in the cockpens at the
back where the owners kept their birds. The crowing was nearly as
loud as the laying of wagers, and we saw the bags in which the cocks
were carried, objects that were often richly worked or embroidered
in the days of the 'fancy'. Here, too, at the back was a lilliputian cockpit, small enough for game bantams to be fought there, though this
was not its purpose. I could not admire any of the Cuban fighting
cocks; or it may be that the cockfighting blood in me is paling. I

cannot have been like this when a main of cocks was fought every
evening in the apse of the dining-room at my old home in Derbyshire. They were grey-breasted greys that my great-great-grandfather
fought a hundred and fifty years ago at Renishaw.

Havana, and the country round it, was all we saw of this island
which is nearly eight hundred miles long, but it would not appear
that the old towns of Trinidad, Camagüey, or Santiago de Cuba right
at the far end of the island six hundred miles away, have much in them,
or, indeed, compare in any way for interest to provincial towns in
Mexico, proving thereby that it is the Indian blood, non-present in
Cuba, that gives to Mexico its especial flavour. It is the Indian or
the *mestizo* that made of Taxco or Puebla, of Oaxaca or Querétaro,
something that is essentially or peculiarly Mexican in style. The
Carib population of Cuba before the Spaniards came were of poor
Indian stock, and probably related to the Indians who inhabited the
Florida swamps. Neither Indian race left any memorial behind it.
But it is the African negro transported to Cuba who, in Havana as in
Brazil and in New Orleans, invented something separate and apart
in popular music.

In the morning below the hotel window in Havana I could hear the
cry of a man selling watermelons, and his call was distinctly and
definitely in the rhythm of a habanera. Manuel de Falla, in an article
on Ravel,[1] calls the habanera 'the supreme element in all Spain'. Yet
it is a negro, and not a Spanish invention, even though cast in the
idiom of Spain. It marvellously suggests and portrays langorous and
enervating heat, with the delights and not the pains of that. Does the
reader know Chabrier's *Habanera*? It is a little masterpiece of evocation,
enough to make one think this musical form 'the supreme element',
but of Spanish-America and not wholly and entirely of Spain. Chabrier
had heard these songs when he went with Manet to Madrid and
Seville for habaneras were then fashionable in the *tertulias madrileñas*
of the day, but as coming from semi-tropical Havana. In Cuba they
have been written and sung for generations. In Havana in 1960 we
heard 'revolutionary habaneras' with words in praise of Fidel Castro,
but still in those langorous and semi-tropical rhythms.

A wine tavern with its dark walls papered with old newspaper
cuttings is one of the cradles of the habanera in Havana. In this setting

[1] *La Revue Musicale*, March 1939.

we heard *Imágenes*, a moving and most beautiful song composed
only a few months ago, and happily non-political in motive. The singer
had a hard tenor voice but of great flexibility. He was accompanied
by a negro at the piano, and a violinist who played with his eyes
shut, and was half-Chinese. A composer of these songs was there as
well. *Imágenes* is a song that haunts the memory, but so does the
little catch or fragment of a habanera sung by the negro selling water
melons under my window. Perhaps the habanera may remain the
'supreme element' in all Havana long after other and louder com
motions have died down and faded away.

Guatemalan village church

Church procession, Guatemala

Dos Pilas, Guatemala; prisoner straining at his bonds. Archaeological site found in April, 1960

Tikál, Guatemala

Chapter Eleven

◆◆◆◆◆◆◆◆◆◆◆◆◆◆◆◆◆◆

GUATEMALA

ANTIGUA AND LAKE ATITLÁN

WHAT A WONDERFUL FEELING TO turn over in the night and know one will be on the way to Guatemala in the morning! What a luxury of anticipation! Ever since reading John L. Stephens' *Incidents of travel in Central America, Chiapas and Yucatán* when I was twelve years old, I have wanted to go there. But while I was young, and much later still, what a journey it would have been, by sea all the way from London to Puerto Barrios which is the Guatemalan port upon the Caribbean! And now we are on the way to Guatemala by air, calling in at one or two more Central American capitals upon the way.

Over the blue Caribbean once more, not for the first time upon this journey, on this aeroplane that continues to New Orleans. And the first stop is at Tegucigalpa in Honduras, where we came down before on the way to Lima. Now I am wishing there was time to get out and stay there. The little airport which I never thought to see again seems quite familiar. The same tiny aeroplane is making practise landings. I look for that impassive, white-clad, sombrero'd Indian at his desk, and find him. Even as late as 1951, this town which is in the neighbourhood of rich silver mines had no railway and had no highroad leading to it. One reason for stopping here, beside its balconied houses painted pastel blue, or rose, or cream, or lavender, would be its cathedral which according to Pál Kelemen has a golden pulpit, 'never reworked or even retouched, and sheathed in pure gold, in a fascinating local Rococo', with a chariot on top of its canopy, all of gilded wood, portraying one of the golden cars drawn through the streets in religious processions. Another and better reason still, would be in order to visit the ruins of Copán, of which more later.

O 209

But our aeroplane waits only for a few moments, and we go on to San Salvador, three-quarters of an hour away. This is a much bigger city than Tegucigalpa, with a larger airport, though El Salvador is by far the smallest of the Central American republics. It seems more sophisticated than Honduras, and even boasts a brand new American hotel. An obstacle race for the passengers is planned by the little Indian soldiers who are on guard, and we re-embark at a moment's notice by an unexpected door. It is but an hour's flight more, over this small state which is alone among the Central American republics in only facing on the Pacific and not towards both oceans, and which is only half as big again as Wales. I have a gangway seat and cannot see any of its volcanoes out of the porthole, and we come down at Guatemala City. We have arrived safely, but there is a good deal of delay at the Customs, and by the time we are through with them the man who had come to meet us had disappeared.

Our affairs are in the hands of Clark's Tours, an American firm that makes all the arrangements for travellers in Guatemala. One of our troubles has been that nowhere have we been able to find a good map of the country, or indeed, anyone who knows anything at all about Guatemala. To ask questions about it is like enquiring for hotel prices in Greenland or Kamstchatka. No one has heard of Antigua although it is probably the most beautiful city in the two Americas. When we mention the name of it everyone thinks we mean the West Indian island which is always pronounced 'Anteega'. (And by this time we are in difficulties already owing to not being able to understand the local accent which much resembles a Welshman speaking English. Some people will tell you this is because the first school-teachers who came to Jamaica three hundred years ago were Welsh Baptists. All this of course in the langorous heat of St Anne's Bay and Ocho Ríos, walking by walls hung with bougainvillaea and past beds of cannas, with chattering negresses in bright cotton dresses carrying bundles on their heads, added much to the excitement of starting for what seemed from this distance almost an unknown land.)

And now we are arrived, and driving into Guatemala City in a taxi, talking to Clark's emissary who had been in the airport all the time, and in a few moments we have discovered from him that Antigua is only some three-quarters of an hour away. By which time we are driving down a broad avenue or boulevard with statues on traffic islands down the middle of it, and the marvellous heart-lifting spectacle of jacaranda trees in full blossom, every here and there, in whichever direction we look. So we have reached Guatemala at just the right moment for one of the most lovely sights in the world. We have driven far enough into Guatemala City to admire them, when we decide for Antigua, turn back to the airport, and are sent off in another car for what seems an altogether excessive price. But, and this must be said in warning, it was as nothing compared to what we had to pay later, on other and longer journeys. It is one of the flaws in this most lovely of countries; and even the privilege of being able to settle for it in quetzals, for the monetary unit is called after the bird with the beautiful green tail-feathers, does not compensate for having to pay so much more than the proper amount.

This, however, cannot detract from the beauty of the landscape which, once we are in the hills, becomes umbrageous like the more lovely parts of Tuscany with the same blue distances and the richest of brown soils. One looks for the snow-crested Apennines and, instead, in a few moments more will be looking at volcanoes. Just now we see Guatemala City far away in the plain behind us, and are among balsam-dropping pine trees. For if ever pine tree was resinous or balsamic it would be here in the wooded glades of Guatemala. Flowers, to this moment are few; and if there is a drawback it is the dusty roads which again remind one of Italy. We could be somewhere near Lucca; or near Ponte de Lima which is in the Minho, the rich and fertile province of Northern Portugal. But now we come down into a valley, and are passing long rows of one-storeyed houses, many of them with tall barred windows. We turn a corner into a plaza with no time to take in its buildings, drive down a long street still of one-storeyed houses, and are in Antigua before one can exclaim out aloud about the flowers.

The hotel is in a cobbled side street and has a long blank wall opposite its door. This wall which, in fact, conceals a garage is almost tumbling or toppling over for flowers; bougainvillaea in several colours and inseparable pale blue plumbago; also, another flowering creeper of which I never discovered the name. Now one knows the one-storeyed buildings are against earthquakes, and looking down the lane there is a church in ruins at the end of it. This, while the luggage is being taken off the car, and now we are led direct into a lovely garden, and down a long roofed-in walk or path with flower beds along it, past several small separate bungalows to the last one of them all which is to be our home during a paradisal rest of several nights and days. I have never been so tired in my life as when we reached Antigua, and it is impossible to conceive of a more lovely place to rest in.

We spent that first evening in the garden, thankful to be safely arrived here after so immense a journey. For it was as though we had come in one stage from Lima, how many hundreds of miles away, and thence along the Altiplano of Peru! The stone idols of Tiahuanaco, and that Megalithic kingdom, where was it beyond Lake Titicaca, in quite another world? Cuzco and Quito and Machu Picchu; what a way we had come! Criss-crossing the Caribbean; and now as a kind of bonus or supplement to the journey, to be in Guatemala which we had not intended, which had never been part of our plan.

The two volcanoes that destroyed Antigua, Agua and Fuego, seen from the garden look but a mile or two away. But we had no time for them that evening because of the pair of jacaranda trees which were in full blossom only a few feet above our heads. And now it was time to go into dinner in the main building where we had our first sight of the Guatemalan costume. Or, at least of one of them, for it is probably the richest and most varied costume in the world today. The distinctive part of this is the *huipil* or blouse which has infinite variations played upon it. One comes in retrospect to look upon the *huipil* as something like the wings and mantle of the bird-of-paradise so entirely does it transform itself, helped, also, by the syllables of its name for there is the hint of preening, of fluttering in them. One or two of the Indian women waitresses in the hotel were remarkably graceful and good-looking, even beautiful, and all wore the identical form of *huipil* which trailed behind their shoulders like a pair of wings.

But in the conviction that jacarandas are one of the lovely sights of the world I could not take my eyes from them. A pair of jacarandas, as I say, were only a few feet from our window. In full blossom, or even a little over that, for the ground under them was thick with fallen flowers. Ever since I saw jacaranda trees in bloom in Lisbon I had wanted to be near one in order to look at it at all hours of the day, and in the evening when the colour must be gone out of it. I have read somewhere that there are fifty kinds of jacarandas but I think there must be but small differences in them. The one sort I have seen, whatever its botanical name, is enough for me. When would there ever again be this opportunity? For the feeling that most of us from Northern countries have for the blue waters of the Mediterranean has its parallel where the semi-tropics are concerned in the jacaranda. The feature of it is that the flowers come out before the delicate fern-cut leaves. The blossoms which are as big as a fox-glove merge or coalesce together into a heliotropic, blue porcelain, powder-blue; a little darker than that but one must not call the jacaranda mauve. It is light when you look into it, and darker when you look at it against the sky; which at Antigua is the blue empyrean in perfection of that, but always with a white cloud or two, caught, or loosed again from the cones of the volcanoes, upon those mornings and evenings of perpetual spring. In the afternoons you could look solidly into them and the jacarandas seemed to have substance, and to be moored or rooted there. But they are strangers and not indigenous. Jacarandas are Brazilian in origin; and wherever planted, in Cairo or in India, in Java or Siam, or here in Antigua, they are surely Brazilian. There are, for instance, large plantings of jacarandas, whole avenues of them in Rhodesia and Kenya, but I cannot believe they look South African. I do not know when the jacaranda was brought to Guatemala, whether it was growing here when Antigua was *la muy leal ciudad de Santiago de los Caballeros de Goathemala*, but it seems unlikely. In Guatemala the jacaranda does not take the scene but complements and fulfils it. A flowering tree that is an emblem or symbol for an Elysium which there has never been, for no one would be drawn or attracted to its habitat in the forests of Brazil. Therefore, it is what it leaves to the imagination that is the fascination of the jacaranda. One finds oneself thinking of all manner of things to carry further its half-hints or suggestions of the paradisal land.

Besides the jacaranda there are many other kinds of flowering trees, purple and blue linda vines, and pepper and orange and tangerine trees, all, or most of them, with orchids growing on them. Also, banana palms and papaya and avocado; and another palm with water running from any hole one made in its stem, which was the far-famed traveller's tree. Quantities of hibiscus, as well, in all colours, but almost relegated here to a back place there were so many other flowers that caught the eye. And a couple of macaws, one scarlet and blue, and the other blue and yellow, tethered under trees, I suppose, poor things, their wings were clipped, but they hopped from bough to bough and called out in their raucous voices. Orchids had planted themselves on these same branches, or been put there by the Indian gardeners. This is macaw country, and indeed they hardly seemed exotic.

We enquired of many persons we met about the quetzal bird of which there is the lovely, lifesize, double folding plate in Gould's *Trogonidae*. I wanted to know if it is true that quetzals are caught when sleeping after a meal of avocado pears, of which they swallow the large and heavy stones, and then regurgitate them. The Indians steal up near to them, and stun them with an arrow from a blowpipe. But this most glorious of the trogons, with crimson belly, green breast, green 'wild man' head, and long green tail feathers from which legend says Montezuma's robe was made, is scarce almost to extinction and, in fact, lives more in Honduras than Guatemala. We met only one person, the Dutch artist living in Quito, who had seen a quetzal. One could wish indeed that there were a quetzal in this hotel garden in Antigua, except that one could not bear to see so noble a bird hop from branch to branch with curtailed wings.

There are other gardens in Antigua, and no reason to think this is the most beautiful of them. But I had the wish of half a lifetime in having a jacaranda morning and evening under my eyes, and if one looked a little further there were the two volcanoes, Agua and Fuego. The one poured down water out of its crater, and the other fire, to destroy Antigua on the fatal day in 1773, but in this clear light of the evening they are like domestic or tame volcanoes. One cannot believe they are capable of doing damage. And now, for it is always dark here at about seven o'clock, the jacarandas look to be of a dark blue powdery being or entity, and one thinks the macaws certainly, and even the quetzal bird to be too strident for them. They are idyllic or heavenly blue islands, harbours of love and poetry against the starlit sky. And we walk across the garden again for dinner, making one discovery when we get there which is that the *huipiles* are worn hanging down like sleeves, and are then tucked up and spread into wings to trail behind the shoulder, for we see the prettiest of the Indian maids arranging her *huipil* in position before serving dinner. It is a special kind of *huipil*, we are told, from one mountain village a few miles away, and all the Indian maids come from that village.

For a day or two we hardly stirred out from the garden which has a wall round it like a little flowering kingdom of its own. We could see the two volcanoes over the wall, and if we walked to the far end of the garden the ruined façade of one of the churches of Antigua, San José el Viejo, stood there in a perspective of flowers. Instead, it was a place in which to gather one's thoughts after so tremendous a journey but, also, the flowering trees inspired one to new ideas. We had been to South America and now unexpectedly and as the result of a last moment decision, to Central America. Now we were in Guatemala which is surely one of the most beautiful countries in the world. What marvellous and exciting latitudes! Reading again in Stephen's *Central America, Chiapas and Yucatán* and looking in the map for Chiapas I find it is the most southern Mexican province, next to Guatemala, and am no longer surprised at Stephen's saying he was about to undertake a journey of a thousand miles from Nicaragua to Yucatán. This was when he had been visiting León and Granada, two old Colonial cities of Nicaragua, and he writes of the former: 'It had an appearance of old and aristocratic respectability which no other city in Central America possessed. The houses were large, and many of the fronts were full of stucco ornaments; the plaza was spacious, and the squares of the churches and the churches themselves magnificent.' That was in Nicaragua, with all of Honduras and El Salvador between him and Guatemala. It is enough to make one ashamed of travelling in aeroplanes.

Here in Guatemala we are near to Mexico, to my taste the most exciting, I do not say the most beautiful country in the world. And thinking of *huipiles* we are not as much as three hundred miles from Tehuantepec where I have wanted to go to see the beautiful Tehuanas who may have a drop of French blood in them from occupation by the army of Marshal Bazaine during Maximilian's Empire. This is what Miguel Covarrubias[1] says of them, or, at least, of the Huave Indians near by: 'At home and for work the women go mostly nude above the waist, but on ceremonial occasions they display beautiful *huipiles*

---

[1] *Mexico South: the Isthmus of Tehuantepec*, Cassell & Co. Ltd., London, 1950, pp. 61, 261, 262, 264. The two villages are called Huamelula and Astata, and the colour of the dye 'changes from lemon yellow to chartreuse green and finally to a beautiful dark purple. Every self-respecting, well-dressed old Tehuana,' says Covarrubias, 'owns a snail-dyed skirt and would not sell it for its value in gold.' The caracol thread has a vile smell, and one wonders if this was so with the purple of Imperial Rome. This is the only explanation I have seen of the 'green-purple' mentioned in connection with the Tyrian dye.

of gauze-thin, homespun white cotton decorated with minute animal and floral designs in soft purple. These designs are woven into the cloth with the famous caracol thread dyed, like the Tyrian purple of the Romans, with a sea-snail' (from two small villages on the Gulf). And he describes, and illustrates, the great-*huipil* or head-*huipil* of the Tehuanas, a little blouse of silk mesh with a border or peplum of starched lace, 'worn on festival occasions with the starched peplum thrown back over the head and forming a glorious head-dress with rays of crisp white radiating from a girl's face in a manner reminiscent of the feather war bonnets' of the Red Indians. The men, in the white shirts and trousers of Mexican Indians, wore hats 'to be seen nowhere else in Mexico, of heavy red felt with an upturned brim and high sugarloaf crown, very expensive because of their trimmings—a rope of twisted silver thread, thick as a ship's cable, worn as a hatband, with a wide band of silver braid bordering the crown'. But never mind about their hats; or, for that matter, those of the aforementioned Huave Indians; 'middle-aged men in their Sunday serge suits with pink silk handkerchiefs tied over their ordinary red bandannas to serve as foundation for a conical head-dress of metallic green cocks' feathers. On their foreheads they wore square mirrors and a fringe of large silver coins; and in one hand they carried rattles of gourds streaming with ribbons, and in the other fan-like wands of long, red macaw tail-feathers set in a wooden handle.'

We are in lands of the macaw and quetzal, and the jacaranda.

The great-*huipil* of the Tehuanas, or *bidamiró* to give the full name, is only at one remove or further stage of development from the winged *huipil* of the Indian maids at Antigua. And Guatemala, we go on, for this is apposite to the setting, has twenty-seven volcanoes in it. Of the view outside a certain town the guide book says that 'from this point on a clear day is seen an entire horizon of volcanoes'. At another place, near San Pedro Sacatapéquez, after passing through forests of pine trees, ten volcanoes can be seen; Agua, Fuego, Pacaya, Acatenango, Atitlán, Tolimán, San Pedro, San Pablo, Zunil and Santa María. But this again is a long way distant from the Gulf of Nicoya as described by Stephens: 'We passed in regular succession the volcanoes of San Salvador, San Vicente, San Miguel, Telega, Momotombo, Managua, Nindiri, Masaya, and Nicaragua, each one a noble spectacle, and all together forming a chain with which no other in the world can be compared; indeed this coast has been well described as bristling with volcanoes.' That was a view of volcanoes from the sea, on a morning that 'the dolphin, the most beautiful fish that swims, played under our bows and stern, and accompanied us slowly alongside. But the sailors had no respect for its golden back. The mate, a murderous young Frenchman, stood for hours with a harpoon in his hand, drove it into several, and at length brought one on board. The king of the sea seemed conscious of his fallen state; his beautiful colours faded, and he became spotted, and at last heavy and lustreless, like any other dead fish.' It reminds one of the poem *L'Albatros*, by Baudelaire.

That was along the coast of Costa Rica.

Let us confine ourselves to Guatemala where Stephens, coming in from British Honduras passed gigantic and roofless churches—'a gigantic church above a collection of thatched huts; another gigantic and roofless church above a few thatched huts; the gigantic church of St John the Hermit seeming to bestride the valley with its red soil of sandstone, and covered with gigantic pines; another gigantic church upon a beautiful table of land; and the village of Hocotán with yet another gigantic church'—the seventh they had seen in that one day, 'all of colossal grandeur and costliness in a region of desolation, and by mountain paths which human hands had never attempted to improve.'

What other facts, fanciful as they may sound, that give the character of Guatemala! That at Mixco, as mentioned by Thomas Gage in *The Anglo-American*[1] (1648) there was pottery of a white earth, 'whereof are made rare and excellent pots for water, pans, pipkins, platters, dishes, chafing-dishes, warming-pans, wherein those Indians show much wit, and paint them with red, white, and several mingled colours . . . which some Creole women will eat by full mouthfuls endangering their health and lives so that by this earthly ware they may look white and pale'. Or that another town is unique in a different way because it has prohibited the sale of alcohol but pays a yearly tax to the government on the amount that a town of its size would normally consume. Or the talking-pond, near Tactic, which starts bubbling and boiling as soon as persons come near it and begin

[1] *The English American: A new survey of the West Indies*, by Thomas Gage, Broadway Travellers Series, 1928, pp. 214, 215.

talking, working up itself to such a frenzy that it will throw logs into
the air, and then quietens as they go away. That it is a land, in short
where in a town near the Pan-American Highway the Indians play
rebecs made of armadillo shell; and where among a list of fruits you
may see pitahaya which is the fruit of the night-blooming cereus.

But one cannot remain secluded for ever in this lovely garden
under the jacarandas, thinking of the wonders of nature in Guatemala.
We must walk into the town to look at its shattered churches. And
now it has to be admitted that their architecture is disappointing. They
do not compare with churches either in Mexico or Peru. The great
convent of La Concepción before the fatal earthquake housed a hundred
nuns and seven hundred servants. The little guide book says of it that
'wandering through its cells the visitor can relive times when in these
very halls, the clasped hands of praying nuns shone in the gloom like
bouquets of white lilies'. And among the nuns was Donna Juana
Maldonado de Paz, of whom there will be more to say in a few
moments, but, truthfully, the ruined churches of Antigua are all much
alike and become confusing. It is a place that is beautiful beyond
words as a whole, but must not be seen too closely. There are seven
or eight of the huge churches, not counting the Cathedral, several of
them with ruined cloisters and fountains in the middle, yet, as Thomas
Gage says of them, 'they are not so fair and rich as those of Mexico'.
The Dominicans, Franciscans, and Mercenarians held a hundred
friars apiece. This English friar from Sussex lodged with the Dominicans; and he tells of their cloisters and gardens, with 'a pond of a
quarter of a mile long, all paved, and a low stone wall about, where
is a boat for the friar's recreation, who often go thither to fish, and
do sometimes upon a sudden want or occasion take out from thence as
much fish as will give to the whole cloister a dinner.'

Next to where Gage stayed was the cloister of nuns called La
Concepción, founded by four nuns from Mexico of noble family, 'in
which at my time there were judged to live a thousand women, not al
nuns, but nuns and their sewing maids or slaves, and young children
which were brought up and taught to work by the nuns. In this
cloister lived that Donna Juana de Maldonado . . . whom the Bishop
so much conversed withal. She was very fair and beautiful, and no
above twenty years of age, and yet his love blinding him, he strove
what he could in my time against all the ancient nuns and sisters

to make her superior and abbess, and caused such a mutiny and strife in that cloister, which was very scandalous to the whole city, and made many rich merchants and gentlemen run to the cloister with their swords drawn, threatening to break in amongst the nuns to defend their daughters against the powerful faction which the Bishop had wrought for Donna Juana de Maldonado, which they had performed if the young nun's father had not entreated her to desist in regard to her young age from her ambitious thoughts of being abbess. With this the mutiny both within and without ceased, the Bishop got but shame, and his young sister continued as before under command and obedience, to a more religious, grave, and aged nun than herself . . . this Donna Juana de Maldonado was the wonder of all that cloister, yea of all the city for her excellent voice, and skill in music, and in carriage. . . . She was witty, well spoken and above all a Calliope, or Muse for ingenious and sudden verses; which the Bishop said so much moved him to delight in her company and conversation. Her father thought nothing too good, nor too much for her; and therefore having no other children, he conferred upon her riches, as might beseem a nun, as rich and costly cabinets faced with gold and silver, pictures and idols for her chamber with crowns and jewels to adorn them; which with other presents from the Bishop (who dying in my time left not wherewith to pay his debts, for that as the report went, he had spent himself and given all unto this nun) made this Donna Juana de Maldonado so rich and stately, that at her own charges she built for herself a new quarter within the cloister with rooms and galleries, and a private garden walk, and to wait on her half a dozen blackamoor maids; but above all she placed her delight in a private chapel or closet to pray in, being hung with rich hangings and round about it costly *láminas* (as they call them) or pictures painted upon brass set in black ebony frames with corners of gold, some of silver, brought to her from Rome; her altar was accordingly decked with jewels, candlesticks, crowns, lamps, and covered with a canopy embroidered with gold; in her closet she had her small organ, whereupon she played sometimes by herself, sometimes with her best friends of the nuns; and here especially she entertained with music her beloved Bishop.'

Whether, or not, we are to believe this unpleasant, renegade friar who on his return to England turned Puritan and was the instrument for delivering more than one of his former companions to the public

executioner to be hanged, drawn and quartered at Tyburn, it is
certainly a picturesque account that he gives of the nun, Donna Juan
de Maldonado. Paler of complexion for she was pure Creole and had
no Indian blood in her, and doubtless more virtuous, she becomes a
kind of companion to *La Pérricholi* in Lima and *La Marichuela* in
Bogotá. Of the convent of La Concepción nothing is now left but the
bare walls, and little more remains of the convent of the Dominican
except that it is a riot of flowers. The Franciscan church and La Compañía of the Jesuits have little to distinguish them from each other in
the memory. The former Sagrario is all that is in use for worship of the
huge Cathedral. Its vast ruins are still there at the back, where used
to be the baldachin over the high altar with its sixteen pillars 'sheathed
in tortoiseshell'. The convent of Las Capuchinas, a nunnery which
had running water in every cell, has become a tenement of Indian
families; La Recolección, outside the town and in the coffee lanes, is
another immense ruin. And there are the many smaller chapels; that
for instance of Santa Rosa in a street lined with old houses and amatle
trees, a convent where the daughters of aristocratic families came, in
the romantic phrases of one writer, 'in many instances to soothe love-
aching young hearts and forever hide their beautiful faces from the
world'.

The palace of the Captains-General of New Spain in the Cathedral
Square with its double colonnades is another dull, but scenically
effective building. It has the escutcheon of Carlos III of Spain over its
door, a testimony at long distance indeed from the palaces this most
heraldic-looking of monarchs built for himself at Caserta and Madrid.
The most charming of buildings in Antigua is the old University of
San Carlo Borromeo, untouched by the earthquake and with a
delightful patio of Moorish-looking trefoil arches in what is decidedly
Guatemalan style. If one is curious to see what the churches of Antigua
were like before the earthquake, there is La Merced at the far end of the
town, and intact so far as the church is concerned though the cloister
is still in ruins with a many-brimmed fountain in the middle of it.
The façade of La Merced in this sunlight, which would make almost
anything beautiful, is one mass of white, repeated ornament resembling
a stencil pattern on yellow stucco, of an effect like marzipan or almond
paste on sugar-icing. By no argument but that of the sunlight could
it be called beautiful. It should be the consolation of Antigua that its

many churches are more picturesque in ruins. The Spanish genius in building that, in part touching the Indians, was the source of unique architecture in Peru and Mexico rose to no comparable heights in Central America. This is the consoling thought, too, in considering the 'seven gigantic churches in ruins' seen by Stephens in his wanderings in the course of one day. They, also, should be looked upon scenically and, doubtless, were more impressive ruined. Though, when searching for a reason why the ancient Mayans abandoned their cities and left them deserted in the jungle, it has occurred to few persons that it was probably for the same causes that the gigantic churches of the Spaniards were already in ruins more than a hundred years ago.

If one takes Antigua in its picturesqueness as somewhat of a theatre scene there is plenty of incident to populate its wings and backdrop of façades and volcanoes. A square in which an open-air laundry is in perpetual use by the Indian women under stone arches. Or, at the end of a long street, the hermitage of El Calvario, a trio of white stucco'd portals, side by side, each with a belfry and a big bell over it. And there are always Indians in their costumes from surrounding villages in the Cathedral Square. Also, the old one-storeyed patrician houses such as the Casa Popenoe, or the Casa de los Leones with a pair of odd-looking heraldic lions flanking two Solomonic columns. The old houses have patio gardens, and nothing could be prettier than the flowering courtyard of the Hotel Aurora. But, again, despite the rich families who lived here before the earthquake, its eighty thousand inhabitants, and its line of thirty-five Captains-General appointed by the Kings of Spain, the results are disappointing if looked at too closely. Antigua has nothing to compare with the Torre Tagle Palace at Lima. It is not only the fault of periodic devastation by earthquake and volcano, but the buildings are themselves to blame. They are not good of their kind. Yet Antigua, just because of its flowers and volcanoes, and the ruined churches, is among the beautiful places of the world. It is restful because we do not have to look at it in detail but as a theatre scene.

What a luxury of thought among those lovely flowers! I recognized the same long-legged, long-winged black birds that hopped about in the garden at Lima, and that we were to see again in Yucatán. And it was only natural that being here in the heart of Central America, and never likely to come here again, I should try to find out if we were missing anything interesting in the other Central American Republics.

But it would seem that Guatemala is unique among them. Of the ol
cities of Granada and León in Nicaragua some little has been sai
already; Comayagua in Honduras is another old Colonial town with
few churches; and for the rest, the flowers excepted, and in the absen
of anything more interesting, attention is drawn to the *alforjas* or sadd
bags with stripes in brilliant colours of a town called Cojutepeque i
El Salvador (they must resemble the *alforjas* of Morella in Spain and a
proof of Moorish ancestry), and to the 'costume village' of Panch
malco, the only notable such village in all Central America out
Guatemala; while in Costa Rica with its predominantly white po[
ulation it is a matter of painted ox-carts, or a mountain village, Escas
where 'some of Costa Rica's most beautiful peasant girls may [
seen'.

After only a short while in Guatemala one may be inclined to tl
view that besides being the most beautiful country on the America
continent it may in the abundance of its Indian life be almost a parall
to Bali in the East Indies. There are not the Balinese dances, it is tru
or the gamelan music, but the costume is unequalled anywhere. Tl
markets are truly a wonderful sight. None of the 'costume village
in either Hungary or Czechoslovakia or Roumania (having seen thos
are on a par with them. Nor is the effect 'peasanty', but, rather, tl
materials and the dresses themselves could be designed by the be
dressmakers. The violent aniline effects of Peru and Bolivia, of Cuz
and Puno and La Paz, picturesque and marvellous as those are in th
high clear light, are replaced in Guatemala by softer, richer effec
achieved, stitch by stitch; not thrown in the dye-pot, and then wor
till they fall to pieces, topped off by a rakish bowler hat. There
perhaps no other place in the world, the Paris dressmakers excepte
where such time and trouble are given to textile materials. As you g
through a small village in Guatemala nearly every house will have
loom at work outside it. The time must come soon, one would thin
when the Indians will buy their clothes ready made at the chain stor
but it has not arrived yet. And surprising as it may seem, some perso
in Guatemala will tell you that the situation has not changed for tl
worse in twenty years. There are rich Indian farmers here, a phenom
enon that does not exist in Peru or Bolivia, or Ecuador; and this Indi
stock which is that of the ancient Mayans has preserved qualities c
individuality and local pride which are not present even among the

ear relations in Yucatán. Perhaps it is this which makes the attitude
f the Indians towards a stranger more akin one imagines, not having
een there, to the angle of the Siamese or Balinese towards a European.
They are neither silent nor self-conscious, and that they are not silent
lone makes them different from other Indians. If you meet an Indian
ountryman, or his wife and children, walking along a country lane in
Guatemala it is no different from passing Tuscan contadini, or Spanish
easants anywhere in Spain. There is no subservience; they are your
quals and comport themselves accordingly.

But in Antigua we never walked further than to the outskirts of the
own. In fact to where the coffee lanes begin, and I have to admit
o not knowing at first that it was coffee which was growing there.
t is said to be the highest grade and best coffee in the world, no doubt
a much disputed title, but one quickly notices how good it is. It was
irst brought here by monks in 1760 and planted in the convent grounds.
Of how many famous vineyards in Burgundy and the Rhineland
has one read that monks planted the first vines! And now that they
hould have grown coffee! This thought, once I was in possession of it,
ecame companion in my mind to having seen tea plants growing in
apan, like little clipped azalea bushes though they are indeed of the
camellia family, and of going from Kyoto to Uji the 'village of green
tea'. How wonderful within two years to have seen tea plantations in
one hemisphere and coffee groves in the other! And now that it was
nearly time to leave Antigua there was the sadness in thinking one
might never see such flowers again. At any rate we were going once
more to higher altitudes where the jacaranda could be coming into
blossom. Having come here it could almost be said that there were
now three zones in one's life of experience and imagination. Born
and bred in England, for a start; and for the little if anything learned at
school, later self-trained having tried to get an education in Italy as so
many writers, painters and musicians have done in every generation;
and now, but only in the last three or four years, experienced a little
of other worlds in more tropical lands, I felt myself much preferring
the palette of Hawaii and Guatemala. Having seen them it was Indonesia
that was now the magnet. And Ceylon and Siam and Bali, and Tahiti!
More than enough for ten lives, and far too much for one.

And now we were to leave Antigua and go to Lake Atitlán. The road
there is out of the town and immediately into the coffee groves, through

a richness and luxuriance of vegetation only equalled in my experien<
by the country I have tried to write of round Kyoto. That is cover<
in snow in winter as though the trees, and roofs and everything els
have another flowering, when indeed it may be at its most beautifu
and a favourite theme with the painters of Japan is the first blossomin
with snow still upon the boughs like the marriage of two world
Here there is neither winter nor summer but the illusion of perpetu
spring. Coffee is grown here with the bushes, and later the cherry-r<
berries under great shade trees to keep the sun off them, and roun
Antigua the favourite shade tree is the grevillea rather resembling
light ilex, without the glitter but dull gloom of the ilex, so that you s<
further into its shadows. It was only when we could see down over th
corn fences to a *finca* by a little stream, where would be a mill i
northern latitudes, that there was a heaped pyramid of some substanc
like finely granulated brown soil, and we knew that this was coffe
the knowledge of it giving another meaning and a new mytholog
to what, not looking too closely, one might have taken for a woo
of ilex trees.

When we emerge from out the coffee groves, out of the shado·
and away from the palisades or fences of maize-stalks, we are in a hug
open landscape of red soil and pinewoods with volcanoes not far away
Agna and Fuego among them. It is a Sunday, and but for the volcano<
we could be on a country road in Tuscany until we notice the ha
of the peasants; straw hats of panama shape but folded into a tricorn<
The whole male population, even the small boys are wearing tricorne
and the men have blue woollen jackets and white trousers. Suddenl
we are in the long street of a village, and as far as one can see dow·
it there are women in bright red and white striped *huipiles*. In Sardini<
where costumes are still worn in the Gennargentu, it is the one or tw
villagers with red costumes that are most admired for it is the rare
colour of all. And here was a large village, almost a town of nothin
but bright red dresses. In another moment we are in front of the churc
and in the market place. It is Patzún where markets are held on Sunday
There is a stone pillar or fountain in the middle, and the square
absolutely crowded with red dresses. The church doors are ope·
and there are kneeling women in bright red and white stripes not onl
up the church steps, but kneeling in serried rows all along the aisl<
This first impression of a Guatemalan market is something added t

ikál, Guatemala; The main plaza, *above*, altar and stela, *below left*, Temple III, *below right*

Tikál, Temple I

Tikál, Guatemala

what one knew before of the world. And again the adjective is lacking
to describe it. As in Peru and in Bolivia it is neither Oriental nor
Asiatic; it is of a ghost-like civilization, called 'Indian' but with no
real name. Anything but ghost-like, though, in this bright sunlight.

And now after Patzún it is a matter of up and down and over hills
by steep curves and corners, at one of which, astonishingly, and it
was at about the most dangerous of them all, we met a car coming
from the opposite direction, and had to stop, and saw among its
passengers two friends of ours. We got out to talk to them, having
no idea at all that they were in Guatemala. It was the means, also,
of making a new friend in the person accompanying them, who lived
in Guatemala City. It was an unlikely encounter by the roadside on the
way to Lake Atitlán. All this time in spite of sharp descents the road was
climbing, eventually coming out onto a ridge or mountain crest along
which it continues till, suddenly, at a certain point you see Lake
Atitlán below you. This is the best view of it. Nothing can ever come
up to this first moment of seeing it below you at its widest expanse,
two thousand feet down, unruffled, blue as a peacock's breast, and rising
to a high horizon across fifteen miles of water, with three magnificent
volcanoes, San Pedro and Tolimán together, so that from certain places
they look to be one volcano, and then Atitlán. It is a view that qualifies
beyond argument to be one of the wonders of the world, though not
altogether or entirely pleasant because its very calm is a little sinister
and threatening. From now on we have other and wonderful views of
the lake, though none so breath-taking, and soon begin coming down
fast towards it, to the bottom of the valley where there are coffee
groves shaded by tall trees, and so through the small village of Panajachel to the Hotel Tzanjuyú which stands right on the lake.

Once here, it is as at all lakes; there is nothing much to do. Sunrise
across the lake as the three volcanoes shed their clouds and mists is a
marvellous spectacle; and even more so is it to look out at them at
night, when the silence of the volcanoes is even a little frightening.
The last eruption of one of them was in 1843, more than a hundred
years ago; but who knows? However, the day's objective, next morning, is to cross the lake and see the other side. Twelve villages on or
near its shores are called after saints, and not, as I had thought before
coming here, after the twelve apostles; and three different Indian
tongues are spoken in them, which is the reason why they have kept

P

their individuality and each village is unlike the other. We crossed the lake in a motor-launch to Santiago Atitlán, the most interesting of the villages, and lying directly opposite at the lake's far extremity. This was a real excursion with a boatful of tourists who had been going round together in a group but it is the same everywhere today, and no different from the morning eighteen months ago in Japan when we left the pine-covered isle of Miyajima on the Inland Sea. Then the vermilion *torii* of the temple had slowly, slowly, faded from sight. Now it was the three volcanoes of Lake Atitlán growing imperceptibly taller as we came nearer. We could not resent the tourists as we were doing exactly the same thing ourselves. The volcanoes have been called 'miniature' volcanoes; and in fact we are at five thousand feet altitude ourselves on the lake surface, while the volcanoes are between ten and twelve so that their cones are not more than five or six thousand feet above us. Their constant shifting of position as we came over the lake is intriguing, and made me long for *A Hundred Views of Lake Atitlán* by Hokusai. His genius haunted by Mt Fuji would have had a quick response to Guatemala. Now we are far enough out in the lake to see the headland we are nearing, and two or three of the villages along the right-hand shore. Are there any fish in the lake? I am told in the hotel there are only freshwater shrimps, but the guide says there are *mojarras* and *pepezcas* that are 'delicious eating', and fresh-water crabs. One would think these waters could be usefully stocked with fish that would improve the feeding of the village population.

There is a kind of gazebo or summer-house on the headland, and now we have passed it and are on a long narrow inlet with volcanoes to either side of us and approaching Santiago Atitlán. From near to it looks nothing much, and one wonders if it will be worth the trouble. There is a little pier or jetty of wooden planks, and only a child or two upon it. Once we have landed, and for the first few steps only, the scene becomes instantly Central African. It could be a village on one of the lakes in Central Africa. This, because of the perspective of conical thatched huts as we climb the stony path, and the fronds of banana-palms rattling and waving in the wind from the lake. A nearer look over the loose stone walls into the huts and we see avocados, and they could be papayas growing, also orange trees, around and at the back of the thatched houses. In another instant we see the first Indian women and children of Santiago Atitlán, and it is no longer Africa.

There is a daily market here, and nearly everyone is in the market-place. But as we go along towards it lengths of woven stuffs are proffered to us over the low stone walls by Indian women of whom we can only see the worked blouses and the red head-dresses like red turbans for they are sitting on the ground. And now we are in the market-place which is so crowded that there is hardly space to walk between them. Now we can look more carefully at their turbans which are made from a headband only an inch or two wide but ten or twelve feet long, as one for sale is held up for our inspection; and this is wrapped or wound round and round their heads to form the kind of flat disk or halo which from its protuberance is like a turban. But, in fact, it is circular like an open hoop or band. Their *huipiles* are of orange and purple stripes on a white ground, and they wear bright red skirts with, maybe, black or white patterns on them. All, of course, are different; no two dresses are the same. One can hardly believe such dresses to come out of the conical thatched huts till one remembers the loom or distaff outside nearly every one of them. There is nothing flaring or of the *flamenco* kind about them. The Indian men have striped shirts and short white trousers, but are soberly dressed compared to the women.

Many of the girls and young women had beautiful, long black hair to their shoulders, or even half-way down their backs, obviously a source of pride, and carefully brushed and combed. Some were beautiful and had soft features. The impression is of an independent tribal life of their own, quite remote and undisturbed, not stricken by poverty, and with enough of lore and tradition of their own to make life interesting to everybody. Marketing was for small heaps or piles of mostly unknown substances, but including coffee, cocoa-beans and sugar-cane. We went into the church which has a wooden roof probably three hundred years old, and some exceedingly primitive, velvet-robed statues of saints. Altogether, I think it is the most primitive-looking Christian church I have ever seen, and returning to the market-place it was curious indeed to realize that all the Indian women sitting on the ground, bargaining and selling, and so content in their own way of life were fanatically Christian, but, also, of the old religion. They still have Chuch-Cajaus or shamans, sorcerers and fortune tellers who carry little woven bags for their insignia, with sacred objects, seeds and stones and bits of jade in them. They could be

described as semi-Christianized witches or warlocks, and are much in
evidence in religious ceremonies at Chichecastenango; still more at
Momostenango, another Indian town, where one authority says there
are as many as three hundred of them, men and women.

When it was time to leave Santiago Atitlán, and walk back to the
boat again followed by a horde of children, we passed two Indian
women who were differently dressed and remarkably good-looking,
and the guide pointed them out to us as coming from Cobán. Apparently the most beautiful women in Guatemala are from Cobán
and their lighter complexions are due, of all unexpected things, to
German blood. Germans came out here two generations ago to work
on the sugar plantations and for the United Fruit Company, and
married the most beautiful of the Queckchí women. It is now a fixed
type; and certainly a young woman of this mixed blood we saw
later on in the hotel in Guatemala City was quite remarkably beautiful.
The return voyage was monotonous and without incident, as only
trips on lakes can be, and it was only sad not to have seen another of
the villages just round the corner of one of the volcanoes. This is San
Pedro la Laguna where for a change the Indian women wear
green sashes, and blue and green skirts, and for some reason or other
many of the Indians have fair skins and light coloured hair and
eyes.

In the evening we walked to Panajachel, passing on the way the
other hotel, the Casa Contenta, one-floored and built like a string of
bungalows, with a garden which it is worth coming a long way to see.
The allamandas, the hibiscus, the bougainvillaea, are riotous and
entirely glorious. One has never seen such a gamut of double-rose and
yellows. Further along there is a garden where the cannas, but more
still the hibiscus, are more full of colour than any garden flowers I
have ever seen. Like those at the Casa Contenta, they are the newest
hibiscus hybrids from nurseries in Hawaii costing, we were told,
fifteen dollars a plant. There were a double-rose, even excelling in
beauty those at Lima; a satiny-yellow of huge size, a yellow flushed
with scarlet, and a cinnamon-coloured or almost a sandalwood
hibiscus.

That night, and for many nights after, they were as a colour tonic
to one's mind and one's whole system. Those flowers, and the memory
of that market at the lakeside village of Santiago Atitlán. I was filled

with a longing to know about the other Guatemalan markets because if this one was at all typical the others must be wonderful indeed. But that it was not altogether and entirely exceptional was proved by the Sunday market we had seen at Patzún on the way to Lake Atitlán. It would seem that the other chief-markets are at San Francisco el Alto, a mountain village nearly nine thousand feet up, with 'private' volcano, near Chichecastenango, where woven stuffs and the renowned striped blankets of Momostenango are sold (the Indian names are a part of the charm of Guatemala!). Chichecastenango, where we go from Lake Atitlán, has a far famed Thursday market, but this can wait till we get there. Sololá, on our way thither, on the mountain ridge up above Lake Atitlán, has its Friday market attended by packmen from all over the country. We had already had onion or garlic fields pointed out to us, the produce of which packmen from Atitlán carry to distant markets. It is a common sight on roads in Guatemala to pass these pedlars trotting along with enormous towers of packages on their backs, secured in place by a band round their foreheads.

Another of the markets is at Palín under an enormous ceiba tree, spreading, it is said, a hundred and eighty feet of shade. Palín is near Lake Amatitlán, a smaller lake than Atitlán, and with a name meaning there are many amatle trees. The finest pineapples are sold at Palín. And it would seem that another and most exciting market is at San Juan Ostuncalco, beyond the second largest town in Guatemala which is Quezaltenango, and almost in Mexico. Naturally enough, this village has its own volcano near it. As well, it is famous for music. It is here that the instruments are played that are made of armadillo shells. How I would have liked to go on a little further into Chiapas! To San Cristóbal de las Casas, the old capital, where every street leads to a plaza with a church, monastery, or chapel. Low-tiled roofs and patios, and grilled windows, with 'dashing *charros* or horsemen in embroidered sombreros and leather trousers' riding in the streets. Bridles and saddles are encrusted with silver, and Las Casas is famous for its silver saddles, worth three or four times as much as a horse. The Indians with their brilliant costumes make a blaze of colour in the market-place. The Zinocantes Indians wear wide brimmed palm-leaf hats with long ribbons; the hats of the Huistecs 'imitate haloes'. These whole latitudes from south of Guatemala up to, say, San Luis Potosí in Mexico, have a marvellous and indescribable excitement to them. And looking in the map I have the name of another village, Huehuetenango, on my tongue. It is near there that 'an entire horizon of volcanoes is visible on a clear day'. It is high up, but there should be many and splendid orchids growing in the heated soil.

✦ ✦ ✦ ✦ ✦ ✦ ✦ ✦ ✦ ✦ ✦ ✦ ✦ ✦ ✦ ✦ ✦ ✦ ✦ ✦

Chapter Twelve

CHICHECASTENANGO

CHICHECASTENANGO WAS TO BE OUR last high altitude in South or Central America. A mere six thousand five hundred feet which is only a little higher than St Moritz, but there were persons living in Antigua who complained it was too high for them. Where we were going was not so very high up after all, but the impression of altitude is given because the road begins to climb the moment we leave Atitlán. Winding up and across *barrancas,* and then along shelves cut out of the rock with little or no parapet between us and the precipice. With the village of San Jorge below us half-way down to the lake, and some of the women from it are walking along the road in their white striped blue skirts. The views of the lake would be wonderful indeed had one not come upon it from the other direction where is the most breathtaking view of all. But a point is reached where one gets the last view of the lake, and where it seemed that another and fourth volcano was coming up behind the others. It must be Santa Clara; and although from now onwards the lake sinks out of sight, the cones of one or other, or sometimes of all three or four volcanoes are visible, and at times Agua and Fuego, above Antigua, are seen again. It is muddling, and impossible to tell one volcano from the other.

It was a sad moment to know one would not see Lake Atitlán again. I had heard of it for so many years, and of the twelve villages round its shores. That it is the most beautiful lake in the world one can neither proclaim nor contradict from personal knowledge, but it does seem likely that this is true. Curiosity is aroused by accounts of a chain of lakes on Celebes, in Indonesia, with waters which are described as being apple or jade green, blue, and bright vermilion, and one would suspect there are volcanoes round them. They could not have the perilous serenity of Lake Atitlán, waters that could be said to have a three or even four-engined Vesuvius around their shores. One cannot but compare it in mind to Lake Killarney in a sub-demi-semi-tropic of arbutus, or to some Welsh or Scottish tarn upon the moors. Those are in their hundreds, but there is only one Atitlán. And it had been an inspiring adventure to watch the market at that village across the lake, and be spectator if only for an hour or so at this new and unknown but ancient world of the Indians. Thinking of which, it was borne in upon me that there is no trace in their costume, that I could see, of Spanish influence. For one is told that in the villages called after the twelve apostles, which is not true in itself, the costumes are derived from dress worn in the sixteenth century in Spain. This could apply more to the men's costume which we hardly saw, though in all the lake villages they are described as wearing short white trousers or pants with, variously, red or purple or black or white thin stripes, perhaps with little figures embroidered down them. This is basically the same as the Indian men's dress in Mexico. It is where knee-breeches, or some attempt at those, are worn by the men that we find an echo of Spanish Renaissance by way of the *Conquistadores*.

Sololá is quite a little town, and indeed capital of a department with a large hospital, I took it to be, on its outskirts. We looked in the church which was most uninteresting. On every week-day but Friday, this town, like many of the villages, is but an empty scene without the actors. For in fact Sololá is famous for its male costume, particularly that of the district mayors or *alcaldes*: red shirts and white pants with red stripes, but the two peculiarities are their black and white knitted handbags and shiny black straw hats. The shamans or Chuch-Cajaus are described as having hats of black-dyed palm leaf, with a gay ribbon and their *tzute* or handkerchief tied round the brim. They, also, wear aprons and red sashes. But of all this there was no sign that day; and a few policemen and some old men hanging about under an arcade seemed to be the only people in Sololá.

The road continued to climb higher past farm-houses with turkeys gobbling at the back, and always, or nearly always, a loom at work in front of the house and in full view from the road. There were pinewoods, and now and then a gully with bigger trees in its hollow which had orchids growing in them. But, in general, it was country not of leaf, but of the pine needle; and in imagination one could hear the wind—a warm wind—blowing through the pine boughs.

Presently we met a procession coming along the road; a local saint's festival, but with exceedingly important-looking Indians walking in front of it. One could understand now what is meant when it is said there are aristocratic Indians in this countryside. They are rich farmers of ancient descent. The dignified Indians walking in front of the shrine may have been *alcaldes* except that they did not carry silver-headed staffs. It is an upland country on top of everything, a kind of pine-clad weald or downs, but with rifts in it, and the distant cones of the volcanoes. We had been wondering where the procession came from for there was no village in sight when, suddenly, a few miles further on we were in a town of low white houses, through an empty square with a church in it, then down a cobbled lane to a doorway, and it is the Mayan Inn at Chichecastenango.

This is an oasis, in no desert, but a land of pines and costumes and volcanoes. Indeed, it takes a little time to recover from the surprise of finding it. In my own experience it is only paralleled by the hotel in the forest of Bussaco in Portugal, also in pinewood country, but I am talking of twenty-five or thirty years ago when hotels were few and far between in Portugal. The Mayan Inn, started some years ago by Mr Clark of Clark's Tours, has a deserved reputation. To my delight a jacaranda was in full bloom in one of the courts, with a captive macaw living in its branches. The hotel is a one-storeyed building spreading over several patios, and we had rooms in the two-floored annexe over the lane. All the rooms have pieces of old Colonial furniture, and there are wood fires in the bedrooms which are very necessary for the nights are cold. Here we came instantly across a change of costume for the houseboy attached to us, who had the sturdy build of a footballer, wore the local dress. We could hear him coming a long way off because his sandals squeaked. He wore dark blue shorts in a peasant edition of knee-breeches quite different from the short pants of Lake Atitlán, and a dark blue jacket with much embroidery. Spaniard like, he was always folding up and throwing his blanket over his shoulder, and his red *tzute* was tied into a turban with the tassels hanging from its corners. He was not in the least Red Indian, but Mongol of feature and like a cheerful, but big Gurkha. I came to think of him as a Gurkha footballer in some kind of fancy dress.

It was curious to be somewhere where the nights were cold again. With a wood fire burning, and more logs to put upon the flames.

As it was early in the week with no market day until Thursday w
had the inn to ourselves. There were but two other persons staying ir
it. We would go up early and sit by the wood fire, and yet all the tim
the jacaranda was in full flower only a few feet away, and the macaw
was 'sleeping out' without an overcoat. But a sad and personal dis
appointment was the marimba music. I had heard a marimba band eigh
years before this playing under the arcades in the square at Puebl
(in Mexico), and from that moment, or indeed long before then, hac
determined in my mind that the marimba music must be one of the
delights and wonders of Guatemala. In the Mayan Inn one coulc
hear it all day long upon the radio from Guatemala City. But no
once did they play a good tune. The repertoire was the cheapest sor
of Central American cinema or salon music. I had hoped for Mexican,
if not local Indian tunes. These must certainly exist; or what othei
music is heard when 'dozens of marimbas from nearby villages' are
brought to the market-place at Chichecastenango for the fiesta of St
Thomas, which is in December, and are played night and day? There
is something peculiarly exciting in the sound of a marimba, as though
it expresses the tropical fruits and flowers and the volcanic air. More
dulcet in tone, it is on the same principle as the Hungarian cymbalon,
only performed on by four players at once, and I have often thought
what exciting music could be composed for it. But in default of that I
had to console myself with reading an interview in a local paper with
one of the last marimba-makers, an old man who gave interesting
details of the rare and seasoned woods he used. The keys are made of a
reddish wood called *hormigo*, frames are of mahogany, and resonators
of cedar; the hammers or mallets are of quince-wood. A year, or even
two years' work is necessary in order to make a good marimba, and
the processes can be little less technical than those required to build a
harpsichord.

It was full moon while we were at the Mayan Inn and the nights
were loud with dog-fights. There had been a particularly noisy 'free
for all' dog-fight at Lake Atitlán which recalled the worst scenes of
bullying at an English private school, the victim being a weak and
inoffensive white terrier which was set upon by four or five big
mongrels, but that was in the late afternoon. At Chichecastenango
zero hour was one a.m. Precisely at that moment for three successive
nights there was loud drumfire-barking in the valley below, followed

by a concerted rush up the hill to try and get into the hotel garden. This was defended by a deep baying bark from the floor below, and a rushing about as though struggling to be over the side and grappling with them; in fact a boarding-party as in one of Nelson's sea-fights. But, obviously, windows and doors were shut and there was no contact. It was some other wretched dog they were after, and with utmost ferocity. If one looked out of the window the moon was not high enough yet and only lit the white houses opposite on the other side of the valley. Its depths were still in darkness. When the barking and yelping had become intolerable I would clap my hands two or three times, as loud as possible, trying to imitate a gun going off, and there would be instant silence on top of a mad scurrying to get away.

Night after night, what had started as a moonlit serenade I interrupted just in time before it became a slaughter. Somehow the serenading of cats is more appropriate to moonlight than that of dogs; but standing at the window in the Guatemalan moonlight what I would have liked to hear was marimba music coming from the square. Both sorts of marimbas; the village kind with a range of little more than an octave, and no half-tones or 'black keys'; and the big marimbas that are played in pairs and cover nearly ten octaves between them. And not only both kinds of marimbas, but as many of them as possible, all playing different Mexican and Indian popular tunes at the same time. I could have listened to that all night long.

In the morning at Chichecastenango there would be twenty or thirty zopilotes on the roofs of outbuildings or hopping about in the backyards. These scavengers or black 'police birds', about as big as a raven only thinner and without a raven's air of wisdom or his glossy feathers, are carnivores, and at night, I suppose, perch in their platoons or posses on the trees. I can hear the flapping of their wings, now, as one of them jumps up and makes a grab for something noxious that another of the zopilotes thinks he has pounced on for himself.

But now for the plaza or market square which is almost empty this morning because it is not market day. There is only a booth selling lemonade and Coca-Cola—in Lima it was Inca-Cola!—and a couple of Indian women who have probably walked all through the night to get here, and are asleep. Nothing, therefore, to delay us in the square and we walk towards the church, which is whitewashed and seventeenth century, and at the top of a flight of broken steps. On the lowest but one of the steps is a square object like a stone box built into the stair, and on top of it there are always ashes smouldering and smoking. It is copal incense that is burning, which is the most interesting thing in Chichecastenango; the copal incense of the ancient Mayans made from cactus, and burning here in front of the church to propitiate pre-Christian gods. I did not like to approach too near though you have to climb within a few feet of it in order to go into the church. It is in fact inconspicuous, and were one not told one might scarcely notice it. There appeared to be a man in charge of it; but at other times it seemed to be unattended, and as though the Indians brought up their own copal offerings and put them on the hot ashes.

How this pagan rite has survived is a mystery perhaps only explained by distance from the nearest Holy Office of the Inquisition. But Guatemala is unique in the Catholic world in this respect, and it is hardly an exaggeration to call the Indians half-pagan and half-Christian. The centres of this bi-lateral worship are here in this village but, more still, at Momostenango, a village near San Francisco el Alto. It is at Momostenango that the striped blankets are made; also, that is where the ancient Mayan ceremony of the Uajxaquip-Báts is held every year on a particular day which comes in the two hundred and sixty day cycle of the Mayan sacred calendar. The name means 'Eight Monkey Day' and fifteen to twenty thousand Indians collect in Momostenango from all over Guatemala for this celebration of the Mayan New Year. The interesting point is that though the Indians have lost everything else of Mayan tradition from their ancestors, their lives are still calculated according to the Mayan calendar, which has been kept only by oral tradition without written records, and is an era of their own, rigorously preserved and dating its beginning from a time unknown. Each eight and a half months the Uajxaquip-Báts comes round again; and the ceremony starts with prayers in the village church on the previous evening, and then the Indians start off at dawn for the pagan altars in the hills. These are a little way from the city at a place called Chuti-Mesabal or Little Broom, and are small mounds of broken crocks and sherds with copal incense burning on them. Here the men and women shamans or warlocks (Chuch-Cajaus) take their red seeds and pebbles of quartz and crystal out of their bags and invoke the world god of the Mayans, acting as sorcerers, witch doctors, and fortune tellers. One would give a lot to see three hundred of the shamans practising their pagan rites at Momostenango, or at another village nearby called Santa María Chiquimula where are copal altars and quemaderos, or 'burning places' for copal, but in the words of one writer 'visitors are definitely not invited to the ancient rituals'.

It must be the oddest and most unlikely spectacle in the whole of the Catholic world to see copal incense burning on the church steps at Chichecastenango. Even as we went up the steps into the church, a shaman lit a twig of copal at the hot ashes and held it in the fire. The whole floor of the church was covered with flower petals, as, later in the year it would be with corn seeds; but this most curious of churches, other than that, has nothing interesting in it. The old Dominican monastery next door has a flowering patio, and was the home of a much loved priest who spent his life among the Indians. Also, one of the few remaining Mayan manuscript books, the famous Popol-Vuh, was discovered there. When we came down the steps, just opposite at the other end of the square a temporary chapel was being built for some church festival. Indians were putting up poles and hanging garlands, and the copal incense was already smoking on a quemadero at the door.

We were given closer contact with the ancient religion on a walk that evening. I shall always remember the experience which amounted to little or nothing, but it had something so moving and beautiful about it. We had been told there was a pagan statue on the hill opposite, before which there was always copal incense burning. We had to walk through the square again, past the little smoking altar, and then down a long lane to the right which soon led out into the open country. Down, down into the valley where the dogs had barked in the moonlight, along a winding stony path, past farm-houses with old Indian women sitting at the door in the evening sunlight, and then between high green banks which reminded me of lanes in Tuscany, with the same smell of pine needles and, but for their embroidered dresses and darker skins, much the same peasants coming home, the day's work done.

Where the land climbed again beyond the valley we had to cross a ploughed field in order to take another path. In a house just here lived, we had been told, a famous mask-maker, and we stopped there to look in at his door. It was like the theatre 'prop' room in an opera house making ready for a pantomime. But the masks much resembled

those we had seen in Bolivia and belonged, so to speak, to the same
mythology. They are used in their dances, and, as in Bolivia, are often
in satire on the Spanish conquerors. Whether true, or not, it is said
that one favourite mask portrays the red hair of the *Conquistador* of
Guatemala, Don Pedro de Alvarado, a phenomenon the Indians had
not come across before. When we set off again from the mask-maker
we were joined by a little girl about nine years old with the romantic
name of Clorinda. A name of ballet association for Clorinda is the
heroine of the old ballet of *Le Diable Boiteux* ('The Devil on Two
Sticks'). Was not our charming maid in Lima, who came from Iquitos
on the Amazon, called Paquita, another ballet name!

And now we set off for the arduous part of our climb. Across another
field, and then to the foot of an exceedingly steep hill. A zigzag
'monkey-walk' climbed about half-way up this hill. And now we began
to feel the altitude and had to take it slowly. Talking, meanwhile, to
Clorinda, who only knew a little Spanish, but had a fair skin and quite
fair hair and eyes, and must have been a *mengala*, as they are called, of
mixed Spanish and Indian blood. But, also, it was exceedingly hot for
the setting sun shone straight across the valley at us. Presently the path
stopped, and an almost vertical zigzag climb came instead, with huge
stones here and there covered with slippery moss and so steep that one
had to cling on to twigs of trees and clumps of grass. It was here that
Clorinda made herself useful holding on to my wife's hand. And soon
walking in front and leading her, stone by stone.

The hill was a pinewood from top to bottom. Walking ahead of
them I got so far in front that I could no longer hear their voices and
only the wind in the branches. But, at last, it was a straight climb and
we were coming to the top. On to a flat plateau with pine trees everywhere and a path, or what looked like one, leading along the flat
ground covered with pine needles. The others joined me after some
minutes during which I had looked round into the shadows and
listened to that sunset wind in the boughs. After waiting a little to
get our breath we hardly knew where to go next, but Clorinda
pointed ahead, and we followed her along that soft earth and through
the undergrowth. The briars might have been those of blackberry
bushes, till one thought of it and remembered why we had come
here and that we were on a hill top in the semi-tropics. There was a
little clearing just ahead and I walked on towards it. Just as I got to

it there was a rustling of leaves and branches and I saw two men who had been stooping in front of something get up and run away. The boughs had scarcely swung back again from their passage when we were in the clearing.

A little, rudely carved stone statue, hardly in human semblance, stood there with heaped twigs and broken bits of pots around it, and there was copal incense burning. The two men must have put it there on the ashes only a few seconds before. It was the altar of Turkaj, the pagan idol of this countryside, upon the Pascual Abaj mountain; and there was no more we could do than look at it, wait for a few moments, and then turn and walk away. It was the descent we dreaded, and the likelihood of a sprained ankle, or worse, which might keep one laid up right at the end of our long journey. But what an unlikely adventure of only a moment or two into the ancient pagan world! I remembered the stone altar at Eaton Hall with the inscription *Nymphis et Fontibus* which belonged to the Roman legion who were stationed at Chester. Was this too, an altar to nymphs and waters of the pinewood? For pagans all over the world have worshipped the primitive forces of nature. And we turned and followed Clorinda through the wood, and down the steep descent, my wife letting Clorinda lead her step by step. Then across the fields and towards home, meeting on the way the old lady who was her grandmother, and with her permission took Clorinda to a shop, near by, where we bought her a bright pink ribbon for her hair.

When we got back, stir and bustle for tomorrow's market had already started. The first of the market people were arriving, and more would be coming to join them through the night. For it has to be explained that Chichecastenango is what is called an 'empty village', that is to say, very few people are living in it for five days of the week. They come into market from the hills but, also, it is a great place for travelling packmen who bring in their loads from all over the country. No one thinks twice of walking the whole night to get here. Going up to my room I looked out of the window to see if the Indian was squatting beside the bell in the church belfry. And there he was. He seemed to be at his post most of the day. Surely he must be another of the shamans, the Chuch-Cajaus, like his companion below who tended the copal altar on the church steps, a shaman and not an ordinary bell-ringer? Now and again he would lift his hammer

and strike out one, or two, or more notes of the bell, which might have
some special meaning. But for most of the time he squatted up there
like a statue of the Buddha. However, he has other duties. On the
fiesta of St Thomas, which is in December, a rope is strung up to the
belfry, and Tsijolaz a wooden figure of a little man on a white horse
with a necklace of silver coins rides up and down it, while squibs and
firecrackers go off in a basket under the horse. This is the prayer-
carrier of the ancient Mayans, metamorphosed. And at this fiesta
the 'flying-game' of the Mayans is to be seen in front of the church
at Chichecastenango. A high pole or volador is set up with ropes coiled
round the top of it. Two Indians at a time climb the pole, and swing
round and round it from the ropes, looping higher and higher till the
cable unwinds entirely and they touch ground. This ancient 'flying-
game' of the time and space-mad Mayans is supposed to have been in
imitation of the movements of the planets. No race of the past would
have been more interested in our space-rockets than the ancient
Mayans! Probably enough so to be mindless of its possible consequences.

Early in the night many Indians have already set up their tents and
stalls in the market-place. In strange silence, though, and without
the shouting and singing that would go on all night long in Italy. But
arrival is in the night air and the excitement makes it impossible to
sleep. I am looking forward to seeing the costume of Chichecastenango,
a more elaborate version of that worn by the Gurkha 'footballer' in
attendance on us. It is a costume with all sorts of symbolic differences
of rank and purpose. Even the tasselled caps have meaning, those with
a white ground being only worn by shamans and by the Aj-Kijs who
are astrologers; while the jackets worn by the local aristocrats, rich
farmers, have purple and orange fringes for rain and zigzag designs to
portray lightning. Corkscrew spirals beginning under the arms and
going up to the throat portend public orators, while a sunburst with a
gold coin in the middle is the sign of a Chuch-Cajau or shaman. And
everyone, whoever he may be, has a folded blanket on his left shoulder.
The *huipiles* of the women of Chichecastenango are red on white,
but there is not such an impression of red as at Santiago Atitlán, and
their skirts are of dark blue stripes, while their *serviletes* or kerchiefs
are in all colours.

But I shall not attempt a description of tomorrow's Indian encampment in the square. It is better left to the imagination. So I close

Mayan Indian woman of Yucatán

Garden of hotel at Chichén-Itzá

now with Chichecastenango, mentioning but one more memory of
it of which is the covering of fresh pine needles upon the floors. These
are renewed every few days in the houses and give a marvellous,
mountain freshness. To see a whole floor deep in the green needles
was a new experience to me. I noticed it particularly in a shop which
sold the local textiles, and as it is new every few days it is much cleaner
than rush matting. I will never forget the pine needles of Chichecastenango. But though I forbear to write about the market, having
said too much already about Indian markets in Peru and Bolivia, I
give some further notes about costumes, for it is in this respect that
Guatemala is unique among South American countries, and indeed
exceptional the world over.

There are an immense number of villages with their own distinctive
costume, perhaps as many as two hundred and fifty of them, all told.
But, of course, a small number of these, perhaps twenty in all, are
outstanding, and it is of these that I now try to give some information,
omitting any that have been already mentioned. A beginning has
been made at recording them by Mr Frederick Crocker, an American
architect living at Atitlán who has restored in beautiful taste several
of the old houses at Antigua. Two albums of his coloured drawings
have been published, and he has made a much greater number of
drawings, but the completion of it is a task which would occupy a
lifetime. There are fabrics of astonishing beauty. In Antigua we were
shown a bluish-purple textile bought off a peasant woman in some
nameless village. It would have been of outstanding tastefulness and
beauty in any age or time. The purchase of such things is often made
difficult for the very reason noticed by Maudslay in his *A Glimpse at
Guatemala*,[1] that the wearer may only possess the one *huipil* she is
wearing, and another still in the making. There are now a number of
shops all over the country that sell the textiles, which are often specially
woven for them, but it is not axiomatic that these projects are in the
wisest hands. When a note of 'artiness' creeps in, the stuffs are doomed
to lose their Indian force and elegance.

The costume villages are all, or nearly all, in a line between Guatemala
City and the Mexican border. One or two of them are near Antigua;
notably San Antonio Aguas Calientes, only four miles away, which

[1] A misleading title for it is a large and handsome work printed on hand-made paper (1899).
It has colour plates of a few textiles.

Q

has a reputation for the finest weaving in the whole country. *Huipiles*
are on white or red or blue, and dresses are pink, green and blue with
black designs. A pair of villages only a few miles from Guatemala City
are San Juan and San Pedro Sacatapéquez. The former village is
famous for its carnations which are carried to market in baskets on the
women's heads. Their *huipiles* are of wide red and yellow stripes with
bright yellow and purple figures on them. A second *huipil* is worn
as a shawl. At San Pedro the *huipil* is white with a tree of life in red and
purple on it, or the double-headed eagle of the Habsburg, Charles V,
in the same colours. A folded *huipil* worn on the head gives the
effect of a turban. Ten volcanoes can be seen from clearings in the
pinewoods.

San Martín Jilotepeque is a village on a road into the mountains
off Chimaltenango, turning off to the right half-way to Lake Atitlán,
through pine woods and orchid country. Here, the most beautiful
according to some opinions of all the *huipiles* are to be seen at the
market, embroidered on white or blue grounds. Comolapa is another
village, near-by, but only to be reached by a cul-de-sac leading off the
main road. Beautiful *huipiles* are worn here, too, generally of red
stripes on white or brown cotton, with bands of designs in different
colours on them. Coming down the high road as far as Sololá, above
Lake Atitlán, there is the remote and unspoilt town of Nahualá, described as being only second in interest to Chichecastenango. This is
where the mill-stones are made which are carried by packmen all over
the country, and the town is famous for its marimbas. At the market,
men are in black, and the women in blue skirts, scarlet sashes, and huge
tasselled head-dresses.

Totonicapán is a large town on the Pan-American Highway beyond
Sololá, and rather more than a hundred miles from Guatemala City.
This is an Indian centre famous for its carved masks, its dances—
and its marimbas. How willingly on this wet August day in England
would I be listening to them! The market must be a wonderful sight;
with white 'ceremonial' *huipiles*, and silk headbands which have
silver-wrapped tassels falling to the shoulder. Beyond are villages,
San Cristóbal with a fine church, silvered saints and golden altars,
more carved masks; and San Francisco el Alto in high, clear air, three
volcanoes in full view, and a famous weaving centre in the tie-and-dye
technique.

Eventually, along the same road we would come to Quezaltenango, called after the quetzal bird, and the second biggest town in the republic, now modernized, but there is an enchanting view of it by 'Mr' Catherwood in Stephen's *Central America* (1841), a view of it which he calls a 'plan'. He mentions the Indians wearing 'large black cloaks with broad-brimmed felt sombreros, and the women in white frocks' (*huipiles?*); 'some wearing a sort of turban of red cord plaited with the hair. The bells were hushed and wooden clappers sounded in their stead. As we rode through, armed to the teeth, the crowd made way in silence'. . . . The 'plan' gives the Cathedral, the colonnade in front of it, 'the stone-paved plaza with a fine fountain in the middle, commanding a magnificent view of the volcano and mountains around'. Quezaltenango, with an eighty per cent Indian population, is still noted for the beauty of its women, who are to be seen in yellow and purple *huipiles* and blue skirts with white stripes. Almolonga, only a mile or two away, where flowers are grown for market, has one of the most intricate and elaborate men's costumes in the country, though rarely seen, and the women are in white and pink *huipiles*.

San Martín Sacatapéquez, better known as San Martín Chile Verde, is a village of very pure Indian blood, on the Pan-American Highway nearing the Mexican border. The men are in long shifts or gowns, cream with red stripes; long black cloaks or overgowns of black wool, and their red *tzutes* or head-dresses may reach down to their knees. Olintepeque, another Indian village, much nearer (only three miles) from Quezaltenango, has women in blue *huipiles* with magenta stripes, and another *huipil* over that, in three panels, bright red with white stripes in the centre, and the colours the other way round in the side panels. There is, confusingly, another and different San Pedro Sacatapéquez featuring yellow *huipiles* with purple designs on them and skirts in different shades of yellow and orange. This is far away from Quezaltenango on another road leading to the Mexican border. Going north again from Chichecastenango, we would come to Sacapulas where the *huipiles* are white, green and blue skirts are worn, and tasselled head-dresses which one authority compares to those worn in the island of Bali. Nebaj, not far from there, has white *huipiles* with men and horses and ducks in blue and green and purple, tasselled yellow and white head-dresses, red and purple shawls, and skirts of red and yellow stripes. And our survey can end, either at San Marcos near the Mexican border where the dresses are yellow which is unusual in Guatemala; or at Todos Santos, far away in the mountains, with the last part of the journey only to be done on horseback. In this village the men wear baggy white trousers with alternate broad and thin red stripes, and a thin vertical red stripe to 'square' them, woollen breechclouts like the Swiss *landsknechts* of the Middle Ages, topped off by a straw hat with cock's feathers in it.

The age and origin of these costumes is difficult to determine, as it is indeed with all folk costume. But two things are certain; that it would be a mistake to look for a strong Spanish influence, and that there is little or nothing that is ancient Mayan in them. They have grown independently of either of these sources, and probably did not reach their maturity till late in the last century. There is a great difference between the accounts by Stephens in 1840 and those of Maudsley, writing fifty years later in 1890, though the one was no more observant than the other. It was the slow growth of centuries which had a sudden flowering. Or was it there when the Spaniards came? One cannot believe this. But, rather, where such things have had their florescence anywhere in the world, it would seem the seeds have lain dormant for a long time, and then of a sudden and for no explicable reason they have sprouted. Thus, there is nearly always something in them that can be traced back a long way, and the rest may be fantasy and new invention. This seems to be the case in countries in Europe where there is local costume, in Hungary, or Czechoslovakia, or Roumania; and it is the same process where there are parallels to it, as with Gypsy *flamenco* music in Spain. Details like the belts or the sandals may be Mayan, but not the whole scheme of things in all their embroidery and colours. The costume of Guatemala is one of the beautiful, living things left in the world; and if the *huipil* has been mentioned too often in the last few paragraphs I believe this reiteration of a name would be condoned by anyone who saw the *huipiles* like a sylph's wings that we first saw at Antigua, and has followed, if only in the reading of them, the Indian variations upon the *huipil* up and down the Isthmus from Honduras to Mexico.

When it was a question of leaving Chichecastenango we were in difficulties because it seems there is only one car in the town, and that was already engaged. We had been charged a quite outrageous sum for the short journey from Lake Atitlán. It was between eighteen and twenty pounds in English money, and now we were forced to pay a like amount for a journey of about the same length from Chiche-castenango to Guatemala City. Nearly forty pounds in all for two journeys of not more than eighty or ninety miles each. Of course, it is cheaper if several persons share the car. But there is no alternative. There are no railways serving these towns; and one cannot travel with a lot of luggage in a motor-bus full of Indians, however beautiful their costumes may be. I had hoped at least that we might be returning to Guatemala City by another road, but with the excuse, first, that the Pan-American Highway was *not* open to traffic and, later, that it *was* open, we found ourselves after a few miles joining on to the same road from Lake Atitlán that we had travelled before. The only consolation was in having been lucky enough to get to Guatemala at all when we had never intended originally to come here, and in the marvellously beautiful landscape. We passed the same cliffs with odd holes in them which were the nests of the beautiful blue pigeons that were flying about, and we picnicked in an idyllic, indeed an Olympian vale of pines and other, orchid-bearing, trees beside a running stream, on a fragrant lawn of pine-needles, and after passing several volcanoes in review, reached Guatemala City early in the afternoon.

We stayed there in the New American Hotel, without contretemps beyond the steel curtain-rod falling within a millimetre of my head and dragging a large section of the wall down with it, when I went to pull the curtain on the first morning. This provoked merriment among the personnel, but could have been more serious. Guatemala City is nearly as difficult for locating an address in as Tokyo. What for instance is to be made of 3^d Ave 14 B 1 Zone 11? But, at least, the streets are numbered. As usual, much of our time was spent in the offices of air companies where, at first, even the existence of the aeroplane we were to travel in was denied. And in the course of these visits we made friends with a little old woman, the top of whose head did not come up as high as the counter. She was a jocular character, full of quips and jokes, and told me she was ninety-six when I asked her age. And this was apparently not far wrong. She lived in one of the convents, and got her livelihood by buying air-tickets for the nuns. A party of them, I gathered, were off soon for Rome but leaving her behind.

Guatemala City has been so often destroyed in earthquakes, the last big one being in 1917, when the whole town had to be rebuilt, that there is almost nothing old in it. The unique address system must date from this rebuilding. Perhaps the most charming sight in its streets is to see a child sitting on the pavement with a dozen or two of small green parrots for sale on his head and arms and shoulders, and in a basket in front of him. And, of course, the flower and fruit market is worth seeing. The churches, even with sugar syrup, cow's milk and white of egg mixed in the mortar to make their walls stronger, are without interest. But the Archaeological Museum, with a few valuable pieces of its own, and its skilful copies of the recently discovered Mayan frescoes at Bonampak, in the forests of Chiapas, gives the opportunity to consider ourselves lucky in that we are going from here to Yucatán.

This was to be our only chance of seeing the ancient Mayan cities. For there comes a moment, which for ourselves was somewhere between the eighteenth and twentieth air flight on this long journey, when one can take no more of it, and must keep the rest of the programme within set limits. We had, therefore, to decide not to embark on the flight to Tikal in the rain forest, where the Mayan ruins are not yet cleared of jungle and can be seen as Stephens and Catherwood saw the dead cities in the forests a hundred and twenty years ago. It is an hour and three-quarters' flight to the airstrip in the forest, and one stays at 'Jungle Lodge' in comfortable palm-roofed huts. We would have seen Flores on its island in Lake Petén, a modern town where nothing ancient is left but where the Mayans remained undisturbed by the Spaniards until 1697; and Tikal with a great open plaza and four pyramids, one of them more than two hundred feet high, as tall as a twenty-storey office building in New York. Deep in the rain forests, the ruins still covered with trailing lianas, and with epiphyte orchids growing high up in the tops of the mahogany and sapodilla trees, while parrots and painted toucans are on the wing. The mysterious, haunted character of the ruins, which is remarked upon by all who have seen them, must vanish under the restorer's hand, however well the work is done. We missed Tikal, and went instead to Yucatán.

Chapter Thirteen

•◆•◆•◆•◆•◆•◆•◆•◆•◆•◆•◆•◆•◆•◆•

CHICHÉN-ITZÁ

OF ALL IMPROBABLE PLACES TO be flying over the wilderness of Quintana Roo! Having passed near to, if not immediately over Tikal, and another Mayan ruined city Naxactún which is a few miles beyond it. Not long after that, crossing the border into Campeche, near to where Laguna Misteriosa spelt out on the map takes up nearly a hundred miles of space. But I would prefer it that we flew due north along the dotted line, that being the hypothetical border of Campeche and Quintana Roo, two provinces of Mexico, but there is both less and more to it than that.

In Campeche, just the name of another settlement Escarcega de Matamoros takes up half the width of the province, while in Quintana Roo there is a stretch of well over two hundred miles with no name marked on it at all. Only last year I had read a book recounting the adventures of two explorers who had pushed their way into this wilderness, seen unknown ruins, fought hand-to-hand with *Sarcorhamphus Papa* the white King vulture in order to secure him for a meal, and nearly died of thirst and hunger. I hoped we were flying over just this area of wilderness, only visited by chicle gatherers and into the border of Quintana Roo. What there may be down there to discover is still unknown. That there are, of a certainty, ruined cities makes it more exciting than any other unexplored area of land.

But the sky was beginning to darken just as the sun was setting, and it was no ordinary gathering of the shadows. A peculiar and smoky obscurity filling the heavens and turning the sunset sinister and lurid. No wind at all, because there was no movement in the clouds, but this premature thickening and darkening as of some unpleasant happening. No lights of Mérida below us but, at last, white houses, the whiter against that darkness, and we made safe landing at the capital of Yucatán.

That smoke-filled sky is in direct descent from the Mayans whose method of agriculture consisted in cutting down and burning patches of forest in order to achieve one- or two-year plantings of maize, by sowing the seed in the ashes, and then allowing the clearing to revert to jungle. This was the time of year (early March), when the process began, and it has often been suggested that the desertion of their cities and the supposed migration of the race from their Ancient Empire in Guatemala to the new Empire of Yucatán was due to this wasteful system which must end in famine. It now appears, though, that both regions were flourishing at the same time throughout the Classic Mayan Era. Every evening in March the sky is darkened with smoke all over Yucatán and there is a smell of burning in the air. It is a lurid, uneasy feeling to come down into this out of the sky.

What an excitement to be touching the soil of Mexico again which to my own taste—the works of art in Italy and Spain apart, and with them, I must own to it, the whole littoral of the Mediterranean—is the most thrilling country in the world! In Mexico again, but not entirely there, for Yucatán is different and apart. It gives one indeed the sensation of being in Yucatán and not in Mexico. From that first moment of coming out of the airport at Mérida with the crowd of other tourists, of being heaped with our luggage on top of us into a very small car, and driven into the town and to the hotel. Yucatán, which for a long time resisted integration with the larger country, is perhaps as different from the mass of Mexico as Texas is from the rest of the United States. Not that it is in any way like Texas. It is wholly Yucatán.

We drove through the streets, past the lit doors of churches to the hotel, or, rather, to the tourist office opposite, where, after some delay and a good deal of needless rushing and sudden luggage alarms, we transferred to a bigger car, for we were not staying the night at Mérida. We were going straight to Chichén-Itzá about seventy-five miles away. Mérida has suburbs which it takes some time to emerge from, and after that we were on the longest, dullest road ever known, straight as a Roman road, and featureless. In the twilight one could see to either side the colourless agave fields, blue-green by day, cacti from which the henequén fibre is made, and once we came through a village with a tall gaunt church which had something of the

Churrigueresque of Mexico about it. Later, there was even a hill with a large and picturesque village with conical huts and many palm trees. Beyond that all was straight again and so it went on for some three hours, until after nine o'clock at night when we saw a huge pyramidal shape against the darkness, and certain other shadowy forms, stopped at a bright lit stair and were in Chichén-Itzá.

There can be few greater changes in the historical scene than between our arrival that night in the manner typical of the modern tourist and the sojourn of Stephens and 'Mr' Catherwood only a hundred and twenty years ago among the ruins. They spent weeks or months in a cell in one of the temples, while we stayed with well over a hundred other tourists in a comfortable hotel. But even that would not be so much of a surprise to them as our means of getting here; that we flew here and came down out of the air. It is this which, as in the parallel instance of talking to Hilary or the Sherpa Tensing of flying over Mt Everest in an aeroplane when they had climbed to the top on foot, makes one a little shy of setting down one's own adventures, especially after the thousands of persons who in recent years have been to Yucatán. But we came to it immediately out of Peru, not yet sated with the megalithic walls of Cuzco; and after an amateur, or, in the older sense of the word, a dilettante appreciation of architecture and works of art all over the world, this was a first contact with the most utterly strange and original architecture in the world. It was this aspect of it that most impressed Stephens and Catherwood who came to Yucatán fresh from Ancient Egypt and the wonders of the Nile Valley; the utter and entire strangeness of the Mayan ruins. Let me, therefore, try to write of them, having seen them with my own eyes and read all I can of them, but in the mood of our having arrived next on the scene after Stephens and 'Mr C.' with no other tourists or other travellers in between.

The hotel at Chichén-Itzá, called the Maya Land Lodge and sprung up out of the jungle, like seaside Arcadia, or pier-pavilion above the storm, as mysterious as that—we have only to think that to the ancient Mayans it would be more interesting than their own temples and pyramids, intact and working—had 'Indian' porters at the door who ran up the stairs like mountain-goats carrying our luggage, and wore, as did all the males on the hotel staff, the ancient Mayan sandals as shown on bas-reliefs and paintings; this, not through affectation but because all the local 'Indians' do the same.[1] It is a hotel in the tropics; like some hotel, I thought, in Malaya or the Dutch East Indies. We are low down, only a few feet above sea level, in Yucatán which juts right out into the Gulf of Mexico. It was hotter that night than anything I have experienced since spending the latter part of August in Kyoto.

The hotel rooms were large with great open balconies that looked onto the garden where under the lights one could see the trunks of huge tropical trees. It being near to ten o'clock we came straight down to dinner, accepting gratefully a complimentary 'Maya Land cocktail' made with rum, and emboldened by that, ordering an oyster cocktail made of oysters, from Campeche, perhaps just because we were told they came from there for the mere name of it. But there is something in the Mexican air that makes one reckless. Eight years before, in Shreveport, Louisiana, and starting that night for Mexico for the first time, we had been warned to eat nothing but fried bananas, and yet on our first evening in Mexico City we ate oysters with no ill results. It was the same in Chichén-Itzá as in Mexico City; and we ate oysters from Campeche all the time we were in Yucatán. But there was one drawback to our late arrival. Thinking the room would be unoccupied, the floor-boy had neither 'flitted' the room nor given us mosquito-nets. And instead of enjoying the restful night we longed for after our travels we were kept awake all night long, and severely bitten, by giant mosquitos. I killed thirteen of them, despatching them against the wall, but next morning when I made a complaint and hoped to show the manager their corpses the floor-boy had removed all traces of them. It can have been little different, I thought, those few days back at Bogotá when Ordóñez and Dominguín had fought *mano a mano* in the bull-ring and between their bouts the arena had been raked afresh with sand.

In the morning we were far too exhausted to join the sightseeing tour which was to start at eight o'clock, the early hour being imperative because of the extreme heat. We had been travelling incessantly for nearly three months and were quite tired out. But in the end, it was to our advantage for the elderly and extremely intelligent guide, an almost pure-blooded Mayan Indian, took us round alone after the

---

[1] In Chiapas the Indian men wear sandals with high leather backs, 'indicating caste', as on the Mayan bas-reliefs.

other tourists had finished and were resting. Instead, we changed our verandah room which I thought must be modelled on those at the famous Raffles Hotel, with its table and chairs on the balcony inviting a clapping of hands and ordering of 'Singapore Slings', for a Gauguin-style, thatched South Sea Island hut with bathroom which was much more comfortable in spite of a bird nesting in the rafters, and which was approached from under a Miltonian banyan:

> 'The fig-tree; not that kind for fruit renown'd,
> But such as at this day, to Indians known,
> In Malabar or Decan spreads her arms
> Branching so broad and long, that in the ground
> The bended twigs take root, and daughters grow
> About the mother tree, a pillar'd shade
> High over-arch'd and echoing walks between;
> There oft the Indian herdsman, shunning heat,
> Shelters in cool, and tends his pasturing herds
> At loop-holes cut through thickest shade.'

We could spend all morning in looking at the tropical trees, first recognizing the same thin, long-legged black birds, of unknown name, we had seen at Lima, and again at Antigua. Here they were splashing and preening themselves by the pool. There were two sorts of flowering trees I had not known before; a huge giant of a tree filling one half of that part of the garden with its enormous smooth-barked trunk and great boughs hung now with some kind of golden cobs or nuts, called, so far as I could make out from the 'Indian' gardener, a *maculín*. The other tree was much smaller and lighter, though it rose to some thirty or forty feet and stood above the first floor balconies. It had a silvery or white stem, and a blossom that was half peach tree and half *laurier-rose* or oleander, made no more intelligible when I was told it was a 'pic', pronounced like 'peach', but apparently this beautiful flowering tree is Mexican. We did not come across it anywhere else and I would like to feel certain of its name. It is of graceful growth; and its soft pink rose colour in a tropical garden would modulate between the flamboyant or the Uganda Flame-tree in their ecstatic tones and the matchless, peerless jacaranda.[1]

[1] Our guide at Chichén-Itzá took me into an arbour in the garden covered with some kind of vine, and showed me the dead husk of one of its flowers which perfectly resembled a miniature parachute or umbrella.

At five in the afternoon we joined the sightseeing party and went to see the ruins. We had missed the first part of the programme but benefited, as I have said, by being shown it later by ourselves. We were taken first by way of some undetermined heaps of ruins to the round tower called the Caracol (Spanish word for 'snail') because of the spiral stair that winds inside it. Even from a distance you know this building had a purpose and was in use for some particular reason. It stands on a high stone platform with a stone stairway leading up to it from one stone landing to another; this stated purposely because one of the impressions of Chichén-Itzá is its dead weight of stone. The stair ramps are stone serpents with projecting heads to confirm that this is the serpent kingdom as much as at the temples of Angkor. At this moment, landed at one or other by a hazard which is now possible though inconceivable before in human history, we might be looking from this platform at other fantastic buildings near by, and for these few minutes we have been among the ruins, it could be that we only know we are among the Mayans and not the Khmers because we see stone serpents but no stone Buddhas.

But now the savage and utter strangeness of all around, become more peculiar still now that it has been expertly restored, strikes in upon one, and it is time to stoop and go inside the stone snail-shell of the Caracol which at once is not a little alarming and sinister in construction. That inner core of the Caracol and the narrow, narrow stairway made obviously for nearly naked 'Indians' of small stature; the slits of windows sited in very particular directions for this was in fact an observatory, and the planning of the Caracol was in order to make the nocturnal darkness darker still for purposes of star-watching; it all begins to leave the impact of the Mayans upon one's mind. After seeing the Caracol at Chichén-Itzá it is no longer so surprising that the collapse of the Mayan civilization may have been due to revolts of the peasants against 'exotic religious developments such as the cult of the planet Venus with its excessive demands upon time and labour in matters of communal building and construction.[1] Astronomy, up to our own epoch the most abstract and inutile of all sciences, was the manic fever and failing of the Mayans.

The strict, if useless though utilitarian purposes of the Caracol called

---

[1] *The Rise and Fall of Maya Civilization*, by J. Eric S. Thompson, Victor Gollancz Ltd., London, 1956, p. 94.

The *Caracol* at Chichèn-Itzà, an observatory built *c.* AD 1000

for no ornament, in which respect this could have been an Inca, and not a Mayan building. But now we come down from the platform, and the next thing we see is what the Spaniards called Las Monjas or the Nunnery because of an old tradition that sacred virgins lived here, and because the number of small cells reminded the Spaniards of nunneries in Spain. That its purpose was almost certainly nothing of the sort does not make Las Monjas any less mysterious, and here we have a building in pure Mayan style of the Classical period for the Caracol is thought to show later, Toltec influence from Mexico. But the mystery of Las Monjas is that like nearly all other buildings of the Mayans it is not really a building at all but only a long covered passage, or, in the case of Las Monjas, two parallel corridors with a cell or two at either end. Such are the mysterious processes of Mayan architecture for they would put up solid masses of masonry with no other purpose than to hold smaller and useless structures on top of them. In other instances they would erect a building with small rooms or cells in it, and then fill them up to the ceiling with loose stones and rubble making of them what the Spaniard called *casas cerradas* or 'closed houses'. Or they would even put up a high wall for no reason at all with symmetrically spaced windows in it, looking from a distance like a blitzed or shattered factory or warehouse wall.

But all such considerations are as nothing in their strangeness compared to the extraordinary nature of the ornament. While it is true that in the Khmer temples of Angkor, also, there are no interiors other than long covered passages and small cells which are hardly even rooms, at least the bas-reliefs of elephants and chariots and warriors and dancing girls are a part, if an exotic one, of the ordinary human repertory, whereas there are things here that are truly out of experience and strange. The eastern façade of Las Monjas which has only one door in it may be taken as an example. This door has two masks on either side of it cut out in a kind of stone mosaic, while above them are larger masks and over the door itself, in a rounded frame of stone, is the seated figure of a man with an enormous plume of feathers on his head.

The little building at the angle of Las Monjas and only a few feet away from it, called too obviously La Iglesia, is even more peculiar. It is indeed the pure and perfect specimen of Mayan architecture, so utterly incomprehensible until quite recently, that no one in the literal sense of the phrase could make head or tail of it. La Iglesia starts off from the ground simply enough, but becomes immensely complicated in ornament and top heavy although it is in fact no larger in bulk than—what shall I say?—a very heavily loaded lorry. Or, to those acquainted, it is about the size of an early Irish stone oratory. Over the door it has a frieze of simple stone squares, and above that huge masks, but it is the hook-nosed protuberances jutting out from the corners that are extraordinary, and at first sight, quite inexplicable. The texture of the stone, and something in the technique of the ornament which is either cut out, or made of other stones applied to the stone bed of the building, gives it an effect as though it was all cast of one piece, and makes one to consider it like some huge and archaic Chinese bronze. For in the light of this it becomes big again, and now those hook-nosed objects are the handles by which to lift it. But in fact 'they undoubtedly represent' the god Chac or the rain-god. Early travellers mistook its hook-nose for an elephant's trunk, and seeing an Indian origin in this, caused widespread archaeological confusion. But, in fact, this long-nosed mask does not at all resemble an elephant's trunk and is more suggestive of some form of bird-abstraction, reversed macaw or toucan in inspiration, as if the rain-god Chac was symbolized as half-god, half-human, in which connection it is interesting to read the reconstruction of Mayan religious ceremonial by one authority, where the priest impersonating the rain-god wears the long-nosed mask of Chac and a head-dress of quetzal plumes to suggest the greenness of young corn and the new leaves green after the rain.[1]

The sky now darkened as on the previous evening, and again for that ancient Mayan reason of their crop rotation, and we were taken to the Temple of the Sculptured Panels which is nothing much in comparison with what we have just seen. This was the end of the day's tour, and while the others returned to the hotel we were able to go back with the guide and were shown some of the greater sensations of Chichén-Itzá. Crossing the road on which we had arrived last evening, the huge shape we had seen in the darkness now materialized itself as the great pyramid of El Castillo, of most formidable and emphatic weight upon the earth and in the giant canon of the Egyptian Pharoahs, but on that evening we only just looked at it and moved on to the Ball Court.

[1] J. Eric S. Thompson, op. cit., p. 196.

Before we reached that, there was another halt at the Temple of the jaguars, a small building in Mexican or rather Toltec style with a chamber under it, the walls and columns of which are all sculptured in bas-relief with traces of the original paint still showing. The interest of the warriors portrayed here is that they are the invading Toltecs who conquered Chichén-Itzá. They came from Tula in Mexico some eight hundred miles away where recent excavation has uncovered temples carved with identical warriors carrying the same weapons. The same cult of the jaguar and the serpent was common to both places; and all this confirms the legend of conquest by the mysterious Itza who were 'foreigners and spoke broken Maya' and were commanded by their leader Kukulcán, the 'feathered or quetzal serpent'. This is reported by Bishop Diego de Landa; while another early chronicler, the sixteenth-century Aztec noble Fernando de Alva Ixtlixochitl (it is irresistible to write down his name), even identifies Tollán, the city of the Itzas, as being on the site of Tula though no one paid any attention and Tula was not excavated until 1940.[1] Kukulcán is Mayan for Quetzalcoatl, the leader or cacique of Tula who was later deified and became god of vegetation and of the planet known to the west as Venus. So in this instance he was in all probability a historical personage and conquered Chichén-Itzá in the epoch ending A.D. 987; or it would be safe to say the city was under Toltec rule from about the year one thousand. Then began the great period of Chichén-Itzá, lasting through the eleventh, twelfth and thirteenth centuries, so that at its zenith when it had perhaps two hundred thousand inhabitants it was Toltec more than Mayan in character. But already when the Spaniards came to Yucatán in 1541 Chichén-Itzá had been almost deserted by its population. The buildings then, the Nunnery excepted, are not in pure Mayan style, and we have to wait for that until we get to Uxmal.

The Ball Court is typical of this Mexican influence which in ancient days was ever bloodthirsty and dramatic. Near by, in proof of that, we will find the Skull Rack or Tzompantli, of grisly *Dies Irae*, *Totentanz* import and association. But to the Ball Court of violent and haunting impression for this is one of the extraordinary places of the world! It is entirely empty on this darkening evening of the smoke-

---

[1] Eric S. Thompson, *op. cit.*, p. 105; and *Maya: the Riddle and Rediscovery of a Lost Civilization*, by Charles Gallenkamp, Fredrick Muller Ltd., London, 1960, p. 161-163.

thrown shadows, for it is the patches of forest afire all over Yucatán that cause this extra darkness and give the feeling that some fertility cult of burning or blood-letting is in the darkening air. We enter to find ourselves in an open space between two high and parallel stone walls giving the sensation that we are being watched or overlooked, not by a huge crowd but perhaps only one soft-tread, feather clad 'Indian'. The arena must be three hundred feet long, at least, and has stone benches along two sides reached by stairways which have ramps in the form of serpents with their heads emerging above the ends of the platform. And we are taken at once to look at the stone relief carved upon the front of what would be equivalent to the president's box, were this a bull-ring. One had best be prepared for something sinister and frightening, and it is difficult to make out the exact purport of the scene, but the players of the two teams are facing one another, seven ball players to each side, and a disk is hanging between them on which a skull is carved with a serpent's forked tongue issuing from its mouth. This is the sign or ideogram for speech. The first player of the right-hand team is kneeling, and has been beheaded by the leading player of the other team who holds an (obsidian?) knife in one hand and the decapitated head in the other. From the neck of the kneeling and headless man blood is flowing which is symbolized by serpents which metamorphose into plant stems that are burgeoning into flower. If we look up from the grisly scene, as always, even in their stone bas-reliefs, a-flutter with quetzal feathers in token of the plumed 'Indies', it is to see the trunk and head of a stone serpent with open jaws, the finial of the ramp above this grandstand.

The game was played with a ball of solid rubber, and the players were not allowed to use their hands, but only their hips, knees and elbows which were padded. Now looking up above us there is a stone ring projecting from the wall, and another one across the arena on the wall immediately opposite. This stone ring, like the other, is formed from the heads of two serpents with intertwining rattles. It would need only an amateur at any ball game to surmise that it would be very rarely indeed that a goal was scored and the ball struck from hip, knee or elbow through the little hole in the stone ring that is close in to the wall. One would guess that as at 'the wall of death' at circus or fun-fair the players would keep the ball running continually along either wall or other to thrill the spectators until the floor of the court

Chac-mul at Chichén-Itzá

Mayan women making tortillas, Yucatán

Above, Uxmal, Yucatán; *below*, Detail of façade at Uxmal, showing Mayan house

lost all importance, and as with 'the wall of death' where the performer circles round and round half-way up the wall of the pit, it was a breaking of the laws of gravity. Only thus could there be a chance of scoring a goal which, if only a few games were held in any one year might occur perhaps only once or twice in a *Katun*, the Mayan unit of time composed of seven thousand and two hundred days, or about twenty years. The ball game of the Mayans had in fact historical, mythological, even astronomical importance. On such occasions as a goal scored or a game won it would appear from the bas-reliefs that the chief player of the winning team sacrificed the loser by beheading him; but the Mexican cult of death and their inculcation with the notion that it was an honour to be sacrificed would make it no less probable that it was the loser who had the duty of beheading the leader of the winning team.

The Tzompantli or Skull Rack is not far away, its long platform carved with a monotonous relief of three rows of skulls stuck or impaled on poles. On other walls are eagles eating human hearts and feathered warriors holding human heads. It is a place of death. The *Conquistadores* were horrified to find these structures in full use when they arrived in Mexico. The Skull Rack at Tenochtitlán was a square block made up of thousands of human skulls threaded together, as in the bas-relief, upon poles. 'In contemporary drawings the black cavities of their orbits and nasal apertures suggest the marks on infernal dice.'[1] This structure here at Chichén-Itzá is a skull rack and there can be no doubt that it was used as such. The skulls of the sacrificial victims were exposed here in Mexican fashion; and were one to embark upon generalities concerning the 'Indians' in all parts of the Americas, it could be remarked that if feathers are their distinguishing mark compared with other races, from the Red Indian chieftain's crest of war eagles' quills falling from the back of his forehead quite down to his feet, to the Aztec Emperor's green cloak of quetzal tail feathers, or the feather tunics of the Incas made from parrots of Amazon, then it would be as true to say that in every race, one and all, they were obsessed with death. The death head or occiput was an important concept with them, from the scalps sought by Red Indians of the plains to the skull rack of the ancient Aztecs, and from the stalls of sugar skulls (*calaveras*) sold in the markets of modern Mexico upon

[1] *The Aztecs of Mexico*, by G. C. Vaillant, Penguin Books, 1950, p. 220.

R

All Soul's Day to the shrunken heads of Putumayo. Not only that, but all over Amerindia, and nowhere more then among the Maya, deformation of the head was practised.

Of which more later. But now it was too dark for sightseeing, and back in the Maya Land Lodge, where more hordes of tourists were arriving, preparations were on foot for folk dancing to be performed after dinner by the hotel staff. Our lilliputian waitress, rouged and mascara'd as any vedette of Odéon or Comédie Française, and with the tiniest hands and feet, was led forth again and again into the dance which seemed one chain of mazurkas, performed with a partner but never touching hands. They danced some ten feet away from each other, and as soon as she returned to her seat the master-of-ceremonies, one of the waiters, would go up to her again, touch her with a knotted handkerchief and she would dance once more with the same partner, exactly as described by Stephens. In fact it was a very pretty form of country dancing and could not but recall to any reader of *Incidents of travel in Yucatán* (1843), village balls described in places such as Ticul, where the cura Carillo was such a delightful character; 'where fresh meat can be procured every day; the *tienda grande*, or large store of Guzmán, would not disgrace Mérida; the bread is better than at the capital; altogether for appearance, society, and conveniences of living it is perhaps the best village in Yucatán, and famous for its bull-fights and the beauty of its *mestiza* women.'[1]

Where was Ticul? It looked on the map as though we might pass through it on the way to Uxmal. Impossible not to fall asleep in that Gauguin South Sea Island hut thinking of Stephens and of Catherwood, who had been a friend of Keats; and of other characters who had involved themselves in Yucatán even perhaps without going there, like the Irishman, Lord Kingsborough, who had ruined himself by publishing among other things the Dresden Codex, one of the only three surviving Mayan hieroglyphic books, in his *Antiquities of Mexico*, which he had printed in nine volumes between 1830 and 1848 at £175 a set, ending his days in consequence in a debtor's prison, and all because he thought the ancient Mexicans were descendants of the lost ten tribes of Israel. Or another strange character, Count Waldeck, whom a ruffianly character known to my family with tragical result, describes in a book of reminiscences as being pointed

[1] Volume I, p. 263.

out to him on the Boulevard des Italiens one summer day in Paris towards the end of the Second Empire with the remark to look carefully at him for he was well over a hundred years old. This was in fact the truth. Count Jean Frédéric Waldeck who was born in 1766, had served under Napoleon in Egypt and in Chile in the War of Liberation with Lord Cochrane, was already sixty-six years old when he became interested in Aztec and Mayan archaeology in 1832. He visited Yucatán, and spent two years digging and making fanciful and not very accurate drawings at Palenque. It was curious at Chichén-Itzá to think I had talked with that horrible person who had seen him. Not long afterwards Count Waldeck died in Paris in 1875 at the age of 109. Killed in a street accident as he turned round to look at a pretty girl. This adventurer, for he was that more than a serious archaeologist, could have been a friend of Mozart or of Casanova.

Deep untroubled sleep, without mosquitoes, made no impediment to an early start next morning for the other ruins. The first building we went to was the great pyramid, the Temple of Kukulcán or Castillo, dutifully climbing to the top of it up one of its four stairs. The Temple has been well and elaborately restored, being a stepped pyramid of nine stages or landings; and it would seem of astronomical import in design for the total of steps on its four sides adds up to the number of days in a year, while the number of stone panels on all four sides of its nine terraces corresponds to the number of years in the Toltec cycle. And so on, for there is much more of that, but there is something compact and finished about it as though it is a clock, or a sun-gauge or water-gauge, and performed some function. But the Temple of Kukulcán has savage attributes to it; in particular, the huge stone serpent heads with open jaws at the foot of the ramps of one of the stairways, and the jaguar that faces you in a cell at the top, a stone jaguar painted bright vermilion-red, with fangs cut out of flint, jade eyes, and circles of jade on its body to simulate its tabbied fur.

Toltec influence is difficult to disentangle from Mayan at Chichén-Itzá, as instanced by no authority wishing to pin himself down to a precise date for the Temple of Kukulcán. Excavation has shown that there is another pyramid under it, but the Temple as we see it must be a thousand years old. Another Toltec-Maya muddle is over the matter of ball courts, for if their presence at Chichén-Itzá is 'one of the most obvious signs of Mexican influence'[1] how is it there are ball courts at Tikal and Copán, entirely Mayan sites, and at other Mayan sites in British Honduras? This Temple of Kukulcán, so many thousands of years younger than the pyramids of Egypt (the Great Pyramid or Pyramid of Kheops was built in about 2700 B.C.), in spite of its impressive shape and bulk is under eighty feet in height (the pyramid of Kheops is four hundred and fifty feet high). Standing at the top, I could hardly believe this was no higher but apparently it is true. Perfect as it now is after restoration, how wonderful it must have looked with trees growing up its sides and out of its summit, as in Catherwood's engravings, in which state it is still possible to see the four huge temple-crowned pyramids of Tikal (one of them, Temple IV, over two hundred feet high), but only for a year or two longer until they, too, are restored and rescued from the jungle.

Our last call was at the Temple of the Warriors, another Toltec building, probably a temple of war dedicated to the Toltec military (and very Red Indian-sounding!) orders of the Jaguars and the Eagles. This is serpent-ridden even more than any of the other buildings at Chichén-Itzá, and where there are no serpents in the carvings, there are beasts and birds of prey. Each of the three storeys of the pyramid has a frieze of jaguars and eagles, eating human hearts. The stairway which leads up, precipitously and without pause or landing, has stone ramps formed from the bodies of plumed serpents whose heads with wide open jaws jut out from the top storey. Once up there, the hook nose of the rain-god protrudes again and again from the corners of the roof-temple, while its interior columns are carved in bas-relief with priests and warriors in huge plumed head-dresses. Still more serpentine and snake-haunted are the twin pillars at the doorways, for an immense snake's head forms the base of each column, its body is the column itself, and its huge rattle forms the capital.[2] In light of which the snake-doorways are in fact thoroughly alarming; while right in front of them, at the edge of the stair, is one of the Chac Mools of which about a dozen have been found among the ruins of Chichén-Itzá. These are statues of semi-feline human beings lying on their backs, leaning on their elbows with their knees drawn up, and their heads

---

[1] *Maya Cities*, by Paul Rivet, Elek Books, London, 1960, p. 166. There are no fewer than seven ball courts at Chichén-Itzá.

[2] The rattle which is in the snake's tail consists of some ten or a dozen round pieces of bone, like pebbles, which are rattled together in moments of anger or excitement.

turned somewhat violently to right or left. The faces are of unpleasant, cat-like expression, and the sex undetermined. Each Chac Mool is holding a kind of offertory-bowl on its stomach, easily enough explained away as 'seeming to have been used to receive the offerings of visitors', but in this setting where even the dumb stone is aflutter with feathers, where the stairs end in snake heads, and the capitals of the columns shake their stone rattles, the offering to this prototype of mid-twentieth-century sculpture is more likely to have been a quivering, pulsing human heart.

We came down from the Temple of the Warriors in that great heat, near mid-day, stone step by step, with still one more thing to see at Chichén-Itzá, the Cenote, which is some considerable walk away, giving time to think of the flowering trees, the *pic* which is decidedly one of the poetical beauties of the tropics, and eloquent of Mexico, as is the *maculín* that other flowering tree. And I have left till now the feature in all these ruins that seemed so strange to Stephens, and that he noted particularly with two other mysterious relics; the wooden beams that have survived in the ceilings of many of the small interior cells under the stone corbelling or vaulting of the Mayan arch which is all they could contrive in interior architecture, and the marks of red hands upon the walls, and of very small hands at that, one of the earliest and most primitive of human tricks or games for similar imprints of hands are to be seen in the caves of Altamira, next to drawings of mammoths and bisons. But the lasting strangeness of these ruins, as of all Maya ruins where there are portrayals of human beings, are the deformed heads.

The effect is of a race of strange and elongated profile, with the forehead sloping back in caricature of the accepted profile of a Red Indian. Over and over again in their bas-reliefs there is this physiognomy which could belong to no other race, and it is the more extraordinary because they had not the copper skins of the Red Indians, but it is as if in concentrating their vision upon themselves in their sculpture they got back to the basic origins of their race. Present-day Maya much resemble their ancestors though without this purposeful accentuation of their features. The Lacandón Indians living in the rain forests of Chiapas are the most direct link with the Maya, and closely resemble the sculptured profiles, although authorities who have lived among them report that they have forgotten all traditions of their past except that of burning copal incense in the ruins.[1] In any photograph these white-robed Lacandón Indians, who are reported to be on the point of extinction and to number no more than one hundred and sixty individuals, with their straight long black hair look like a group of actors. Like actors who had grown their hair long in order to impersonate the Maya; either that, or they are a company of ghosts.

Deformation of the skull was practised by several Red Indian tribes, notably with the Flatheads whose foreheads were compressed with wooden boards from childhood; but this is further confused because among the near-by Crow Indians, who were distinguished by their great height and their dresses of white deerskin, there was a form of head peculiar to themselves, the semi-lunar outline which gave them half-moon or baby faces. In fact they must have resembled the mysterious baby-face statues of the ancient Olmecs of Veracruz. This practice of the Flathead Indians was exactly paralleled among the Maya. When the new born infant of either sex was only a week old its forehead was compressed between two boards, one in front and the other at the back of the head, and the pressure was increased from time to time in order to produce the desired effect. It so happens that in the frescoes at Bonampak in Chiapas, where the best preserved and the most aesthetically perfect of Maya paintings were discovered as lately as 1946 among Lacandón Indians who still go on pilgrimage to burn copal incense in the ruins, this very process is shown in detail. There is a group of important personages, all portrayed in profile with the approved distortion and wearing head-dresses of extravagant size, and to one side of them on a dais or platform a figure is standing holding a child in its arms with its head between the compressing boards (pl. II of *Maya Cities, op. cit.*). What must have made the finished product of a Maya profile more peculiar still, a squint was a sign of beauty with them, and this was induced by attaching a ball of resin to the front hair to dangle between the eyes and cause both eyes to focus on it. This reads also like a quick means to self-hypnosis.

They also seem to have shaved the front hair in order further to accentuate the sloping profile, leaving enough of the hair to grasp

[1] *A Glimpse of Guatemala*, and *Biologia Centrali America*, by A. P. Maudsley, 5 vols., London, 1889-1902; *A Comparative Study of the Maya and the Lacandones*, by A. M. Tozzer, New York, 1907; and Charles Gallenkamp, *op. cit.* pp. 126-131. A photograph of Lacandón Indians as ghosts in the ruins of Bonampak is on p. 17 of Paul Rivet's *op. cit.* This group of four smiling Lacandones in their white robes with the American archaeologist J. Eric Thompson is a strange and haunting document.

with one hand like a carrot-head (notably in a sculptured detail from a throne at Piedras Negras in Guatemala)[1]. The head in question could be the perfect presentation of a Red Indian brave. We have now, after only a day or two in Chichén-Itzá, seen enough to be familiar with the Maya warriors in their jaguar skin tunics with their nose-plugs and spear-throwers. The head-dresses that are often so inexplicably extravagant and huge on the Maya bas-reliefs become credible in the paintings at Bonampak, where we can see that the chieftains or priests are wearing whole heads of deer, antlers and all, jaguar heads, totem ornaments, animal masks as still in Bolivia and Guatemala; or even what I take to be on the analogy of the 'eccentric flints' and pieces of obsidian worked into profile heads, plumed serpents, and so forth, in order to be put into the heads of ceremonial staffs, 'eccentric' *objets trouvés* in the form of pieces of whittled down or hollowed wood, doubtless of some especially friable soft-timbered tree.

But all else of their head-dresses whether on carved stelae, or bas-reliefs, or in the paintings at Bonampak, pales before the huge plumes of quetzal feathers. In the copies of the Bonampak frescoes in the museum at Guatemala City attendants are carrying what appear to be immense frames or wings of the green feathers, probably for fixing on the shoulders, as was the case in the seventeenth century with the Winged Hussars of Poland who had frames of eagles' feathers attached to their shoulders. But there the intention was that the beating and flapping of the wings should frighten the enemies' horses. In this particular painting one important personage seems to have a pair of the quetzal wings upon him, with a few separate tail feathers to nod and wave above that. In another of the frescoes where the captives are awaiting their fate, the King or chieftain in tunic and boots of jaguar skin has just one superb jet or plume of quetzal tail feathers streaming from his head-dress. In other paintings there is mad profusion of quetzal plumes, indeed plumes with no one to wear them and to no purpose, culminating in two extraordinary scenes of dancing which are awave and awash with the green feathers in a delirium of movement. The dancers appear to be holding patterned cloths in their hands; or else those are their skirts that flare out in the dance. One or two of them are holding fans with that tell-tale red hand outlined upon the fan—

[1] Charles Gallenkamp, *op. cit.* pl. opposite p. 85. The 'eccentric' flints mentioned below are illustrated in J. E. S. Thompson, *op. cit.*, pl. 22.

but what tale does it tell? That they are paintings dating from our eighth century according to a stela which carries a date corresponding to A.D. 785? At which point they have become like towering bearskins of green feathers, and in the excitement it is no longer possible to make out what is happening. Great quetzal masses with antler-like quetzal plumes waving from them, and quetzal tails, and a confusion and crescendo of green quetzal feathers.

What a pity it is that not one shred of a feathered cloak has been found, and that here among the Maya 'there is no arid region comparable to the coast of Peru which would have saved such treasures!'[1] But the Bonampak paintings are a hopeful sign of what may yet be discovered in the wildernesses of Chiapas and Quintana Roo. For Bonampak, which had to be christened by the archaeologists with a word meaning 'painted walls' in Mayan, because it had not even a name, can never have been more than a small obscure town near the larger Yoxchilán, and the painter or painters of Bonampak probably came from there. What a mystery that these works of art by a great painter—of what stature?—shall we say as great a painter as Sôtatsu?—should be found in the jungle several days journey by mule from the nearest airstrip, in just the locality still haunted by the white-robed Lacandón Indians, the direct descendants of the Mayans, and the only group of Indians which has kept entirely remote from white civilization! In fact the dance scenes at Bonampak are strangely reminiscent of Sôtatsu's pair of screens and of *Court Dances* in the Sambôin Temple at Kyoto, seventeenth-century works of art which are among the greatest works of art in Japan. On one of the screens a group of four masked dancers performing a round dance with their hands on each other's shoulders has a strange, archaic formality in its movements. Sôtatsu was painting a *Bugaku* dance of the seventh or eighth century (still performed at the Emperor's Palace in Tokyo) and the cloaks with wide sleeves or skirts, and the masks and head-dresses are completely in the spirit of the paintings at Bonampak.

One could imagine or dream of bringing this great artist to see the three painted cells in this remotest part of Mexico. And of how, like ourselves, he might be surprised more than by anything else by the sloping profiles. By ten *caciques* standing in a row with nose and fore-

[1] J. E. S. Thompson. *op. cit.*, p. 185. The frescoes at Bonampak are reproduced in *Mexico, Pre-Hispanic Paintings*, Vol. X. Unesco World Art Series, text by Jacques Soustelle.

head nearly in a flat line; by three women sitting on a stone dais, 'undoubtedly of high descent', with the same foreheads, shaved temples and tufts of hair; by the three young women on another throne, a dais painted green with red circles on it, and they have the same foreheads and tufted hair; or by the warrior below them who looks like nothing else than a Red Indian brave, Crow, Mandan, Sioux, or Minataree. So little can be presumed where all is mystery. But in fact how does this compare with what was going on in England in A.D. 785? Or in 1960? Would paintings of the United Nations or the Labour Party Conference be works of art? How long did the languages of the American-'Indians' take to evolve from the speech they brought with them over the Bering Straits? Is four or five thousand years enough for this? And how did the small ethnic groups of only a few hundred or thousand individuals, as with some of the Amazon tribes, or even a few of the 'Indian' tribes in Mexico, evolve their own language? These are questions that are unanswered. But neither is it known what tongue was spoken at Stonehenge, or in the underground oracle of the hypogeum at Malta; any more than it will ever be discovered what was the language of the cave-painters at Lascaux or Altamira. It is no more and no less of a mystery than the Mayans.

And now in the heat of mid-day we are to see the Cenote of Chichén-Itzá. Readers of Stephen's *Yucatán* may remember the account of his descent into a cavern Cenote down a series of wooden ladders, to a depth according to his calculation of four hundred and fifty feet, down to the water basin which he states was some fourteen hundred feet from the entrance to the cave. 'This was the only watering place of one of the most thriving villages of Yucatán, containing a population of several thousand souls; and yet for an unknown length of time, and through a great portion of the year, files of Indians, men and women, were going to it every day with *cántaros* on their backs, and returning with water.'[1] And 'Mr C.' contributes a Piranesi-like drawing of this subterranean scene at the Cenote of Bolonchen, which I take to be the modern Bolonchenticul on the borders of Campeche and Yucatán.

But the Cenote of Chichén-Itzá is of another sort, and no less than the sacred well into which the Mayans threw their virgins. 'The Indians and principal personages of the land had the custom, after sixty days of abstinence and fasting, of arriving by daybreak at the mouth of the

[1] Vol. I pp. 145-156.

Cenote and throwing into it Indian women belonging to each of these lords and personages, at the same time telling these women to ask for their masters a year favourable to his particular needs and desires. The women, being thrown in unbound, fell into the water with great force and noise. At high noon those that could cried out loudly and ropes were let down to them. After the women came up, half-dead, fires were built around them, and copal incense was burned before them.'[1] But in fact this tradition is not entirely true. Bishop de Landa adds: 'They had the custom of throwing live men into the well during the dry season, and although the men were never seen again it was not felt that they had died.' The dredging of the Cenote by Edward Thompson, and later by the Peabody Museum of Harvard brought up an immense number of jade articles, gold ornaments, and other objects, and about fifty skulls and remains of skeletons; thirteen men, twenty-one children including babies, and only eight women. In fact there were as many children as adults at the bottom of the Cenote.

Lying in some seventy feet of water, with ten feet of mud below that, and a drop of sixty-five feet before you reached the water, if you were being thrown in, that is to say, and it is difficult not to think of that standing at the edge of the Cenote which is some two hundred feet across. Looking down into it, there is no way out of its waters unless you are hauled up on a rope. Obviously at some time or other its edges have been artificially steepened, and it has perhaps even been made bigger. The ten feet of mud at the bottom may be the earth that fell in before it could be taken away. So the Cenote has been made worse than it need have been. Its waters are a horrid green colour even now that they have given up their secret. In this land where there is neither lake nor river it would be strange indeed were there no superstition attaching to this sudden opening in the rocky plateau, to this orifice in the bony surface of Yucatán filled mysteriously with water.

The objects found down there include a piece of carved jade bearing a Maya date corresponding to A.D. 706, and a jade bead of A.D. 690 which is thought to have been brought here from Palenque. Other metal objects, since the Mayans scarcely understood the working of metal, must have come here from Colombia and Panamá. So the Cenote was a sacred place of wide renown; and it may have continued

[1] Don Diego Sarmiento de Figueroa, Alcalde of Madrid. He went to Yucatán in the late sixteenth century. Edward Thompson's account of the dredging of the Cenote is in *People of the Serpent*, 1932.

to be sacred for nearly a thousand years, in which case it is true that the number of sacrificial victims found in it is remarkably small. It is in dispute among archaeologists as to whether these jade and other objects found in the Cenote were thrown into it in the eighth century, or kept as treasures for many hundreds of years and thrown in at some time of crisis. Who will ever know? If no one was left alive down there, 'the master and his companions,' we read, 'threw heavy stones into the water and fled away, shrieking.' In silence I had already thrown in a stone which dropped, plumb-down into the green waters. And we threw in another stone, and walked away.

Chapter Fourteen

❖❖❖❖❖❖❖❖❖❖❖❖❖❖❖❖❖❖❖❖❖❖❖

UXMAL

IN ORDER TO GET TO Uxmal we had to go through Mérida again. Upon a Sunday evening when the Yucatecas were to be seen walking the streets in their white dresses, with white cotton shifts worked with green leaves and roses, and their hair tied with coloured ribbons. The embroidery of roses is of Spanish accent; the rest is Indian, Mayan-Indian, and not Mexican. Many hundreds of them, all alike, but we were only long enough in Mérida to be off again, out through the suburbs and past the blue-green fields of agave, mile after mile of those along the road to Uxmal. Just missing Ticul, as I had feared would be the case, since it lay a little further along the same road, but where I had wanted to go, having read of it in Stephens. And reaching Uxmal about an hour before dark, with the sight of pyramids and ruins as at Chichén-Itzá, but now their substance and not their shadowy shape, for it was still daylight.

There is an almost brand-new hotel to put to shame readers of Stephens and other early travellers, with Viennese waltzes relayed all round the garden and into the big cool bedrooms as we arrived. With the hotel-macaw of all Central American macaws tethered, or, rather, pinioned to the boughs, and a swimming pool in the middle among terraces of flowers. A little further away under a kind of kiosk a potter was at work, with a sleeping babe in a hammock beside him in an attitude of purposeful and determined repose, the Mongol strain showing clearly in its uncreased, tight-shut eyelids. No one could doubt the Asian ancestry after seeing that sleeping baby. But, also, the hammock was interesting. Passing the one-roomed, conical-roofed huts in the villages, and wondering how a whole family could live in them without beds or furniture, the mystery was explained. They string up their hammocks at night, and probably their ancestors lived little differently a thousand years ago. Again one wishes there were some other adjective than 'Indian' by which to describe their huts under tall palm trees, with nearly always a few turkeys gobbling away in the back garden.

At an early hour next morning we were in the ruins of Uxmal. And at the first of the ruins we came to, we met our guide from Chichén-Itzá just coming out from them with a family of French tourists. They were leaving in a hurry because they had just seen a black panther (jaguar?) prowling through the bushes. The guide said he had never seen one before in a lifetime spent in the Mayan ruins. Perhaps it should have been accounted as some kind of omen or portent. Unfortunately, we saw no more of the black panther; though a rustling in the bushes and something large and heavy darting up a wall and into a crevice proved to be a big iguana which stayed hidden with only its tail showing.

The building out of which the black panther had emerged was long and low, and yet another of those cores filled up with rubble which are one of the mysteries of Maya civilization. Building for the sake of building, and as idle of other purpose as a child's house of cards. Through the doorway in the middle of it we came into a huge area of tumbled stones, scrambling about on them in the blazing sunlight. Quite large sections of Uxmal are still unexplored in the sense that they have not been cleared of jungle, nor given systematic excavation. This is certainly one of the areas in question, and from its debris an idea can be formed of how much patience is required in restoration. For Uxmal like Chichén-Itzá is, largely speaking, restored or museum-proofed, that is to say, though there may still be the finished results to show, no more sensational discoveries are likely to be made.

According to the archaeologists Uxmal dates from the tenth and eleventh centuries which makes it some three or four hundred years later than the golden ages of Palenque and Copán. At the same time it is in purer Mayan style than Chichén-Itzá and without sign of Toltec or Mexican influence. I think one can detect this for oneself for it is without the death's head, skull and crossbones motifs of the Mexicans. But, also, although 'the buildings at Uxmal are distributed in quadrilaterals without any settled plan,'[1] it is on the contrary just

[1] Rivet, *op. cit.* p. 159. Nevertheless, there is a frieze of nothing other than skulls and cross-bones at Uxmal in the building, known because of this, as the *El Cemeterio*.

the signs of deliberate planning that give one the sensation, perhaps for the first time among any ancient remains on the American continent, that this is ordered architecture and that the Mayan ruins could be on the scale of the temples of Angkor.

This, on emerging without warning into a huge quadrangle with four carved and sculptured façades; or, in Stephens' account of it— for no one could describe it better than this first explorer to look upon it with intelligent eyes: 'We enter a noble courtyard with four great façades looking down upon it, each ornamented from one end to the other with the richest and most intricate carving known in the art of the buildings of Uxmal; presenting a scene of strange magnificence, surpassing any that is now to be seen among its ruins.'[1] The Spaniards called this square Las Monjas though there is no reason to think virgins or nuns lived in it, but it is certainly not only a plaza, cloister, quad- rangle, call it what you will, but a centre of civilized life over many generations of human beings. With no wheeled traffic or beast of burden for they had neither, but had to carry their own burdens and move upon their own feet. Not a market place, for the litter of that would not be tolerated in this place of orderliness and authority. The four buildings cannot have been temples but, rather, this is the piazza or capitol or Campidoglio, the feathered 'Indian' equivalent of the Place Stanislas at Nancy, or the Piazza of St Mark's.

One side has 'rain dragons', masks of Chac the rain-god, in profusion, and now as 'rain dragons' their hooked noses begin to make sense. At Kabah, another of the Maya ruined cities in Yucatán, not far from here, there is a building called agreeably the K'odzp'op with a façade con- sisting of nothing but stylized masks of the rain-god, and with a mask of Chac looking like a rolled tongue for the doorstep. Kabah must be an extreme case of this obsession, made credible when we read in Stephens that 'there was one strange circumstance connected with these ruins' (at Uxmal). 'No water had ever been discovered nearer than a mile and a half distant. The sources which supplied this element of life had disappeared . . . the discovery of these wells or reservoirs would, in that region, be like finding a fountain in the desert.' We begin to understand the throwing of young virgins into the Cenote.

---

[1] 'Count' Waldeck had preceded Stephens at Uxmal by two years, but his 'large folio edition, with illustrations fancifully and beautifully coloured' published in Paris in 1839, pertains, as hinted by Stephens, less to the realm of fact than fiction. The rain gods of Kabah, mentioned lower, are illustrated in Rivet, *op. cit.* pl. 15 and 16.

It is difficult to penetrate into the mind which so stylized the rain-god, which invented this imagery, till we remember that even the birds of the air of the Mayans were hard-billed parrots, macaws, toucans; and recall as a perfectly natural motif 'the stone parrot heads, deeply tenoned three abreast on the side walls,'[1] of the ball court at Copán.

But the other buildings in the square are no less extraordinary, and at first sight incomprehensible in their ornament. This is indeed, the most foreign of all languages and the most difficult imagery to understand. Little by little, however, it can be explained and it is grasped that it is another world, a new world without historical connection with anything we have seen before. The northern of the four buildings has strange carvings over the doors which are formed of a quartet of masks of the rain-god, one on top of another, with a frieze to each side consisting of the hook noses in juxtaposition over each other, either the right way up, or upside down, in light of which what was meaningless now comes to have its meaning. Other doors have curious little structures over them which are nothing else but stone models of little Maya huts. The eastern end of the buildings has three tiers of masks of the rain-god at its corners and over the central door, and a fill-in of stone trellis work with an over-lay of stone bars or grids, eight of them, diminishing in size from top to bottom so as to form a pattern like a triangular portcullis on the stone trellis.

The southern side of the square which is the largest of the buildings, with a high vaulted doorway in the middle, has more of the stone trellis work, and the smaller doors along its façade have the simple, but baffling little stone huts over them. For are they just ornament, or have they some deeper meaning? But the building on the western side is the most careful and painstaking of all, and but for its having only seven little rooms or cells in it, would be taken for a palace. There is a throne with a canopy or baldachin over it, above the central door, and a seated figure which is much damaged and difficult to make out, though one can still see swirls cut in the stones round it to suggest quetzal plumes. There are smaller thrones over the doors to each side, and there the seated figures are easier to distinguish. The end doors have the little huts over them, and the background of the façade is made up of squares and lozenges and twined serpent bodies which look like cables; also, snakes 'on the crawl' over the field of trellis.

[1] J. E. S. Thompson, *op. cit.*, p. 79.

Perhaps the seated figures are not so much portraits as tribal totems, or some concept like a personal device, or even a coat-of-arms.

We noted with what pleasure the guides, who were of Mayan origin, showed these buildings, pointing with pride to this western façade as the palace of the Xiu who were builders and rulers of Uxmal. It was now we heard of the 'Queen of Uxmal', an old lady living in the next village who has lately been identified as last descendant of the Xiu family (pronounced 'Shoo'). Her pedigree can be traced back through successive generations for eight hundred or a thousand years. Apparently this was well-known locally, but not thought to be of any interest until her descent was investigated and proved true (by Mr Eric S. Thompson?). She is a poor old woman living in a hut in one of the villages, with children and grandchildren, although her name dies with her; and a source of pride to the local population but not to the far away Mexican government who will not give her a pension. There was talk of her coming to live in a hut built for her by the hotel, where incidentally, there is a splendid and touching photograph of this old 'Indian' lady, last descendant of the ruling family of Uxmal.

Knowledge of her existence somehow brings the ruins nearer and makes them credible and human. In Stephens there is a similar story of an Indian family living near another of the ruined cities, and descend-ed from the ruling chiefs. Yet, taking a last look at this square of Las Monjas, certainly the most impressive of 'Indian ruins' that we had seen, and looking more particularly at the building on its western side, or House of the Xiu, with the serpent cable motif on its front, this whole piazza or capitol, as I have called it, seemed more than ever outside and beyond all experience. To those readers who have been there it may bring a momentary reminder of Manoelino buildings in Portugal, and in particular the Convent of the Order of Christ at Tomar, but there is no more to it than noting a fortuitous resemblance to some European in an Indian or Chinaman. It is there all the same, in the twisted cables that are the bodies of serpents, in the canopies over the seated figures, in the colour of the stone. And now the en-trance to the piazza, which is the corbelled doorway in the southern building, magnifies itself into an architectural invention, forgetting for the moment that this is where the Mayans stopped and could get no further. For it is this very invention of the Mayan arch that limited them to the roofing of small cell-like interiors. They could contrive

Above, Chac-mul; *below,* Uxmal, Yucatán

Uxmal, pyramid of the Dwarf

long ranges of buildings, or even one card-house storey on top of another, but always they had to build solid or fill up with rubble. The cells with little tell-tale *zapote* beams, still in place, could never have been lived in. Perhaps for some great occasion they may have hung up their hammocks, lit a fire and spent the night much as did Stephens and 'Mr C.' when they slept in the ruins. These were not cities or towns but ceremonial and religious centres. Among them all there is not a single house or human dwelling. Nevertheless, the 'Mayan arch', under which we came into the square, now takes on a character of its own. It is in a language or individuality apart; as much, or nearly as much so, as the fretted arches of the Alhambra, or the Mogul arches of the 'Pearl' Mosque at Agra.

The huge three-storeyed pyramid of Uxmal, or Casa del Adivino, stands just at the back, and it is supposed that these buildings 'served as residences' for the priests. But even with their frugal wants this seems unlikely. This 'house of the prophet', surely a silly name for a pyramid a hundred foot high, has not one but two temples on top of it, being rather taller than the Temple of Kukulcán at Chichén-Itzá but less impressive because the site has not been cleared. The temple on its first storey has again the obsessive rain mask at its corners, seven of the hook-nosed faces one above another, and a door formed out of a rain mask with its teeth for the lintel; the hook noses at the corners being a little different in outline, I thought, not so curling and like an up-turned elephant's trunk—though those we had seen at Chichén-Itzá had more resemblance to a conventionalized wild boar's tusk—but these at Uxmal were like a turtle head.

We were now taken to what has been called 'the most impressive building of pre-Columbian America'. This is the Palace of the Governor so called, though we may well be at a loss to know what it was really intended for. No photograph does it justice because of its extreme length, and probably it will never show to such advantage in any publication as in Catherwood's folding frontispiece to the first volume of Stephen's *Yucatán*. There it unfolds to all its length on its enormous terrace. This must represent labour almost on the Pharaonic scale for it is a solid base or core of masonry with another platform on top of it on which the building stands, itself over three hundred feet in length. There are, in fact, a number of small rooms or cells in this, and even two rooms or salas sixty feet long in one of which Stephens and

s

'Mr C.' took up residence and put up their hammocks. It was from 'the south end apartment' that they took away the carved beam of *zapote* wood, 'the only sculptured beam in Uxmal', which was unfortunately burned in the 'conflagration' at 'Mr C.'s' Panorama in New York. Stephens describes it as 'a sculptured beam of hieroglyphics', and on the analogy of the panel in sculptured wood from Tikal, now in the museum at Basle, it may have been very beautiful. This, which is of 'a type of medlar tree called chico-zapote'—and how distant we are from the quinces and medlars of an English kitchen garden!—is carved with a serpent with open jaws. A *cacique* or chieftain, probably someone even more important than that, a *halach uinic* or hereditary ruler, is seen in profile with enormous ear-plugs, holding a spear, while a quetzal with spread wings is above his head, its plumes coming down to the panels of hieroglyphs at either side.[1] This wooden panel which dates from A.D. 750 is one of twelve lintels from temple doors at Tikal, and may give some idea of what is missing from the bare bones of Uxmal.

It was on the interior walls of this Palace of the Governors that Stephens particularly noticed 'the prints of a red hand with the thumb and fingers extended. . . . He who made it had stood before it alive as we did, and pressed his hand, moistened with red paint, hard against the stone. The seams and creases of the palm were distinct in the impression. There was something lifelike about it that waked exciting thoughts, and almost presented the images of the departed inhabitants hovering about the building. And there was one striking feature about these hands; they were exceedingly small. Either of our own spread over and completely hid them.' This building, though impressive by its size, did not seem to be as fine in detail as the House of Xiu; but what Stephens has to say of it is true, that 'if it stood at this day on its grand artificial terrace in Hyde Park or the Tuileries, it would form a new order, I do not say equalling, but not unworthy to stand side by side with the remains of Egyptian, Grecian, and Roman art'.

The façade is ornamented with stone trellis and key patterns, has the hook-nosed rain-god at its corners, and seems ready for its stone to break into feathers at any moment. Which it does above the central door, where there is a seated figure on a throne with a head-dress of

---

[1] Illustrated in Rivet, *op. cit.*, pl. 125. Another panel of the same series carved with a chieftain on a throne with a jaguar over him, is in the British Museum.

gigantic plumes of feathers, parting at the top and 'falling evenly to each side until they touch the ornament on which the feet of the statue rest'. In fact this mysterious personage or bird-man is entirely swathed in quetzal plumes, springing from high above his head down to his feet, while his throne rests on that same triangular, portcullis grid-motif on the stone trellis of the background. Right in front of this building in the middle of the terrace is a large stone object that Stephens describes in cautious language: 'from its conspicuous position, it doubtless had some important use, and in connection with other monuments found at this place, induces the belief that it was connected with the ceremonial rites of an ancient worship known to have existed among all Eastern nations.' Or, in other words, this is a phallic symbol, and it was interesting to see the thinly disguised enthusiasm with which the guides dilated on this topic to the tourists, and in particular to a pair of American maiden aunts travelling together who were quite unable to grasp its import.

We had now seen all the important buildings in both Chichén-Itzá and Uxmal, and there are a few last moments in which to gather and correlate the impressions that they leave.

It is an unforgettable experience to come upon these relics of plan and order in the midst of the Central American jungle. There is evidence that Chichén-Itzá was still inhabited, probably by only a small population, when the Spaniards reached it, but most of the Mayan cities had perished and were empty of inhabitants long before that, and for their golden period we have to go back to the seventh and eighth centuries, some twelve hundred years ago. The interest of Uxmal, which is a little later in date than that, and indeed contemporary to our Norman and Plantagenet Kings, lies in its purity of the Mayan style. There is no aura of human sacrifice clinging to the ruins, and only one ball court where at Chichén-Itzá there were seven. This is supposed to show there is no influence from Mexico; and even if this is no place for moralities we may remind ourselves that if the Aztecs had their holocausts of human beings, the Romans had their circus games, and the Christians their *autos-da-fé*. Uxmal leaves an impression of orderliness without suffering and bloodshed, and although the Maya may not have been too gentle in themselves we must be thankful on their behalf that they escaped the greed of the *Conquistadores*. The mystery of why their cities were deserted may never be explained, but is after all no more mysterious than the deserted temples of Angkor. However, there is one thing altogether missing from Chichén-Itzá and that is the carved stelae, the absence of which in some of the Mayan ruins is as conspicuous as would be Bernini's Rome without the fountains. But neither is Uxmal a place in which to look for stelae. They were the sculptural invention of the Mayans, and set up at the end of every *atun* or period of twenty years in accelerating progress as they took more and more pride in their chronology, from the fourth century A.D. until shortly before A.D. 900, but they hardly occur in Yucatán. For the carved stelae one must go to Tikal, Copán, Quiriguá, Piedras Negras, all cities of the Old Mayan Empire which lay chiefly in what is now Guatemala, but proves to be contemporary with the New Empire in Yucatán.

It is the carved stelae that emerge to such marvellous effect in the engravings from Catherwood's drawings, and that have never been bettered in any modern photograph. In the first volume of Stephens' *Incidents of Travel in Central America, Chiapas, and Yucatán* there are no fewer than seventeen engravings of stelae, all from Copán, which we may recall is in Honduras, and about three-quarters of an hour by air from the capital, Tegucigalpa. More stelae have been uncovered since Stephens' day, but how wonderful and mysterious is the frontispiece, a huge stone of a standing man, his feet and sandals clearly shown, his hands folded on his breast, 'Indian' countenance with enormous ear-ornaments, and towering hieroglyphic head-dress. And now the whole succession of them, in most cases twenty-four to thirty feet high; an 'idol' emerging from a jaguar mask, its belt hung with human faces like the trophies of a scalp-hunter, and the stone steps of a mysterious staircase in the background, overgrown with trees; another, still more convoluted of ornamented as though caught in a tangle of stone lianas; now, one with mask head-dress and quetzal plumes, wearing a kind of quilted apron; and the back of this, or of another—for some of the stelae have both sides sculptured—one mass of masks and hieroglyphs framed in quetzal feathers. Next follows another, half-dug out of the ground 'when we first discovered it, it was buried up to the eyes', with its hands under its chin as though trying to assist its own return into the light of day; and what seems to be a bearded 'idol', 'with open mouth and eyeballs starting from the sockets, the intention of the sculptor seeming to have been to inspire terror', and the back of this, beautifully carved with hieroglyphs in a surround of quetzal plumes.

The series continues with a stela of a human figure, unmistakably Red Indian, and of no other race, with its back carved with two parallel rows of picture writing, in nearly every instance including human features, standing in front of a 'colossal altar' or carved boulder with a flat top, and representing a huge death's head. An engraving of this 'altar' follows with the statue standing behind it under the trees. And we come to another stela, broken in two, its stone feet still on the ground, and the upper half of it lying on its side, face and rustling head-dress to the earth. The procession closes with another king or *cacique*, or astronomer, the back carved with hieroglyphs, and at the top of those a figure sitting, cross-legged, in a huge head-dress; and last of all, a stela, in front, back, and side view, no less mysterious than all the others, and of the same continent, demonstrably, as any Alaskan totem pole. It must certainly be the 'idols', as Stephens calls them, 'which give the distinctive character to the ruins of Copán.' But the wonder of Copán must be the Hieroglyphic Stairway, rising to ninety feet and leading from the lower to the upper city, with each of its treads carved with the mysterious symbols, and six more than lifesize statues of gods or priests set at intervals up the middle of the stair. And what would seem to be splendid and unique at Copán must be the stone sculptures of the doorway in Temple 22; relief sculptures of a huge skull on which sits a mysterious 'Indian' personage, for he is obviously that and of no other race, with an extraordinary tangle of animals and human figures, running up the wall behind him like a fantastic head-dress; and the stone framework to match it, but the aforementioned of the sculptures is the better and more perfect of the two. This stone doorway, but more still, the Staircase of the Jaguars which has to either side of it large sculptures of jaguars, standing on their hind feet like human cats, with bits of obsidian put into the stone to simulate their tabbied fur, these must be the wonders of Copán. The date of these extraordinary objects is the eighth century and they would seem to be like nothing else on earth.

Many of the stelae were originally painted and still have traces of red or blue colour adhering to them. In their pristine state it must have much increased their basic totemic character. At Tikal, in Guatemala, where the four huge pyramids with temples and roof-crests on top of them are hardly cleared yet and rise above the jungle like the cones of volcanoes, there are more of the stelae set up in rows, twenty to thirty feet high, in the great ceremonial court; and there are others at Uaxactún, another site in the rain forest not far away.[1] It was at Quiriguá which is in this group that Stephens noticed 'the monuments were of the same general character with those at Copán, but twice or three times as high'. However, the feature peculiar to Quiriguá would seem to be the huge sculptured rocks or boulders carved with snakes and tortoises, so worn now that they have come to resemble the stones off lake beds set up in old gardens in China.

If carved stelae are the feature of Copán the finest bas-reliefs are at Palenque. This ancient Mayan site in Chiapas, in a tropical landscape closely resembling that which surrounds the temples of Angkor, was the scene of a remarkable discovery in 1952, when a magnificent, carved monolithic stone slab in the Temple of the Inscriptions was lifted up and a subterranean chamber came to light in which the skeleton of some personage of great importance lay, decked with jade, the first burial ever found in a Mayan pyramid. The bodies of six youths killed in sacrifice were lying near to him; and a curious feature was a kind of air-pipe or duct emerging from the tomb, in the form of a serpent's head and leading up the wall to the temple floor, like a breathing tube or communication between the living and the dead, between the darkness of the tomb and the world outside.

It is in the bas-reliefs at Palenque that the 'Indian' physiognomy is most marked. Stephens noticed it immediately, commenting upon one relief in which 'the principal personage stands in an upright position and in profile, exhibiting an extraordinary facial angle of about forty-five degrees. The upper part of the head seems to have been compressed and lengthened, perhaps by the same process employed upon the heads of the Choctaw and Flathead Indians of our own country. The head represents a different species from any now existing in that region of country; and supposing the statues to be images of living personages, or the creations of artists according to their ideas of perfect figures, they indicate a race of people now lost and unknown.' And in his very next sentence, just as we would expect: 'the head-dress is evidently a plume of feathers.' A little later,' . . . the subject consists of two figures

[1] The largest number of stelae at any known site is a hundred and three, of which most are carved, at Calakmul, in Campeche. There are eighty-six stelae at Tikal, but sixty-five of them are plain.

with facial angles similar to that in the plate before given . . . each has hold of the same curious baton, and opposite their hands are hiero-glyphics which probably give the history of these incomprehensible personages'. Later still, '. . . the physiognomy is the same as that of the other personages'. And excessively curious it is indeed. In another of the reliefs the hair is bunched together with a ribbon, or something of the kind, tied round it.

But that is from another site, Piedras Negras; and perhaps some of the oddest of all are from Yaxchilán, a site in Chiapas, where they are in the form of stone lintels. In one of them, which has become famous in illustration, a kneeling personage in an enormous and complicated head-dress, with many rows of necklaces, is making a blood offering by passing a cord strung with thorns through a hole in his tongue, a painful process which must have ended with a tongue badly swollen. The drops of blood dripped from the mouth onto strips of bark paper which were offered to the deity. The sting from the tail of a stinging ray was used for the same purpose, but this was only by priests, and sting-ray spines have been found buried with the bodies in Mayan graves. The deity at whose feet he is kneeling holds some object over him which is like a flowering cactus pole, and both of them, god and man, have the sloping profile, *le front fuyant*, to a pronounced degree. In another of the stone lintels from Yaxchilán, a man holding a jaguar head is in converse with someone, quetzal-plumed, of major importance, and the head deformation with both of them is so marked that it has become freakish. Visually, the Mayan must have been one of the oddest of all human cultures. If one is to think of it in terms of aesthetics one cannot but prefer it to the stereotyped Egyptian, accord-ing to the same canon by which we rate the temples of Angkor higher than those of Luxor. It is one of the supreme losses to human experience that there is no account at first hand of the Mayans. This is hardly to be endured when we are told that at Tayasol, the island in Lake Petén where the Mayans from Chichén-Itzá were undisturbed by the Span-iards until 1697, there was living, shortly before its capture, a red-haired man, married to an Itza woman, who had a book with him conjectured to have been a Bible, and it is thought that he may have been an English buccaneer from the pirate stronghold at Belize.

But the most living relics of the lost Maya are certain pottery statuettes, only a few inches high, of which there are specimens in the

Robert Woods Bliss Collection of Pre-Columbian Art, now on loan to the National Gallery at Washington.[1] A number of them are in fact clay whistles. One figure, with arms outstretched and upturned hands, leaning back on his feet, with his hair dressed in a series of odd spikes, and the three beads on his forehead to induce a squint, is evidently an orator. He could be nothing else; the eternal orator of a cartoon by Daumier. Another, kneeling figure, with the Mayan nose, looks down in contemplation and wears an enormous calabash—shaped turban. There is a standing warrior in a leaf head-dress for it is surely that, although the catalogue says the head-dress is most unusual, and that it cannot be stated of what materials it was made. But it is as when on a hot August day a child will shield his head with a rhubarb leaf in a northern garden; and for the return to a tropical clime the warrior wears a curious device like a false nose to improve his squinting. Another man in a pale blue kilt and yellow tunic, with his hair in the spike arrangement, wears an animal head on top of that, which in a phrase explains those incomprehensible head-dresses on Mayan stelae and bas-reliefs and in the frescoes at Bonampak when the catalogue says that 'Guaymí Indians still wear stuffed animals for ceremonial adornment'.

Other of the pottery figures are no less curious and revealing. A bearded man with folded arms, and the cross-eye inducer between his eyebrows; but it is his head-dress which rebuts all explaining till the compiler of the notes suggests that its odd-shaped tubes are the leg bones of jaguars with the ends sawed off, which the Mayans made use of to extract poison or disease by suction. So this is a shaman or *chuch-cajau* wearing the implements of his trade in his hat, and we are at no distance from his present day descendants in the market place at Chichecastenango. An amatory group of an old man embracing a young girl has its topical features of time and place for he wears a deer's head mounted on his own head, and we can tell from the beads above her nose that she is squinting playfully into his eyes. A man sitting on his haunches, but wearing a spiked cloak which defied all learned explanation, has a peaked, pointed hat and is very little different from the 'Indian' you might see trudging the road in the Guatemalan highlands.

---

[1] Reproduced in colour in the *Phaidon* volume devoted to this collection (1957), pl. LXIX to LXXVII. Text by S. K. Lothrop.

But perhaps the most tell-tale of them all is the pottery whistle which looks so much grander than that in spite of its small scale, and could easily be some kind of Buddha. His balloon-head-dress is enormous and weighed down with ropes, and there is dark blue paint on his head-dress and his clothing. But the upper part of his face, and his neck and hands and feet are painted a lighter blue. It is as though he is wearing a blue mask. His nose and chin have tattoo marks and both lips are cut and mutilated which gives him a changed shape of mouth. Blue was the ritual colour of the Mayans. Their sacrificial victims were painted blue, and the stone altar on which they were immolated was smeared with blue. So it may be that he is a Mayan ready for sacrifice. Or, if not that, he is at least someone who has undergone deep ritual penance.

If there be persons in our own time in this middle of the twentieth century prepared to undergo the ordeal of training and have themselves fired into space in a rocket, there may well be others willing to be killed in sacrifice in order to have seen the Mayan ruins as living cities. To have lived but a day or two in Copán or Palenque and then be painted with blue and laid upon the fatal stone! Nothing else than their cities lying in ruins brings the living Mayans so near to us as the pottery figures just described. We had been lucky to see Chichén-Itzá and Uxmal with our own eyes, and now it was time to be leaving. The long journey which had taken us to the Altiplano of Peru and to Lake Titicaca was ending.

It seemed a smaller world when we came back from all our wanderings to the hotel at Uxmal. With a last wish to be able to go one day to the island of Cozumel where the 'armament' of Cortés made rendezvous in 1519 a few weeks before he invaded Mexico. An island with a tropical climate and many turtles, lying off the coast of Quintana Roo, and where this same hotel company is opening a new hotel next spring. Instead, we must start for home by way of New York, where the bronze Seagram Building and the green-blue Steuben Glass are wonders of the modern world. They may be torn down in our lifetime to make room for other, maybe glass, pyramids or teocallis. But no skyscraper of North America will be as long-lasting as the Mayan temples, or the walls of Cuzco that once glittered to the first Spaniards in that cold sunshine with plates or spangles of pure gold.

INDEX

126 TO FINIS 281
58 TO 64